A SCOTTISH LIFE

A SCOTTISH LIFE

Sir John Martin, Churchill and Empire

Michael Jackson

Edited by
Janet Jackson

The Radcliffe Press
London · New York

Published in 1999 by The Radcliffe Press
Victoria House, Bloomsbury Square
London WC1B 4DZ
175 Fifth Avenue, New York NY 10010

In the United States and Canada
distributed by St Martin's Press
175 Fifth Avenue, New York NY 10010

ISBN 1–86064–416–3

A full CIP record for this book is available from the British Library
A full CIP record for this book is available from the Library of Congress

Library of Congress Catalog card: available

Typeset in Sabon by Oxford Publishing Services, Oxford
Printed and bound in Great Britain by WBC Ltd, Bridgend

Contents

Illustrations

Illustrations

Acronyms and Abbreviations

ADC	aide-de-camp
ADO	assistant district officer
AKEL	*Anorthotikon Komma Ergazomanou Laou* (Progressive Party of the Working People)
ASP	Assistant Superintendent of Police
BA	British Adviser
B.Litt	Bachelor of Letters
BOAC	British Overseas Airways Corporation
CB	Companion (of the Order) of the Bath
CCC	Corpus Christi College
CCTA	Commission de Coopération Technique pour l'Afrique du Sud
CIGS	Chief of Imperial General Staff
CO	Colonial Office
CPA	Commonwealth Parliamentary Association
CRO	Commonwealth Relations Office
CSA	Commission Scientifique pour l'Afrique du Sud
CVO	Commander of the Royal Victorian Order
DO	District Officer
EOKA	*Ethnike Organosis Kyoruakou Agonas* (National Organization of the Cypriot Struggle)
FCO	Foreign and Commonwealth Office
FMS	Federated Malay States
FO	Foreign Office

Acronyms and Abbreviations

GFS	Girls' Friendly Society
GH	Government House
GOC	General Officer Commanding
HC	high commissioner
HE	His Excellency
HH	His Highness
HMG	His Majesty's Government
HMOCS	Her (*or* His) Majesty's Overseas Civil Service
HQ	headquarters
ICS	Indian Civil Service
JCR	Junior Common Room
KCMG	Knight Commander of the Order of St Michael and St George
KL	Kuala Lumpur
KOSBs	King's Own Scottish Borderers
KP	Kuala Pilah
MCS	Malayan Civil Service
NAAFI	Navy, Army and Air Force Institutes
NATO	North Atlantic Treaty Organization
OTC	Officers' Training Corps
PM	Prime Minister
PMC	Permanent Mandates Commission
PPS	Principal Private Secretary
RAF	Royal Air Force
RMA	Royal Marine Artillery
SBA	Sovereign Base Area
SofS	Secretary of State
TUC	Trades Union Congress
UMCA	Universities' Mission to Central Africa
UNESCO	United Nations Educational, Scientific, and Cultural Organization
UNO	United Nations Organization
UNRRA	United Nations Relief and Rehabilitation Administration
UNSCOP	United Nations Special Committee on Palestine
USS	United States Ship

Acronyms and Abbreviations

V	*Vergeltungswaffe* (German reprisal weapon) as in V-1 and V-2
VE	Victory in Europe
YWCA	Young Women's Christian Association

Introduction and Acknowledgements

Reassessment and revision are historians' delights. The present slips away to feed the past; guesses about the future tend to be wrong but the past is always with us and is infinitely malleable. New evidence emerges; new assumptions are made; the certainties of previous generations are questioned and rejected.

In the two decades after the war, colonial territories moved rapidly to self-government and to independence, a majority remaining in the loose association of the British Commonwealth. It would be wrong to suppose that this was forced upon the British governments of the period. Many years before the war the policy was adopted of preparing colonial territories for self-government and independence. The Second World War, however, hastened the process. The war had weakened the British economy so that the cost of maintaining a worldwide empire and a worldwide military commitment was prohibitive. Further, the war encouraged the spirit of nationalism. There was neither the power nor the desire in government to hold on to reluctant populations.

In the *fin-de-siècle* 1990s, there is an opportunity for the revisionist historian of the British Empire to look back at the century in which it came to an end and to reassess it. The twentieth century began with the empire at its peak. It survived the shocks of the First World War and was to enjoy a twilight glory to 1939. Thereafter, came the period of rapid change. The red map of a quarter of the inhabited earth had by the 1970s become multi-coloured.

Introduction and Acknowledgements

The revisionist questions are to do with value and benefit, as well as with practicality. On what values, assumptions and principles was the empire built? What benefit did colonial territories receive from the mother country and what did it receive from them? What benefit did empire give the world? Who were harmed by empire and how? The practical questions are to do with government, administration, law and the management of economies. How was the empire run? By what processes did it come to an end? Ideologies play a part in answering such questions.

Empire claimed the lives and services of British people over many generations in government, the armed services and all other agencies required to run territories dispersed around the world. It was a dimension of life in many families with parents, children, uncles and aunts in the service of the empire. Many took the opportunity to emigrate to empire territories. The story of empire is written in lives.

The lives of the empire builders, pioneers and empire maintainers in the middle generations of empire are readily available and to hand. Yet, the twentieth-century stories are of those whose duty it was to bring the British Empire to an honourable close. It is of particular interest to see how they acted, what they thought of the tasks they had to carry out and what they felt about the empire in its last years.

The life presented in this book is that of Sir John Miller Martin, KCMG, CB, CVO, Deputy Under-secretary of State at the Colonial Office, born in 1904, leaving the Colonial Office at the end of 1964 for two years of diplomatic service as high commissioner to Malta. His war service was in Winston Churchill's private office where from 1941 to 1945 he was principal private secretary, a key figure in Churchill's 'secret circle'. He was then at the heart of things, accompanying the Prime Minister on the majority of his journeys and prolonged visits to see and confer with British and Allied commanders and political leaders.

John Martin saw himself as essentially a servant to his country through his Colonial Office work in two long periods, 1927–40 and 1945–64. He saw the British Empire in its final prewar glory. At the CO he was at the nerve centre of the empire. Early in his time there, he was sent to Malaya for three years to gain experience in the field. After the war, in more senior positions, he had responsibilities in the process of decolonization and of preparing colonial territories for independence and, mostly, for membership of the British Commonwealth.

Some months after John Martin's death at Easter 1991, his wife Rosalind let me see the many papers and letters he had kept and collected in his long and active life. She encouraged me to work on them to see if a life of her husband could be written. It was a most entertaining and interesting task. In these pages I have sought to show in the life and work of John Martin a man of Christian commitment and moral integrity in the service of his country and of the British Empire at times of change, threat and danger.

He was uncle to my wife. I had known him for 40 years as a much-loved and much-admired member of the family. Yet, he was not one to talk easily of himself and certainly in the last years of his working life he was much burdened with the final acts of decolonization. I did see him in action once when I spent three days in Malta in 1966. This was a revelation of the way in which diplomats pick up and assemble information; every event was a diplomatic occasion. It was also clear how people enjoyed working with him. So it was that his life then, and mine for many years after, made it impossible to explore what he had been doing and where. Towards the end of his life, there was more opportunity to draw him out. Yet, a lifetime of restraint and discretion had made it difficult. If you looked for analysis you were likely to get a good-humoured anecdote. He, now departed, has left his letters and papers to speak for him.

John Martin was an assiduous letter writer in the tradition of a son of the manse. His parents kept his letters to them, which run up to his mother's death in 1947. His marriage in 1943 gave him another correspondent for his wartime journeys with the PM and his many tours and duties after the war in the Colonial Office. Most of these letters have survived, as has much of his correspondence with contemporaries in Edinburgh, Oxford and elsewhere, along with other miscellaneous correspondence in defence of Churchill's reputation and of the British Empire. In addition, JM kept many papers and documents from his CO days. These letters and papers provide twin-track documentation. One consists of contemporary letters and papers written at the time of events, and the other of thoughts, comments and reflections on earlier events and actions, often in response to questions or requests to give lectures, addresses or help make TV programmes. This has made the narrative rather like some Western music, when one voice answers or complements another in a series of interweaving themes. This is particularly true of John Martin's experience of the general strike of 1926, Malaya, Palestine and the Churchill years and, after the war, of Cyprus, Africa and the United Nations.

I am particularly grateful to Lady Martin for the opportunity to work on these papers and for her encouragement and interest, and to her son David for his help. The late Professor Kenneth Kirkwood, former professor of Race Relations at Oxford University, gave a considerable amount of help on colonial matters, while Martin Gilbert, justly praised for his great work on the life and papers of Churchill and other subjects, has been helpful and encouraging on matters to do with the war years and Palestine.

I have also had an opportunity to meet or correspond with John Martin's diminishing band of wartime and Colonial Office contemporaries and thank them for their interest. I am grateful also to the authorities of the Edinburgh Academy, the library staff of Corpus Christi College, Oxford, the staffs of Cambridge University Library, the Bodleian Library, Oxford, in particular the Rhodes House Library, Nottingham University Library and the Public Record Office at Kew.

M. J. Jackson, 1994

This life of my uncle John Martin was researched and written by my husband before his death in 1995.

It has been my responsibility to prepare the text for publication. My thanks are due to Maureen Edwards, and to Gary Entwistle for his help in preparing the maps, which were drawn by the Cartography Department of Nottingham University. In these maps John Martin's own spellings have been preferred when on occasion they differ from present-day agreed versions.

J. E. Jackson, 1999

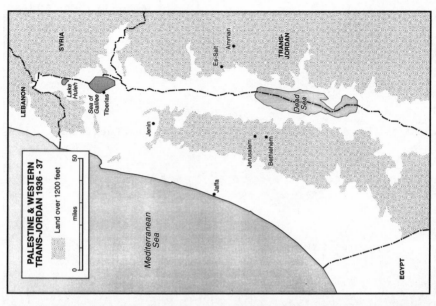

PALESTINE & WESTERN TRANS-JORDAN 1936 - 37

Land over 1200 feet

miles
0 — 50

LEBANON

SYRIA

Lake Huleh

Sea of Galilee
Tiberias

Es-Salt

Amman

TRANS-JORDAN

Jenin

Jaffa

Jerusalem

Bethlehem

Dead Sea

Mediterranean Sea

EGYPT

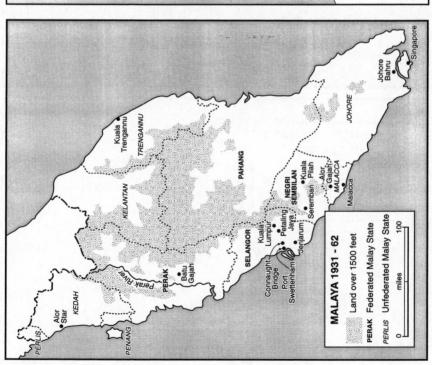

MALAYA 1931 - 62

Land over 1500 feet

PERAK Federated Malay State

PERLIS Unfederated Malay State

miles
0 — 100

PERLIS

Alor Star

KEDAH

PENANG

Perak River

PERAK

Batu Gajah

Connaught Bridge

Port Swettenham

SELANGOR

Kuala Lumpur

Petaling Jaya

Jenjarum

NEGRI SEMBILAN

Kuala Pilah

Seremban

Alor Gajah

MALACCA

Malacca

KELANTAN

Kuala Trengannu

TRENGANNU

PAHANG

JOHORE

Johore Bahru

Singapore

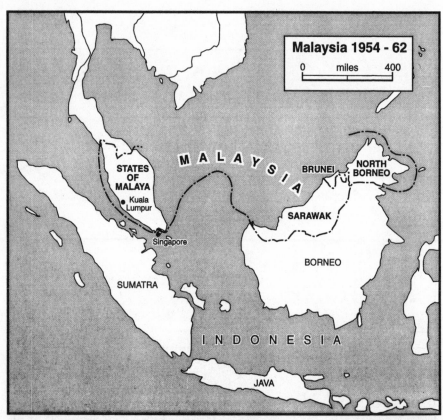

Malaysia 1954 - 62

0   miles   400

STATES OF MALAYA

Kuala Lumpur

Singapore

SUMATRA

MALAYSIA

BRUNEI

NORTH BORNEO

SARAWAK

BORNEO

INDONESIA

JAVA

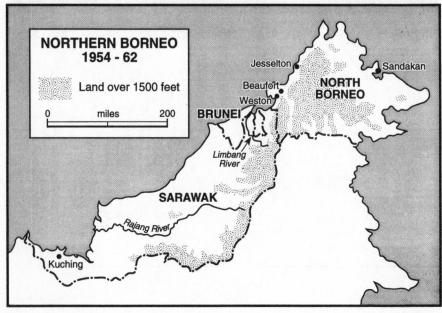

NORTHERN BORNEO 1954 - 62

Land over 1500 feet

0   miles   200

Jesselton

Sandakan

NORTH BORNEO

Beaufort

Weston

BRUNEI

Limbang River

SARAWAK

Rajang River

Kuching

1

Edinburgh, No Better Place
to Live, 1904–23

John Miller Martin was a son of the manse. The plain living and high thinking of his early years set the framework for his whole life. His father, also John Martin, was minister of Free St Paul's in Dundee at the time of John's birth, on 15 October 1904. He was the son of a Perthshire 'pendicler', or farm labourer. Like so many Scots of his generation from humble homes, John Martin senior had a passionate love of learning. As a child, he would walk three miles to Crieff, through all weathers, to seek out the 'dominie', or teacher, with the best reputation. From the age of 13, he was a pupil teacher; only after ten years could he go to study for the ministry in Glasgow.

John's mother, Edith Godwin Miller, was the only child of an Edinburgh lawyer. Before her marriage, at the age of 35, she had had a record of public service in Edinburgh. From her home in George Square, Edinburgh, she had studied with the Edinburgh Association for the University Education of Women. She was a rent collector for the Edinburgh Social Union, a charitable housing association and, in 1898, had been elected parish councillor for the George Square ward. The Scottish Parish Council's duties at that time corresponded to those of the Guardians of the Poor in England, that is, 'the spending of the Poor Rates on behalf of the destitute and broken-down'. In her first year, council records show she made ten visits to two poor houses, attended 88 committees, and visited many 'boarded out' children, once going on a two-day expedition to visit 150 children boarded out in 39 cottages.

She was in demand as a speaker and, in 1900, spoke knowl-

1

edgeably to the Glasgow Council for Women's Trades on opportunities for women in public life. As well as the predictable Girls' Friendly Society (GFS) and Young Women's Christian Association (YWCA), she spoke to the Women's Liberal Federation, concerned with women's suffrage, and the Women's Industrial Council. She deplored the lack of women sanitary inspectors, at a time when infant mortality in Edinburgh was 600 children under five in a total of 1600 deaths in a three-month period.

Her marriage, in 1901, was a happy one. John Martin senior was a widower, whose first wife had died in 1899 after childbirth; their daughter, Jessie, always known as Detta, was then five. Peggy was born in 1902, and two years after John, the youngest, William, was born in 1906. Both Peggy and William became doctors, William in general practice in Peebles and Peggy with the Edinburgh Medical Mission in India.

During John Martin's ministry in Dundee, his forte was evangelical preaching. His stirring appeal attracted so many that the membership rose during five years from 500 to almost 900. The strain of such a large congregation, unfortunately, was too much for his health and, in 1905, he accepted a call to Callendar, according to a history of the church compiled in 1938. The family remained in Callendar for the next five years. Here, it was commented that John Martin found a church 'like the inside of a railway carriage' and left it 'a most beautiful house of God, which fills every worshipper with joy'.

Further deterioration in health led to John Martin's early retirement to Edinburgh, but before that the family spent a winter in Cannes, and photographs record the children of the manse, much behatted, among the splendours of the Edwardian Riviera. Young John, then aged six, thus had an early taste of foreign travel.

Returning to Edinburgh in 1911, they settled at 34 Inverleith Terrace. This was an impressively large house at the end of the terrace, facing up to the Royal Botanic Garden. Edinburgh Academy was only ten minutes' walk below; both boys were entered there, while the girls went to St George's High School. For the remainder of their schooldays the children had both parents at home, both keenly interested in their academic progress.

The household of 34 Inverleith Terrace was lively. Father, in his premature retirement, was at home. He knew the value of education and the hard work necessary to attain it. His liberal Presbyterianism was an encouragement to thought about Christianity and he himself administered its disciplines with a gentle touch. These disciplines included daily family prayers. Even though 34 Inverleith Terrace was a retirement home for John's father, it was a substantial property for a growing and maturing family. Every summer the entire household, including crates of hens, took the train to St Fillans in Perthshire for long holidays, with walking, boating, fishing and, sometimes, golf.

Their mother's notes on Sunday observance survive. She herself was to have 'a sunny face', there was to be 'nothing unworthy, no newspapers'. Sunday was to be 'different from weekdays, Sunday clothes and behaviour. No porridge. Sunday School lesson at worship. All help in the household. All to Church. Church occupations. Writing and pricking texts. Sleep. Family dinner.'

In 1911, John entered Edinburgh Academy. Founded by Sir Walter Scott and other Edinburgh lawyers in 1824, in 1923 the school had 659 pupils: 443 in the upper school and 216 in the preparatory school. The Edinburgh Academy was set up as a rival to the Edinburgh High School, with the purpose of providing a classical education with a prominent place for Greek. There were no clergy among its founders nor was provision made for religious education, but it was assumed that the school's religious policy was that of liberal Presbyterianism.

In John's time at the Academy, the rector was an Englishman, Reginald Herbert Ferard, an old Etonian and a graduate of Exeter College, Oxford, and an inspector of secondary schools before taking up the post at the Academy. John admired him. 'His inclination to the humanities was infectious: he was an excellent teacher of Classics with highly civilized standards in all things.' The staff were almost all graduates of Oxford and Cambridge.

The classical tradition was at the heart of the founders' hopes for the school. Dr Williams, the Academy's first rector, said at the inauguration on 1 October 1824 that, in looking to the times when the youngest new boy had reached the top form class, 'they would no longer shrink from comparison with Eton in Latin versification — nor with the Charter House or Winchester in Greek.' The Academy's motto, composed by Dr Williams, stands in Greek on the facade of the portico of the main building: H

A Scottish Life

ΠΑΙΔΕΙΑ ΚΑΙ ΤΗΣ ΣΟΦΙΑΕ ΚΑΙ ΤΗΣ ΑΡΕΤΗΣ ΜΗΤΗΡ –
'Education is the mother of both wisdom and Virtue.'

For John, the games side of the school was unimportant; walking, fives and golf came into the story but there was little relaxation in his school years. His parents arranged extra lessons for him on Saturdays instead of games. John prospered in the Academy's Officers' Training Corps (OTC) under Sergeant-Major Atkinson, became a sergeant and was awarded his Certificate A, which then was a passport to a commission in time of war. The Academy OTC wore the uniforms of the Seaforth Highlanders. John's military achievement inspired him to offer himself to the London Scottish Regiment in 1939, but his part in the war was not to be a military one.

The First World War of 1914–18 dominated the middle years of John's schooling with its changing news of battle, not only in Europe but in many parts of the world. The empire was engaged and brought into prominence. The sad reports of casualties were brought to the school. Magnus Magnusson, the historian of the Academy, wrote in *The Clacken and the Slate* (p. 295): 'As the annual list increased of medals and decorations for gallantry won by Academicals, so did the toll of war dead, until it reached 298 by the end of the war — 298 out of 1539.'

Some of John's school essays survive. At the age of 16, he had to write on what he would do were he a millionaire. He reveals that he would continue to live in Edinburgh, 'no better place to live in', he would buy a country estate, build an observatory, improve the Edinburgh tramway system, build up a library, tour Mediterranean countries first and then in his own steam yacht tour the world, and make an annual payment of £100,000 to the League of Nations. In marriage, he would avoid 'Americans and dukes' daughters'. He had a lot of fun writing this. The only point on which his master fell out with him was his intention to give money to 'deserving and undeserving charities'. The master thought he had a duty to discriminate.

By the autumn of 1920 John was 16. He had entered the seventh class; all his energies had to go into his academic work and later into preparing for Oxford. In December 1922, a letter came from Corpus Christi College, Oxford, telling John of his election to a classical scholarship.

4

Edinburgh, 'no better place to live in', had many attractions. There were its history and traditions; there was its church life and contemporary leaders of thought. Within the United Free Church, there were prominent names. To the younger generation one of special attraction was the Revd Dr John Kelman, whose obituary John kept. Kelman, who was the minister of St George's United Free Church from 1907 to 1919, had a strong influence on students and young people. He wrote *The Faith of Robert Louis Stevenson* and drew on the life and examples of contemporary leaders of thought like Browning, Tennyson and Carlyle. The obituary says that he came with 'a more joyous outlook on human nature, with a sympathetic interest in the arts and refinements of life, with less of a conviction of the corruption of human nature and its occupations, and a greater sense of the possibilities of realizing the Christian ideal in the everyday efforts and occupations of the body of the people'. He retired through ill health to 7 Inverleith Place, not far from 34 Inverleith Terrace and, like other colleagues, came to the retired John Martin, minister, for consultation, advice and prayer.

John made a lifelong friendship in Edinburgh with Colin Hardie, son of William Ross Hardie, professor of humanities at Edinburgh University and younger brother of William Frances Ross Hardie, a fellow and tutor in philosophy at Corpus Christi College, Oxford (1926–50) and its president (1950-69). Colin was to be director of the British School at Rome (1933–36), official fellow and tutor in classics at Magdalen College, Oxford (1936–73) and public orator of Oxford University (1967–73). John was best man at his marriage in 1940 to Christian Lucas. Colin, like his father and brother before him, was at the Edinburgh Academy, a year behind John, and succeeded John as dux of the school in 1924. The friendship developed towards the end of their time at the Academy. In an early letter of 2 May 1923, John wrote to congratulate Colin on being awarded the senior scholarship at Balliol.

John's Edinburgh Academy years began after the family's winter in Cannes and ended with a European tour. The first part of the tour in Italy was arranged by a United Free Church youth organization. It took John to Rome for four days and to Florence and Venice, the most beautiful of all he thought. For the rest of the tour he was on his own, first in Paris and then in Tours. In each of these he followed a course at the university, attending lectures at the Sorbonne and in the foreign visitors' programme at Tours University. He found his own accommodation in hotels and pensions and delighted in the mixture of people he met. To Colin he wrote:

> the greatest thing has been my wealth of cosmopolitan experiences; it is most illuminating (to use a horrid grown-up word) to see repeatedly and have conversations with Swedes, Czechs, Moslems, Egyptians, Americans (Northerners and Southerners). Then plenty of leisure to read *The Times* has been a great boon: particularly good debate on disarmament and, to an imperialist like me, speech on the colonies.

The course at Tours stimulated him to journalism. He sent an article about it to the *Scotsman* which printed it on 25 August. 'I see that the *Scotsman*,' he wrote to Colin:

> has published today (Saturday) on the middle page an article I wrote on the course at Tours: I wonder if you have seen it. It is horribly penny-a-lineish, I am wondering how much they are likely to give me for it. My first earnings! I haven't had time to read it yet, to see what havoc the printer has made.

In the article, John sets out the content of the course, the variations in its activities and the costs in some detail. He himself kept a careful financial record of his whole tour in a small red notebook. He was much in favour of the course.

> These French courses have a greater value than the mere giving of language instruction implies ... it is impossible to return from such a course with any trace of anti-French feeling; at least it becomes easier to look at international questions more sympathetically and from a double point of view. One can rub shoulders daily with American and Swiss, Spaniard and Italian, Swede and Czech — though the friends one makes are but as 'ships that pass in the night',

one cannot part without something being added to that common stock of friendship and fellow-feeling that is the only hope of the world. I recall one afternoon spent out walking with a Czech for, as we talked, Czecho-Slovakia no longer was a mere strange-sounding name — the breaking up of the ramshackle Empire [Austrian] seemed no longer a mere incident in the making of the peace. It is impossible to forget that boy, his eager face and quick, stumbling French — as he enthused over his country, poured out the woes and injustices of its past etc.

This writer could never have accepted Neville Chamberlain's 1938 reference to a 'far away country' with 'people of whom we know nothing'.

John's years at the Academy were happy and profitable ones for him. He had received through the classics an excellent education and enjoyed living in Edinburgh. He was aware how much he owed to his parents. His European tour in the summer after leaving the Academy broadened his experience and came as a climax to his school years. John attended the school's centenary dinner in July 1924 and continued to keep in touch with the Academy. In John's thoughts and actions, some great virtues were beginning to appear — gratitude to his parents for his family tradition and education, loyalty to his family and school, and responsibility in his conduct, which he had carried as dux of the school and which was a promise for years to come.

In 1952, the year he received his knighthood in the New Year honours, the Academy invited him to chair the upper school exhibition. In his speech, John drew attention to the new Elizabethan age then beginning and pointed out that, for Scotland, it would be the first Elizabethan age. He stressed the importance of parents in the running of the Academy, knowing how much he valued his own parents' part in his education. He would like to have awarded a gold medal to the 'dux of the parents' for those who could best 'implant firmly in his or her boy's mind that true standard of values, those sound beliefs (and I do not mean only religious beliefs) by which alone a good and happy life can be guided'. He then gave his hearers a motto, '*pulsantibus aperietur*', 'knock and it shall be opened unto you'. John saw this as 'expressing the truth that in life effort is rewarded and that the rewards cannot be expected without it'. He took this further and showed the motto to be a great Christian truth.

> Remember them when you are up against religious difficulties. Christian faith is not always easy. It is not easy for finite minds to comprehend and approach the Infinite. But it is part of the Christian belief that God comes to meet men and my motto is matched by that other saying 'Behold, I stand at the door and knock.' If then, when baffling questions arise in your mind, you are ready on your side to receive the answer there is One who is only awaiting your readiness to give it.

These remarks come from his mature years. Oxford was to be a time for reflection on his Christian faith and strengthening it in talk with others. It was also to be a time of preparation and decision for the future. It was certainly where his own motto, *pulsantibus aperietur*, would prove true. John was more than ready to go.

2

Corpus Christi College, Oxford, 1923–27

The Oxford of the mid-1920s, which John was to know, had lost its ex-servicemen and had returned to its intake of pupils directly from schools. A new generation with the Great War, the war to end all wars, behind it looked to a new world in which security lay with the League of Nations and democratic governments. In the east, the successful communist revolution had overthrown the tsar and established the Soviet Union with its messianic message of world revolution, a destabilizing factor in most Western countries. British industry was uneasy, with a series of strikes culminating in the general strike of 1926. It was all very different from the seeming solidity of the prewar Edwardian world. By 1923, the immediate postwar period of plunge into pleasure by bright young things seemed to be over, although the intellectual equivalent of this in 'aestheticism' had a place at Oxford, as Evelyn Waugh's *Brideshead Revisited* revealed. It stood for a life and theory of beauty detached from harsher realities. There is little sign that this had any attraction for John.

When John entered Corpus Christi College in October 1923, his fellow classical scholars were George Abell, with whom he was to share lodgings at 23 Iffley Road, Nalin Bakhle, Philip Boas, John Greenwood and Edward Southby. In addition, a scholarship in modern history went to Eric Schroeder. Correspondence and papers survive in John's collection concerning all of these.

Corpus Christi is small among Oxford colleges, but has a distinctive character set by the founder, Richard Fox, Bishop of Winchester. His statutes of 1517 envisaged a college 'in which the

9

scholars, like ingenious bees may day and night make wax and sweet-flowing honey to the honour of God, for the benefit of themselves and all Christian people.'

By 1923, the college had grown. The president had nine fellows, a bursar, an assistant bursar and three honorary fellows. The college booklet for Michaelmas 1923 named 25 other academics with teaching responsibilities in the college. There were 72 undergraduates, of whom 32 were scholars, 4 exhibitioners and 36 commoners. There were two graduates preparing for the Indian Civil Service (ICS) examination and one reading for a B.Litt.

The life of a conscientious undergraduate in 1923 was demanding. There were lectures and tutorials to attend and preparations to be made for three examinations. The first, a divinity examination set by the college, came in the first year, after which there were two public examinations. In John's case, reading Lit.Hum. (*Literae Humaniores*), known as Greats, he would sit Mods. (Moderations) in the second term of his second year and a final examination, known as Schools, at the end of his fourth year. He would be required in his first two years to attend chapel or roll call four times a week, three times in his third year and beyond that he would be exempt. All were required to attend at least one service on a Sunday. Scholars were required to say grace in hall in their turn. The college gates were closed at 9.05 p.m. A list of those going in and out after 9.05 p.m. would be sent to the president and dean. Charges were imposed; after 12.00 these rose to 2s. 6d. University rules forbade undergraduates to visit the bar or lounge of any hotel, public house or restaurant, to play billiards before 1.00 p.m. or after 10.00 p.m., to loiter about the stage door of any theatre, or to attend any public race meeting. A growing problem was recognized in heavy type under the vice-chancellor's instructions: 'Special regulations as to motor vehicles are displayed in all Colleges and Halls, and all persons in *statu pupillari* are expected to make themselves acquainted with them.'

With no skill in any ball games, John found a sporting outlet in membership of the college boat club. In his first year he rowed; later he coxed the college boat in the Torpids and in Eights week the *Pelican Record* of 2 March 1925 applauded John's coxing. 'Martin at the helm successfully combined racing experience with native coolness of judgement.'

John mentions in his letters that he occasionally played golf and tennis and that he tried his hand at fencing. He also took riding lessons. His friend in Rome, Sarah Lewis, wrote in January 1927 to applaud him. 'I should have approved too of the riding lessons — you can't become a horseman in a few lessons but you would learn a little about it — which is easier to do while you are still young and if ever you were obliged to take it up, it would probably come a good deal easier in consequence.' A few years later, in Malaya, John had reason to be glad that he had had some instruction in riding. In his lodgings, John could hardly escape sport. His co-lodger and friend at Iffley Road, George Abell, came to Oxford from Marlborough with a great reputation. He acquired cricket and rugby Blues, captaining the Oxford XV. Outside Oxford, Abell kept wicket for Worcester County Cricket Club and played rugby for Blackheath.

John found Oxford a great place for developing friendships. He dined from time to time with his 1923 classical scholars, and gave them a dinner for his twenty-first birthday at the Clarendon. They usually signed the menu card and for the Clarendon dinner John wrote 'Hurrah! Hurrah!, I'm twenty-one today, if my head had been stronger my speech had been longer.' John was a member of a college club, the Wasps, and of the Sundial Society, which read and listened to papers on four Sunday evenings a term. John was vice-president of the Sundial in June 1925 and president in December. John was elected president of the Junior Common Room (JCR) soon after his college had provided one. Previously, it had been a smoking room. One of the president's duties was to restrain the young men from breaking up the furniture. In his last speech as president, John warned members against 'ill-advised demonstrations of high jinks and youthful horse-play'.

Some Corpus friendships became lifelong. Two fellow classicists, George Abell and Nalin Bakhle, the Indian, went from Oxford to the Indian Civil Service. Bakhle wrote interesting letters to John in the early part of his service there until his early death. George Abell became a lifelong friend, continually in touch. When Abell married Susan Norman-Butler in 1928 at Chelsfield parish church, John was best man and was later godfather to their elder son.

Another Corpus friendship that became lifelong was with Edward Muir, who also came up in 1923. He was to have a

11

distinguished career in the Civil Service. He wrote entertaining and informative letters to John in his Oxford vacations from the southern states of the USA in 1925 and from Greece in 1926. His mother wrote to John in 1924, applauding him for speaking on behalf of Liberal candidates in Oxfordshire in the general election. 'Tho' I am a strong conservative and don't at all wish your side to get in, I wish *you* all success in your efforts — and only wish more young people would take the problem of their country's Government seriously.'

In John's first year, his letters to Colin Hardie, still at the Edinburgh Academy, are revealing about his tutors. His tutor to begin with was Livingstone, then classics lecturer and dean, but on his departure in 1924 to be vice-chancellor of Queen's University, Belfast, was replaced by Phelps, assistant tutor and classics lecturer. 'He is an odd sort of man with none of Livingstone's refinement, though a good Mods tutor. He speaks his words in little batches of 5 or 6 at a time, with long pauses between the batches.' A few weeks later John is warm in his praise of Phelps.

> [Phelps] is a splendid tutor, as far as practical instruction is concerned, and a very good fellow. Last week he took me out in his car. Our lunch was a picnic in a forest and Phelps produced a bottle of beer for each of us. This we drank from the bottles in a very undignified fashion. Can you imagine Pickard-Cambridge so behaving?

In the college, there was an easy relationship between under-graduates and dons, especially the younger ones. John also wrote about his lecturers. 'Of my lectures the most practical have been Cyril Bailey's on Lucretius and far the most brilliant and inspiring Pickard-Cambridge on Aristotle.'

The Union was a great interest for John; he became a life member and served on its library committee. He enjoyed the debates and took part in them from his first term. He wrote to Colin Hardie:

> Speaking at the Union is rather an ordeal. One has, when a beginner, to wait till about 11 o'clock when every possible argument has been exhausted, when the audience has

thinned to a chilling 40 or 50 who don't listen to your scin-
tillating oratory but are all busily rehearsing their own
remarks and gasping for a chance to get them out.

The *Cherwell* of 24 January 1925 reported Mr Martin (CCC) as
'witty and good. He enlarged on Mr Matthew's Latin and the
Bible's dogs.' It is hard to see the connection of this summary with
the motion that 'This House welcomes the intention of His
Majesty's Government to build a dock at Singapore.' In June
1925, John was called to speak first to oppose a motion that
'Politics do not offer any scope for a useful career.' The *Cherwell*
of 13 June said that 'Mr Martin is restrained and dignified in
manner; his speech was free of erudition and always well phrased.
He did not quite succeed in deceiving the House into believing that
his speech was extempore, but we felt that the midnight oil was
not ill spent.' The *Oxford Magazine* of 18 June 1925 reported him
as contending that politics were 'the very reverse of self-seeking in
the modern world. He dealt with the religious objections to what
is regarded as a materialistic solution for the evils of society. It
was a sincere speech — just a little too long.' Mr Lennox-Boyd of
Christ Church, who was later to become colonial secretary, 'condemned a business career'. John was to work closely with him in
later years and much admired him.

The affairs of the Union did not always run smoothly. The secretary had to write to him over 'a stupid mistake — will you speak
for the motion on Thursday? In favour of "general enforcement of
compulsory vaccination". If you have begun to prepare to speak
against your convictions it will be a help to you perhaps in meeting your opponents' arguments.' Yet, John was energetic in
recruiting new members of the Union. The president thanked him
for persuading 12 of the 24 freshmen at Corpus in 1924 to join.

As a loyal Scot, John attended dinners of the Oxford Academical
Club and the Caledonian Club. John Buchan, later Lord Tweeds-
muir, was secretary of the latter in 1923 and in 1924 became
honorary president. John's signed menu cards of club dinners
survive.

Many of his contemporaries thought John Martin would go into
politics. He was an active member of two university Liberal clubs,
the Liberal Club and the New Reform Club. It became clear that

the choice of career for John lay between the law and the Civil Service. The case for the law was put by John Buchan, whom John had met at the Caledonian Club and who took an interest in Scottish undergraduates, especially sons of the manse.

In the summer of 1926, when he had no public examinations to face, John was to have an experience that influenced him greatly. On Saturday 1 May, in the course of a bitter dispute, the miners were locked out by their employers and the Trades Union Congress (TUC) announced a general strike in support of the miners to begin at one minute to midnight on 3 May. John, writing home as usual, wondered 'whether it would be right to help in any strike-breaking, but, if things go so far as many people fear, it may be necessary to do something'.

By the time of his next letter of 11 May, he was in Hull, having decided, as the majority in the university had, to support the government and to help keep the country going. He was driving and conducting trams, accommodated in a small hotel, *The White House*. Oxford undergraduates had taken on various kinds of work and some like George Abell had become special constables. Of the contingent that went to Hull, most worked on the docks. By the time John arrived on Sunday 9 May, new arrivals were assigned to the trams.

John described this work the following day, 12 May, which was the day the TUC called off the general strike.

> I was on as a Tram-conductor (I can't call them cars in 'Ooll) yesterday afternoon, from 1 till 7.30, and today from 1 till 7.30 (with a short interval of driving). It is monotonous and dirty work but a very easy way of earning a living. There were constant breakdowns and minor collisions and much confusion in turning trolleys etc. Our efforts were watched by large crowds, many people shrieking jeers and abuse — telling us to go and get more Glaxo etc. and worse. Others were more jovial: others again quite overwhelming in their thanks, calling us ''eros' etc!

Though the general strike had been called off, it took some days for normal routine to return. John found that the tramway strike, as he told his father on 13 May, was turning into a local dispute.

It is an unsatisfactory and uncertain position, as it seems as though the continuation of the strike were a merely local affair and not our business. However we appear to be staying at least till tomorrow. The work is often monotonous and a little wearing; but interesting at the same time. The crowds who watch us are now smaller and never threatening. As a matter of fact, the 'ooligans were kept quiet by the firmness of the magistrates at the beginning of the week. A man who had kicked an undergraduate on the leg was given three months. I've met with nothing special; one woman pinched my ankle and ran off making faces and a boy threw some orange-peel but there has been nothing beyond that.

This sequence of letters ended with his reflections back at Corpus on Sunday 16 May.

Here I am back in my own room again. We felt no compunction in going — though we were supposed still to be working on the trams — since the dispute was now only a local one, in which the Tramway Committee seemed to be out to use this opportunity to down their employees. The special constables are back here now, but most of the dockers are still away. Abell had been at once promoted to be Inspector and had one of our dons under him! But the Specials had had rather a dull time. They were mostly billeted in the homes of the aristocracy near Hyde Park.

It seems an age since last Sunday and it is very strange to look back on our feelings when we stood waiting for buses outside the Town Hall only a week ago. There had been rumours of troopers mutinying and bad riots, and I almost expected there to be a revolution in the next few days. It seemed so foolish to be leaving Oxford in the middle of the summer term, and nobody knew how many weeks it might be before we saw it again.

As we approached Hull we had the wind up rather, as we passed two companies of troops marching in with tin-hats, saw all the cars coming out protected with wire-netting, and read of bad riots in the city and many people in hospital. In

Hull itself there was great excitement, with big threatening crowds in the chief streets. County police had been rushed in and had great difficulty even in getting directed to the Town Hall.

His 'Recollections of an Undergraduate' give his later thoughts, contributed in 1971 to Brian Harrison of Corpus Christi for an article, 'Corpus in the 1926 Strike', which appeared in *Pelican* (Michaelmas 1972, vol. 2, no. 1).

My information about the Strike came mostly from news-papers and from listening to broadcasts, which one could hear in one of the rooms of the Union. I think that, like most people, though I had some sympathy especially with the Miners (of whose harsh conditions of life I had read a good deal), I took a pretty grave view of the possible conse-quences of a General Strike, even fearing that it might lead to red revolution. [The Russian Revolution was, of course, recent history.] After some preliminary hesitation I accepted what was, I think, the general view at Oxford at the time, that it was a patriotic duty to support the government in suppressing it. There was a surge of emotional, patriotic eagerness to do something and a feeling that, at such a time of threat to the state, it was impossible to carry on with ordinary academic work. Men went off to queue at the office set up in the Town Hall to offer their services.

The strongest impression to remain with him was of some of the hostility he met.

We were subjected to a good deal of jeering by strikers and their wives (shrieking *tricoteuses* whose bitterness I remem-ber more clearly than almost anything else), especially in the city centre, where we turned the trams. We also saw some quite violent rioting in the streets. By their dress and general appearance Oxford undergraduates were strangely con-spicuous. I remember a group of us going into a large tea-room where a hush fell on the citizens of Hull as they stared at their strange visitors. In a few days the General Strike was over; but the tramway strike continued and we were asked to stay on. We did for a day or two; but had an uncomfortable feeling that the employers were using the opportunity to down their employees so my party of four left before the end.

I won't deny that we found it fun playing with trams and did not mind the discomfort of our living conditions (sleeping two in a bed and canteen meals) for a day or two. But the hate in the eyes of those women was a shock and a hurt and I did not take to the people who were running Hull. How the arrangements were organized, I don't remember; but I think it must have been done by the City Council.

His experiences in the strike opened his eyes to 'the gulf between the "two nations" — to the bitterness of feeling among many of the "workers" and their wives and also to the existence of an unpleasant hardness of attitude towards their employees among sections of the employers'. His mature conclusion was that he had been right in what he did. 'In the light of subsequent experience I do not repent of my action as a strike breaker. I still think that the General Strike was a threat to the state which had to be resisted.'

At Easter 1926, John was attempting a novel. He had a new scheme, he wrote to Colin Hardie, told as his own story and much to do with the loss and recovery of faith.

I am born *c*.1902. On the same day a mob of strikers marches to my father's house; (he is director of the works concerned); a brick is thrown at him and kills him. Often I have visions of an army of poor and angry men. I can't be happy unless I'm trying to right the wrongs of society about which I am morbidly sensitive.

Although this outline of loss and recovery of faith is set out as his own story, it is no more true than his father being a director of an industrial company. Yet, there is a reflection in it of Corpus life, the opportunities to question and debate all topics, especially those of faith. In the midst of these debates, John remained firm in his own faith, received through the Presbyterian tradition of Scotland, and in the value of a national church. His mind was alert to

17

the social problems of the times, division in society, poverty and harsh conditions of work. He was in favour of practical rather than Utopian politics. The outline of the novel was partly a reflection of his continuing religious debate with Colin Hardie and partly a summary of the topics he was turning over with his other friends in the college, the Union and elsewhere in Oxford.

John took the opportunity in his Oxford years to broaden and deepen his understanding of the Christian faith. Rooted as he was in the Presbyterian tradition, he was glad to explore the faith and worship of others. The Orthodox Easter was on the Sunday before the general strike. John gave his father a vivid description of the Holy Saturday and Easter ceremonies of the Russian Orthodox Church in London, which he had attended with his friend Zvegintzov and his family and for which he wore evening dress.

Theological discussion by letter ran on for some years between John and Colin Hardie. From Marburg in 1925, John sought to explain in a long letter the concepts of 'following Christ' and 'communion with God'. With the first, he laid emphasis on the moral qualities of the Christian life and with the second he set out his view on prayer, worship and repentance. In a letter of 15 April 1928, when Hardie was still at Oxford, John wrote of his visit to Gloucester Cathedral with Phelps, his Mods tutor: 'It is one of the places that reminds me of what he, though more than a bit of a sceptic I think, said of Durham — "There must have been something which would make men build a place like that".'

The correspondence was at its strongest in the two post-Oxford years. In it, John appeared as the pastoral theologian and Colin as the philosopher. At the same time, Colin, like John of Presbyterian origin, was exploring other traditions. In a letter of February 1929, when Colin was attracted to Roman Catholicism, John set out his view of Rome.

> The Church of Rome is an intolerant Church, essentially. It has a hard and fast drawn creed and those who will not subscribe to every letter of its creed are left without hope in the world, save only for 'the infinite mercy of God', a convenient intervention *ex machina*. Tolerance of course is neither easy to define nor to practise. It is perhaps the characteristic virtue instilled by Oxford into her children

and no less characteristically often their vice. The essence of it seems to be a singular humility in judging the opinions of another, an unwillingness to reach unfavourable judgements in the absence of overwhelming proof, a realization that variety is as much a feature of the nature of things as unity, above all, in the supreme business of finding God, the belief that *Uno itinere non potest pervenire ad tam grandum secretum*. This does not mean that anything will do for *me*. I, if I am to reach the heart of so great a mystery, must strike consistently and persistently along one road: only I am not to deny the validity of other roads.

By July 1929 Colin was looking towards the Church of England. On 21 July, John wrote:

> The most interesting news is of course that you think of joining the C. of E. 'The only church for a gentleman' said Matthew Arnold, but I don't do you the injustice of my jesting that you look on it in that way. I have a lingering fear that you are not altogether fair to the Church of Scotland, which represents the Church Universal in Scotland [and] has as good [a] historical basis for its presbyterian form of government as England for episcopacy, a very noble history of its own from the early beginnings to this day (the Reformation being no real break in the continuity), and has a notably well educated ministry — though few of the English public school or Oxford type.

John himself was later to become an elder of the Church of Scotland. Yet, living in England, he also worshipped in and supported the Church of England.

Meanwhile, at Oxford, examinations had to be faced. The first public examination was Mods to be taken in March 1925. This was a resounding success for John and his fellow classics scholars at Corpus; all five were placed in the first class. John had already written of the excellence of his Mods tutor, Phelps. This is borne out by other witnesses. Hilary Sinclair remarked that Phelps made great contributions to Mods and reported meeting Phelps one day after he had retired from Corpus and was then doing a part-time

Mods job at Christ Church. He had said 'they have never seen anything like it, they are getting more firsts than ever before.'

The second public examination fell in June 1927. This was Schools, or the finals of Lit.Hum. This time, there were no firsts for the classics scholars of Corpus of 1923. Abell, Boas and Greenwood got seconds, while Bakhle and John secured thirds. Among the firsts in Greats in 1927 were such obvious high fliers as Oliver Franks and Dorothy Emmet. Yet, John had some interesting company among the thirds, including Cecil Day-Lewis and J. H. S. Wild, who later became Dean of Durham.

His third was a cruel blow for John. The sudden death of his father in the January of that year may have been a contributing factor. Because of his father's early retirement, John had seen much of him, held him in high regard and valued his interest and advice. He was able to speak and write freely to his father so that his death removed a pillar of his life. Many of John's Oxford friends had stayed in Edinburgh with his family and they rallied round him in his bereavement.

Of his 'third', John wrote to Colin Hardie on 10 August: 'I've got over the first stunning shock now, but shall never get over my disappointment and haven't the pen of a Saintsbury to defend myself.' Before the exam, he said he had lowered his sights to a second. On 7 September, he said in a letter to Colin:

> I have learnt from the disaster of Greats at least the necessity of cutting one's coat according to the cloth. Till it was too late I didn't realize that at the rate at which I was going the whole ground could never be covered. Indeed the whole fact of *ars longa vita brevis* is hard to learn and it is necessary to get reconciled to being interested much in only a few things.

It was not only that he had spread himself too widely; it was also that, by 1927, the classics grind, which had occupied him for many years at Edinburgh Academy and for four years at Oxford, had lost some of its interest. He had grown out of it. Life had broadened for him. He had travelled a good deal; he had learned other languages; political matters had become important to him; and his experience of the general strike had taught him much about the world in which he was to work. In retirement, he was able to return to the classics with enthusiasm, but now a wider and changing world called him.

The question of career had resolved itself before the Schools examination. Perhaps the strongest influences upon him in his choice were his developing Christian faith and sense of public duty. John was heading for the Civil Service and had put in his name for the August Civil Service examination. The disappointment of June turned there into a triumph. Among the hundreds of candidates for the home and Indian Civil Services, John came first on the Indian list and second on the home list. He was headed only on the home list by Christopher Eastwood. On the Indian list, Philip Mason was second to him. Among his Oxford contemporaries on the home list, Hilton Poynton, later to become permanent under-secretary of state in the Colonial Office, was seventh. His fellow classics scholar, Greenwood, was eighth and Edward Muir, tenth. Philip Boas was seventeenth and went into teaching. Out of the candidates, 10 were selected for the home Civil Service, 50 for the Indian Civil Service and 26 for Eastern cadetships.

The Oxford years were formative for John, years of laying the foundations of friendships, ideas and principles. He kept in touch with his college. It was in Oxford some years later that he found his wife and in Oxford that they married. In retirement he turned to Oxford rather than to Edinburgh, making his home within easy reach of Oxford. He then served his college as a secretary of the Corpus Association, became a member of the Senior Common Room and in 1980 was elected an Honorary Fellow.

3

The Colonial Office, 1927–40

A part from the war years, John Martin's working life was to be spent in the Colonial Office, or on overseas missions in its service. He was to know the British Empire from its zenith in the 1920s to its postwar dismantling and reconstruction following decolonization.

Historians of the British Empire often mark three stages or periods of the empire. The first runs up to the loss of the American colonies on their independence at the end of the eighteenth century, leaving the Caribbean colonies, Canada, Newfoundland and the commercial penetration into India through the honourable East India Company to form the nucleus of the second empire, which expanded greatly in the nineteenth century. British settlers in Australia and New Zealand created an extension of Britain under the crown. In India, the transfer of administration from the East India Company to the crown created the one territory where the crown was also emperor; elsewhere the monarch was *rex*, not *imperator*. The colonies of the Mediterranean, Africa and the Far East, acquired mainly by treaty, rarely by conquest of arms, completed a pattern that showed a quarter of the world's territory coloured red on British maps.

By the time John Martin joined the colonial service, the third stage had already started, that of a commonwealth under the crown. It was a process by which countries of the empire became self-governing dominions within the British Commonwealth of Nations under the crown. The Commonwealth was a voluntary association. At a later stage, some dominions chose to become republics, yet remained in the Commonwealth. The empire at the time John came to serve it was not a stable entity. Change was in the air, gradual at first, but the Second World War and its consequences made change more rapid. Colonies that were not dominions looked for independence. Much of a colonial servant's work was to prepare them for it.

Though changes were in progress, for anyone entering its service in the 1920s the British Empire was a massive fact and a British achievement of which to be proud. Unlike the colonies of France, which were extensions of the metropolitan country and therefore seen as permanently linked to the mother country, the countries of the British Empire were held in trusteeship for future independence. The speed at which independence could be achieved depended on many factors — political maturity, levels of education, economic development and the wishes of the population. In the 1920s and 1930s, it was thought that, apart from the dominions, the speed would be slow and in some, the fortress colonies, British military requirements would put independence in the distant future. After the war it was very different. Expectations of independence were more urgent and British military requirements were reduced, especially after the Suez affair of 1956.

The British Empire had two classes of enemy, low-minded and high-minded. The low-minded wished to replace it by their own rule. The Russian revolutionaries of 1917 sought, through the actions of worldwide communist parties, to subvert not only the British Empire but the world itself. This failed initially and the Russian régime fell back on extending its empire over adjoining territories and, after 1945, over the countries of eastern and central Europe. The end of this century has seen its collapse. A more subtle example of low-minded enmity to the British Empire was in the USA's attempt, during and after the war, to replace the political rule of empire with its own economic dominance of these countries. John Martin was to meet both communist and US hostility to empire in the United Nations after the war.

The high-minded enemies of empire belong to the academic, intellectual world. Imperialism is wrong; nothing good can be said of it, as Edward Said demonstrates (*Culture and Imperialism*, 1993). In a revealing paragraph the author calls a footnote, he 'insists ... on the necessity of a rigorously anti-imperialist position' (p. 291). The remark is in the context of an attack on low-minded anti-imperialism, which he rightly sees as dishonest and corrupting. Yet, what establishes the necessity of the anti-imperialist position? Surely more than the need to be an honest anti-imperialist? Moral exhortation will not do it, nor will the anecdotal evidence and argument the author assembles. These are all contingent; it may sway some minds but it cannot establish necessity. Said has given the reader a statement of faith, which cannot be sustained by the case he puts forward. Suicide by footnote is a rare example of the death of a theory. Empire is a form of government of greatly varied circumstances. Edmund Burke put well the different approaches of the statesman and the academic:

> A statesman differs from a professor in a university; the latter has only the general view of society; the former, the statesman, has a number of circumstances to combine with these general ideas, and to take into his consideration. Circumstances are infinite, are infinitely combined; are variable and transient; he who does not take them with consideration is not erroneous, but stark mad — he is metaphysically mad. A statesman, never losing sight of principles, is to be guided by circumstances; and judging contrary to the exigencies of the moment, he may ruin his country forever.

John Martin's philosophy of empire and of the processes of colonial rule was certainly in the Burkean tradition. His work was not only to put into practice the policies of statesmen but also to help formulate them. He was not one to lose sight of principles or fail to be guided by circumstances; nor was he a romantic about colonial rule; there were mistakes and errors among its successes.

After the war, there was an ideological shift in Great Britain over the empire. Before the war, the beneficial aspects of empire were predominant; after the war its negative aspects were stressed. Exploitation rather than trusteeship seemed to many to be the purpose of empire. The ideological shift weakened the desire to retain empire and strengthened movements towards independence. After the war, Britain had neither the will nor the resources to retain an empire against the will of the natives and local residents. Moreover, India's rapid move to independence in 1947, creating also the state of Pakistan, sent a strong signal to other parts of the empire that were not yet enjoying dominion status. The handling of the move towards self-government within the Commonwealth was an administrative success story in which John Martin played his part. The process depended on consultation, conciliation and agreement. Burma sought immediate independence outside the Commonwealth; South Africa left it in the face of the Commonwealth's disapproval of its policy of apartheid. The changes were brought about by due process. Although there were periods of conflict in some of the colonies in the postwar years, it was only in Aden that Britain withdrew from a territory to the sound of gunfire, which was very different from the French departures from Vietnam (Indo-China) and Algiers through military defeat.

In 1969, two years after his retirement, John agreed to a recorded interview with Charles Carstairs, a former colleague in the Colonial Office, for the Oxford University Colonial Records Project, in which he looked back on his career in the Colonial Office over the changing years. Memory can distort, but John was scrupulous about the truth and his replies to Carstairs's questions give a fascinating picture of the prewar colonial service. Asked why, having no family connections, he had joined the Civil Service, he said:

> I think it was mainly because it was a tradition of my college, Corpus. In spite of its small size it had produced a comparatively large number of Civil Servants through the years, many of whom had reached high office. ... People in the Service said that it offered interesting and intellectually stimulating work with agreeable colleagues. Another attraction they described, which was not confirmed by my own experiences, was that the Civil Service offered ample leisure in which to pursue literary and other spare-time interests.

His first choice would have been the Treasury, regarded then as the top department. However, the practice at the Treasury became one of filling vacancies by transfer of proven highfliers from other departments, a practice through which, John told Carstairs, 'we lost several outstandingly good young men from the Colonial Office.' Learning that the Treasury offered no vacancies, he chose an opening in the joint establishment of the Colonial and Dominion Offices, the Dominion Office having been set up in

1925. The separation of the two offices at that time was more nominal than actual. There was a certain amount of 'eye-wash' about it, John thought, 'because there was still the same Secretary of State and, though there were different Permanent Secretaries and different Parliamentary Secretaries, otherwise it was the same staff serving both Offices. The name "Colonial Office" was put on one side of the door and "Dominions Office" on the other side.' It was a new department to look after relations with the dominions' governments, which had had their status very recently defined in Balfour's famous words as 'autonomous communities within the British Empire'. Also, the Dominions Office was proposing to set up high commissions in the capitals of the dominions and the prospects of working in such places as Ottawa and Wellington seemed to him, at that time, attractive. It was diplomatic work overseas but in British surroundings. Moreover, it was made a condition of admission to the joint establishment of the Colonial Office and Dominions Office that one accepted a liability to be sent for one tour of service overseas. 'When our time came to be sent overseas most of us counted that period one of the happiest in our lives,' John said.

John had never thought seriously of the Foreign Office (FO), not seeing himself as belonging to the social class from which members of the FO and diplomatic service were drawn, nor having private means. John also explained why he had not taken up the Indian Civil Service option, having come top of the ICS list.

Already the time had come when the ICS, which had been such a great service in the past and had taken some of the most brilliant men coming out of the Universities, had changed. I had been rather active in Liberal politics in Oxford and therefore had some familiarity with the agitation for *Swaraj* [self-government] and it seemed to me that the prospect of time being left for a career for British Officers was now small — and that, indeed, is how it turned out.

During his early years in the two offices, John, corresponding with Corpus friends, received from them first-hand accounts of their spheres of service. Their reports widened his own understanding. Both Bakhle and Abell reported from the ICS. If the views of Bakhle, an ardent Indian nationalist, were right, a career in the ICS could not last long. Yet, his own career was cut short by his death in 1935. Had he lived, he might well have been prominent in the new India. In two long thoughtful letters, Bakhle revealed himself to John as 'English in tastes and Indian in sympathies'. He treated John to a careful analysis of his difficulties with membership of clubs in India, a topic important to John because the empire could be said to cohere around clubs. On Christianity, Bakhle said he was less an opponent of Christianity than of all religion, particularly Hinduism. He thought the conflicts of religion in India would be harmful in the future. This line of thought was to lead to the partition of India and the creation of the new India as a secular state. A remarkable feature of this correspondence is Bakhle's confidence in revealing his innermost thoughts to John. The Abells reported their interest in the Simon Report, which came out in 1930. It was a further step in drawing Indians into government.

After only a year in the Dominions Office, John obtained a transfer to the Colonial Office. Contrary to his early hopes, he had found the Dominions Office 'a sort of glorified Post Office, which passed on messages from Whitehall to the Dominions Governments.' The dominions were fully independent sovereign states, a fact Whitehall departments were slow to learn. Much of the work of the Dominions Office was 'to turn into more polite and constitutionally appropriate language messages which, as phrased by Whitehall Departments, might have seemed rather peremptory when they reached, shall we say, Ottawa.' Further, John found that in the Dominions Office there was little contact with people. In the Colonial Office, the geographical departments, which composed most of the office, were in close touch with the colonial governments with which they were concerned, and it was customary to have many personal dealings with officers of these governments and others, when they came to London. This was intensely interesting and the members of these geographical departments took a close personal interest in the affairs of what they regarded as their territories. The work in the Dominions Office, in comparison, was very impersonal. Another difference, perhaps stemming from the nature of the work, was that the control of work in the Dominions Office from higher authority was very much stricter than in the Colonial Office. Drafts had to be referred upwards far more than in the Colonial Office and a Dominions Office junior would never have expected to sign a letter going out from the office nor to have approved it on his own authority; as the drafts went upwards they were examined with a meticulous eye by the more senior officers and altered and re-altered as if drafting a Latin prose. This was rather discouraging to the young. In the Colonial Office, he found that the freedom given to the juniors almost made him giddy. There was far less control from above, it being impossible for higher authority in the office to control in minute detail the varied work of the several geographical departments.

Once in the Colonial Office, John was appointed to the Far Eastern department. The Far Eastern department was responsible for the affairs of the Straits Settlements, the Malay States and Hong Kong, and for British relations with the Borneo territories. These at that time were not under British control; North Borneo was administered by the North Borneo Chartered Company and Sarawak was the personal possession of the Brooke family. Reflecting on that phase of colonial history in the late 1920s with Carstairs, John commented:

> The fact that colonies could be handled in a series of separate Departments like this, does, I think, illustrate the fact that control from London, and indeed, administrative help from London, was comparatively limited. The Secretary of State in London didn't try to run the colonies, they were run by their own Governments and the policy of the British Government of those days can be summed up as being simply to ensure that they were well administered and this was done first and most important by selecting suitable British staff, expatriates, to run the administration and man also the professional and technical services. And also, by control of the Civil Service, by ensuring the promotion of the right people so that efficiency of administration was maintained, and also by keeping some control over finance and legislation, to ensure that they were in accordance with British ideas and that Colonial Governments did not

become bankrupt. But, looking back, I don't think there was much thought in those days about the development towards self-government. No doubt, if the question was asked, it was assumed that in the course of time these territories, at differing paces, would move forward in the same way that the old colonies of British settlement had moved forward to self-government; but the question I think was not often asked in those days, and the policy of the British Government was to provide an efficient, honest, good administration for the territories.

However, as a consequence of tidying up the colonial service in 1930, creating a uniform colonial service and the separation of the Dominion and Colonial Offices, a greater emphasis was to be placed on preparing colonies for independence. In a letter to the *The Times* of 14 January 1972, Sir Arthur Benson (Governor of Northern Rhodesia from 1954 to 1959) wrote of his experience of this policy:

I was selected for the Colonial Service in 1931 long after it had become common knowledge that the job of those selected would be, not to 'govern others', but to help the people whose servants they would become learn the difficult job of governing themselves. This was the key-note of my repeated interviews: and the year's training ... which I then underwent hammered the truth home throughout its syllabus.

I was taught as much as I could absorb in England in a year about how the people of the protectorate I was assigned to lived, and what on, and how they produced it; whence came their religious, political, legal and social institutions ... and what were their aspirations; and in regard to all these how I, as a continuing learner (and only because I had had the advantage of some education — much more than most of them) might help them to develop their institutions as they themselves might decide would be in their best interests having regard to the place they must take as soon as possible in the modern world as independent nations.

This is an utterly different concept, and at the same time a much more difficult and exciting one, than 'governing others'; but during the ensuing 28 years in different African territories I never met a member of the Colonial Service, recruited contemporaneously with or later than myself (other than Africans), who gave me cause to doubt that his outlook, his training, and his gospel was different from that built into me.

Carstairs asked John about the ideas and doctrines held in the Colonial Office in those days; he mentioned dual mandate and *mise en valeur*, which John went on to explain as ideas developed after the First World War, partly through the new League of Nations, which instituted the mandate system, and partly through a more general international interest in colonial questions. The mandate system implied trusteeship for the people ruled by mandatory powers. It was a trusteeship designed to promote their benefit and bring them to political maturity, self-government and independence, a trusteeship also to advance the economic well-being of such territories and their development. He mentioned that, at that time, *mise en valeur* was sometimes expressed as harnessing the tropics.

> When it came to be realized what enormous natural resources the colonial territories contained, minerals, agricultural products like rubber and cocoa and so on, it seemed necessary to apply the new scientific knowledge, new methods to improving production of these, not only in the interest of the inhabitants of the territories, but also in the interests of the whole world, the promotion of world prosperity and trade.

The first Colonial Development Act (1929) put forward a doctrine of development, a change of policy that had more to do, John thought, with relieving unemployment at home than with development in the colonies. It gave the Treasury more flexibility in financial assistance to the colonies. A colony no longer had to be on the verge of bankruptcy before the Treasury could help. John added that the rules of Treasury control had previously been extremely restrictive. He had seen something of this at work in his first years in the Colonial Office. 'I shared a room with a man who was handling the correspondence with the Western Pacific and some of these territories, if not all of them, were under Treasury control and, therefore, could spend nothing unless it was in their approved budget without special reference to the Treasury.'

> No latitude was allowed. I remember seeing many proposals that would come up, shall we say from the Gilbert and Ellis Islands, from some remote District Officer there, saying a storm had damaged his pier and it was essential to add 10 feet at the end of the pier at a cost of perhaps £50. He couldn't spend the £50 without sending a despatch to London and in those days there was no air mail. A very formal despatch was typed out and tied together with chocolate-box ribbon, sent to the Governor of Fiji (who was also High Commissioner of the Western Pacific) to get his approval, then sent by sea to London. Then in the Colonial Office a letter had to be drafted to be sent to the Treasury and weeks would pass before approval was received. Possibly it might be telegraphed out, but as often as not the despatch was sent back by the slow shipping route, and the wretched man in the Gilbert and Ellis Islands had spent all these months without a pier because he couldn't get authority quickly to spend £50. It can be imagined how destructive it was of good administration to have such a slow and detailed control from remote London. The pettiness of the system was very bad indeed for relations.

One controversial issue the Far Eastern department had to face was the opium trade in the context of the League of Nations' campaign against drugs. When sent to Malaya in 1931 one of John's first tasks was to attend a regional conference on opium at Bangkok. John set out the British government's policy on opium at that time.

> In those days opium was still smoked by the Chinese in our Far Eastern territories and was, in fact, the source of a considerable amount of revenue, notably in the Straits Settlements, and the method of control applied was that of state

monopoly. There was a Government monopoly of opium and it was believed that this was the best way of bringing the traffic under official control, with the idea that in course of time consumption could be reduced and restricted and finally completely prohibited. There were undoubtedly people in the Colonial Service in the Colonial territories who thought that the idealism of those who conducted the fight against opium internationally was unreal and that to the Chinese opium was, as some people said, no worse than beer for the English working man. Be that as it may, it was certainly the policy of the British Government to bring the trade in opium to an end as soon as was practicable, and in the meantime by various means to prepare the territorial finances to take the shock of the loss of the revenue that was derived from opium smoking.

Relations between the colonial service and the Colonial Office were always matters of importance to John. At the time he joined the Colonial Office, they left much to be desired, but measures were in hand to improve them, measures from which John himself would benefit.

Relations could hardly be described as cordial. They were the relations you found in the Army, for example, between the front line and the staff. A feeling on each side of criticism of people at the other end of the line, a lack of understanding. It was often forgotten that these men were men of very similar upbringing, background ideals and principles and so on, and that A who was in the Colonial Office, if he found himself in the place of B who was in Nigeria, would have acted in exactly the same way as B did. But somehow there came to be — often was — a feeling that they were a different kind of animal and this was not true.

Selection was part of the problem, as John pointed out; a more unified system of selection was soon to come into effect.

The Colonial Office man was selected by examination whereas the Colonial Service man was selected by a different process, with the one exception that the Eastern Cadet-ships in Malaya, Hong Kong and Ceylon, were filled by the same examination as the Home Civil Service and the ICS. The Malayans in those days took much pride in the fact, but it is only fair to say that it was most unusual for anyone to take an appointment in Malaya unless he came too low down in the list to be accepted for Home Civil Service or for the Indian Service. And so I've heard it unkindly said that these cadets were rejected rather than selected by examin-ation. That was unfair because they had to be up to a reasonable standard to pass and there were many men of very considerable ability in the service. All other appoint-ments in the Colonial Service were filled by a process of personal selection without written examination. This was not primarily a test of intellectual ability, like the Home Civil Service exam. In the Colonial Service brains were taken into account, but there was special emphasis on per-sonal qualities and character. This difference in methods of selection reflected the difference in the duties falling to a district officer in the field and to a clerk in Whitehall.

In my first years in the Colonial Office there was not nearly as much personal contact between the man in the Colonial Office and men in the overseas service as devel-oped later. It was partly this curious suspicion in the service about the Office. I've heard it said that there were Gover-nors who gave definite instructions to their men that when on leave they were to go nowhere near the Office, and in those days men in the Colonial Office did not travel over-seas. Travel was, of course, much more difficult, the days of air travel had not come and it was only occasionally, per-haps as secretary of a Royal Commission or otherwise, that a Colonial Office official would visit the colonies. As I say, this did not prevent them from having a very minute knowl-edge in many cases of the affairs of these territories — quite extraordinarily minute. I remember being told by someone in Fiji that the man who handled Fijian affairs in the Colonial Office and who had done so for many years was so familiar with the geography of the place that he could tell you what buildings you would see on the right and the left as you walked from the wharf for three or four miles inland in Suva. He had never himself been there, never thought of going there, never wanted to be there.

Lack of contact caused suspicion. The solution was to bring colonial service people into the office and to send office people overseas. John described how it worked.

The Warren Fisher Committee, which enquired into the future of the Colonial Service in 1929 and had recommended the loose unification of the service, laid stress on the importance of increasing contact between the Colonial Office and the Service by this method of bringing Colonial Service men to serve in the Colonial Office, usually for two years at a time. They were rather oddly known as beachcombers, but there was never anything opprobrious about this, it was a sort of technical term. In reverse, the policy was accepted that the young men in the Colonial Office should be sent out for one tour of service overseas. Sometimes they would go as a Private Secretary — Private Secretary to a Governor — sometimes they would serve in the Secretariat of a Colony and there were several who went as District Officers, who served in the field in African territories. ... The policy was to work towards the situation where it would be the normal thing for a junior in his early years to have this service overseas. It gave him an idea of what things looked like at the other end, it gave him the feel of colonial administration on the spot and it helped him to form personal friendships with many of his contemporaries in the overseas service. By this two-way traffic the barrier between the Colonial Service and the Office was, over the next few years, very largely broken down. It was accepted that the type of work in the Colonial Office was very different from much of the work in the Colonial Service, so that it would hardly have been reasonable to have had a unified Colonial Office and Colonial Overseas Service; but they worked together as colleagues in a sort of joint enterprise.

In 1930 there were changes in Colonial Office structure.

A Personnel Division was created and separate Economic and Social Service Departments were also established. Thus a double organization of subject Departments and geographical Departments replaced the former almost exclusively geographical organization.

The geographical Departments still continued [to be] responsible for the general administration of their particular territories, but it was also their duty to see that the subject Departments were brought into consultation on any particular matters that affected their territories. The subject Departments were to lay down general practice so far as was appropriate and necessary and to bring in expert advice and assistance from the United Kingdom for the various territories. Also advisory committees of all kinds were developed ... the Medical one, a Labour Advisory Committee ... and a whole series of such committees composed of experts in their respective fields. A large body of advisers was formed. Medicine had already led the way in this: several years before there had been a medical adviser in the Colonial Office. Secretaries of the Education Advisory Committee gradually became, in effect, advisers; in time there was an appointment of Education Adviser. There was a Financial Adviser ... by the time of the years after the war there were so many advisers one couldn't from memory have drawn up a list.

From 1931 to 1934 John was in Malaya, which is the subject of a separate chapter. On his way back from Malaya in 1934, John Martin wrote with an urgent request to return to the Colonial Office rather than to the Dominions Office. The request was not granted. He was first to spend a year in the Dominions Office as private secretary to Permanent Under-Secretary of State E. P. Harding, which brought him a small increase in salary, before he rejoined the Colonial Office with a promotion to principal. The 1930s were years of continuing change and development in both offices and particularly in the Colonial Office. Although seconded to serve as secretary to the Royal Commission on Palestine in 1936 and 1937, he was able to observe these changes and to have some part in them. In the 1930s war clouds were gathering.

His months in the Dominions Office were not happy. He described himself as 'a sort of glorified bell-boy'. Four aspects of his work did interest him. The first was keeping the British high commissioners abroad posted with up-to-date information on foreign affairs, sending weekly Foreign Office print-outs, or selected items from them. The second lay in the close contact with Buckingham Palace. At that period, when the implications of the new dominions system were being worked out, under which the King of Britain was also the King of Canada, there was a good deal of contact between the permanent under-secretary in the Dominions Office and the King's private secretary. This contact was useful experience for John when he went to the Prime Minister's office in the war. Third, John had to keep a file for each of the Australian states, not themselves dominions, so as to keep in touch with their governors and to help in their selection or appointment. The fourth area of interest was John's work as secretary of a small interdepartmental committee of enquiry into the affairs of the Empire Marketing Board, set up as a result of the Ottawa economic conference. The board's task was to increase knowledge of the empire in Britain and trade with the empire.

Yet, he was pining for the day he would return to the Colonial Office. It came after about eleven months as private secretary to Harding. He went back to the Colonial Office to the geographical department that dealt with Palestine (the Middle East one). In those days, Palestine was one of the colonial secretary's most awkward responsibilities. It took up much of his time. There were a great number of parliamentary questions being asked about it and the department had to draft replies to these, often as many as 20 in a single day, not to mention the endless memoranda that had to be drafted for cabinet committees. These responsibilities helped to fit John for his secondment, in 1936, as secretary to the Palestine Royal Commission — the subject of a later chapter.

On completion of his service to the Palestine Royal Commission in 1937, John returned to a Colonial Office geographical department. H. F. Downie, an assistant secretary, was head of the Middle East department and John worked under him in dealing with Palestine, for which Britain held its mandate under the League of Nations. John had various dealings with the Permanent Mandates Commission (PMC). His later conversation with Carstairs noted the differences between the PMC and the Trusteeship Council of the United Nations, which replaced it after the war.

> The members of the Mandate Commission were experts in colonial matters, in colonial administration, appointed by their Governments for that reason, and not simply as representatives of the Government. They were people of high standing. Our own representative Sir Malcolm Hailey, later Lord Hailey, was a quite outstanding administrator from the Indian Civil Service. Then there were such figures as Professor Rappard, the Dutchman Baron Van Asbeck and others ... people whose views were bound to command respect; when they examined the British Government's representative regarding the operation of the British-held Mandate (in Palestine) they did so with responsibility. No doubt we sometimes found the Mandate Commission a tiresome body ... but by and large it was accepted as a reflection of the genuine and legitimate international concern and interest in the manner in which colonial responsibilities were conducted.

John's experience after the war working with the Trusteeship Council of the UN was to be very different. His tribute to the League of Nations' PMC was also based on experience and on friendship with its members.

His work changed again in 1938. He was put in charge of the promotions branch of the Colonial Office's personnel division.

> It handled all the transfers in all branches of the colonial service, that is not only the administrative service but the various professional services and the like. ... We worked a paper system. We had individual reports on the various officers and annual reports on them were sent home by the Governor which were filed in London.
>
> In the early days the ordinary man, except perhaps at the very top, spent his whole life in the territory to which he was posted; but later it came to be seen that there would be advantage in giving opportunities of transfer, of cross-fertilization between the territories, so that, whenever a vacancy arose in any particular territory, not only the local

candidate was considered but also eligibles from other territories; but no-one was compelled to leave his own colony.
... Some people saw disadvantage in the system in that it
bred careerists, people who were no longer so immediately
concerned, so deeply involved in the affairs of their territories. The traditional administrator of the British Civil
Service was tied up in the affairs of the people for whom he
served. Now you got a man who perhaps started off feeling
like that in the Gold Coast but then he went to Malaya and,
before he had learned a great deal about Malaya, he was
then promoted again back to Africa. There were cases of
people who were more interested in their careers than in the
affairs of those they served, but this was a small price to
pay, I think, for the advantage of the greater mobility, the
greater possibility of choosing the best man for the job. And
also, of increasing the attractions of the service for recruit-
ment, which this system undoubtedly did.

There was a disadvantage in a paper system, John thought, that
not all officers in such a large service could be known personally.
They tried to improve it by inviting 'noted officers, those worth
consideration for promotion' to call at the Colonial Office for
discussion about their work and future. This gave the Colonial
Office a chance to judge the man partly in amplification of what
his governor had told in his report.

John also felt that they did not always know enough about the
wife of an officer, an important matter, 'especially in a small
community where people had to get on together and very specially
when a man was in high rank, perhaps the head of his Department, where his wife could be a great help or hindrance to the
job'. John also remarked that they had a special task in the last
year or so before the war.

It lay in drawing up a register of recently retired people
with special experience and qualifications who might be
employed in the event of war; this was in the years 1938
and '39, when it was already apparent that war was hanging over us and was likely to come and there would be a
great expansion of the business of Government in the event

of war, and so it was very desirable to have a central register of people with special skills and knowledge. This took plenty of work and I remember devoting many long hours to it. ... I can only hope that some use was made of it when the balloon went up eventually.

In 1935, John had had a holiday in Rome with Colin Hardie, then director of the British school there. The following year he wrote to him from Peebles where he was recovering in his brother William's house from the removal of his appendix.

You must feel unsettled about the future of the School in Rome. The arrogance of the Romans will be fairly intolerable now and there are points against pitching one's tent within range of the fire and brimstone that may be expected to fall on that satanic government.

Don't you — for once resembling Mr Baldwin — feel a bitter, personal humiliation about the fate of Abyssinia? It was in our power to stop the war and it was our plain duty to stop it and it was also in our ultimate interests to stop it. The hesitation to play the part of leader in the councils of the nations, for which our power and position in the world so clearly fit us, seems to have become a fatally dominant mark of all our statesmanship. We never give the stars in their courses a chance to fight on our side because we resolutely refuse to take a side.

This is a very Churchillian paragraph from the pen of John with its sense of personal humiliation at a duty not fulfilled nor the risk taken to fulfil it. The letter shows a sense of demonic powers at work to be bravely confronted by those who had the power and courage to do so. Italian aggression against Abyssinia and the weakness of the League of Nations were dangerous portents, which did not escape John. Colin Hardie, like George Abell, served as an extension of John's antennae.

'Has the new Roman Empire reached its Limen or does Musso already envisage a whole series of new maps for the Via del Impero? In any case the propaganda in Palestine and Malta and elsewhere will be redoubled.' Peebles redressed the balance for John.

In all this I have found Peebles rather cheering in the immense stability of everything, the solid houses, the solid people — healthy, ordered, well-dressed, well-fed — the fields thick with lambs, the quiet Sunday morning till the resounding tramp of processions to the various churches (where religion, whatever it may be elsewhere, is certainly not an opiate). The air of prosperity, I should add, is due to overtime in the tweedmills on military supplies.

The new Roman empire would seem a poor and unworthy thing compared with the great Roman Empire of Antiquity with which Greats minds were familiar. To the Greats mind, that empire was beneficial, an upholder of law and a bringer of civilization. Moreover, to the Christian mind, the old Roman Empire had a place in divine providence as an agency through which Christianity spread and prospered. The Peebles example of stability and good order has something of the Roman Empire. The rejection of the Marxist opiate view of religion is double-handed. There is no sign of a heartless world there nor are its people in need of narcotics.

The balloon did go up in September 1939, quietly at first for the British in the months of the 'phoney war', phoney except at sea. John remained at his work at the Colonial Office, but in May 1940, when the war was no longer phoney and there was a new prime minister, he was called to 10 Downing Street.

What did he take with him? In addition to his intellect, with its sharpness of mind and personal qualities of honesty, loyalty and agreeableness, he took 13 years of valuable experience. He had learned how government worked at home and overseas. He had learned administration, not only in the Colonial Office work but in the Singapore Trade Commission and the Palestine Royal Commission. He had learned how to deal fairly and pleasantly with a wide range of people across the social range and from different cultures and races. His mind firmly grounded in Christian belief had sought to bring all his thoughts and actions not only within the range of that belief but under its judgement. This was shown not in a parade of religious language but in the quality of his life.

4

A Golden Age: Malaya, 1931–34

In 1931, the Colonial Office had begun to send promising young men for attachment to the colonial service. John, from the Far East department, had been selected to go to Malaya, but the initial response from Malaya was unfavourable. Malaya was suffering from the world recession; times were hard; it would be better to postpone the attachment, it was said. The CO was not put off by this and used a little sleight of hand to ensure that John went. A request had come in from a British delegation to an international opium conference to be held at Bangkok in November 1931 to supply a secretary to the delegation. John was chosen for this task and his presence in the Far East was used to confirm the decision to attach him to Malaya. The opium conference was of a sort convened from time to time to review an intractable problem on which little firm action could be taken but which provided for John's pen the opportunity for Noel Cowardish and Somerset Maughamish accounts of the conference's sideshows.

From Malaya, he sent weekly letters to his mother, letters she kept, which filled a large box. They are a young man's letters, full of enthusiasm and fascination with the new world opening up before him. They are slanted towards his mother's interests in links with Scotland, church going and his health. They give a good picture of an apparently stable empire at its best, portraying a world now quite gone with assumptions now little understood.

The United Kingdom opium delegation was headed by Sir Malcolm Delavingne of the Home Office; John sailed with him for Malaya on 3 October 1931 in the P & O's SS *Rajputana*, shortly

41

before his twenty-seventh birthday. He reported that Delavingne was invited to sit at the captain's table but refused, 'so we sit together at meals. He isn't very exciting company but is affable and very friendly.'

The company he kept in the dining-room included 'a talkative old vice-consul from Morocco, a Hong Kong cadet with one or two HK friends of his, a very nice young police-probationer just appointed to Malaya, the FMS [Federated Malaya States] Warden of Mines whom I'd met in the CO'. Until after Port Said the day went in vigorous exercise in deck games, John claiming he had never been so fit, and in the mornings 'reading opium'.

Among the passengers was the wife of the Governor of Malaya, Lady Clementi. John sought to keep his distance from her. 'Lady Clementi is rather a terror, though in some ways I like her. With her long hair tied up loosely in a sort of turban, she marches round and round the deck very fast and is apt to seize one as an audience for her loud and continuous conversation.' Lady Clementi was to be generous and kind to John in Singapore.

Gibraltar gave John his first sight of empire. He had had the authorities there notified of the ship's arrival. He reported that 'as soon as the *Rajputana* cast anchor the Colonial Secretary [Colonel Beattie, whom John had met at the 1930 Colonial Conference] came on board and took us ashore on a police launch.' The colonel's car took them around the town and high up the rock into the forbidden area. 'I was duly thrilled', he wrote, 'by my first sight of Colonial Empire and we agreed that it was worth coming round by sea (as opposed to overland to Marseilles) for the visit to Gibraltar alone.'

Port Said brought the change from West to East. 'People appeared in their tropical clothes, so did the ship's chairs, the stewards changed into white, coffee became iced and ices replaced the morning soup.' At Aden, the Resident's ADC came on board to collect Delavingne and John for breakfast at the Residency. There they met the governor of Bombay and his wife, Sir Percy and Lady Sykes, Aden being a dependency of the Bombay presidency. 'The Residency was the coolest place we had been in for days — wide empty rooms with overhead fans.

Arabs handed round iced barley-water and cigarettes.' A six-course breakfast followed.

The next empire call was Colombo, where John met various officials on board including the inspector-general of police, the head of the medical service, the secretary to the minister of health, the head of the CID and the governor's secretary. Ashore, there was a discussion about opium and the illicit drug traffic and a visit to the depot where government opium was prepared for sale. From Colombo, Delavingne and John were taken in the Government House Daimler to Kandy, the ancient capital, 70 miles away.

The outward voyage reinforced John's respect for the empire, which he expressed in a letter to Colin Hardie some weeks later, his 'Good Friday creed', written on that day in 1932.

> It is of critical importance to ourselves and to the world that we should act worthily of and maintain the dominating position to which the efforts of the Victorians brought us. This is not jingoism: it is simply the realization of our responsibilities. Our position is one which may very easily be lost ... but it is impossible to travel down the red corridor by Gibraltar, Suez, Aden and the Red Sea and on to Ceylon and the East and to see British administration at work in a country like this, without believing that if the power of the British Empire were to crumple it would mean taking the keystone from the arch of civilization and the loss of powers for good which are tremendous beyond calculation and which would not be replaced. All of which will sound bombastic, so please don't show this to anybody else as a material for mirth, for it is my creed.

The Good Friday creed, drawn from the red corridor vision of the voyage to Malaya and from what he was beginning to observe there, was the understanding of empire John was to test out in the prewar years, first in Malaya and then in Palestine, as well as in his other Colonial Office work. It carried a conviction of the benefit the British Empire brought to the countries and people it ruled, 'the keystone of the arch of civilization', yet was aware of the risks posed by its enemies. Military enemies brought down empire in Malaya in 1941–42, while the voices of ideological enemies were never silent. After the war, while holding his creed of the good which the British had brought and still could bring, amid changed circumstances, John had to prepare for and put into practice self-government in a large part of the empire.

The country John was approaching and where he was to spend almost three years had a complex political organization. In 1931, the bulk of the Malayan peninsula was composed of nine Malayan states, which had entered into a treaty with the British government. Four — Perak, Selangor, Negri Sembilan and Pahang — composed the Federated Malay States (FMS). The FMS had some central control from Kuala Lumpur with a British Resident in each state. The rest, Johore, Kedah, Kelantan, Trengganu and Perlis, were unfederated states. These had a measure of self-government supported by a British adviser. In addition, the colony of the Straits Settlements consisted of Singapore, Malacca and Province Wellesley, which included Penang, as well as Labuan in North Borneo.

The chief officer in the Malayan Civil Service (MCS) was entitled the Governor, Straits Settlements and High Commissioner for the Malay States, based at Kuala Lumpur. The MCS provided a variety of legal, administrative and other services, with some of the senior posts combining functions in Malaya and Singapore. Others had duties in both federated and unfederated states. The main field officers were Residents, advisers and district officers. It was to them that John would be usually attached. The MCS list for 1931 shows that appointments in the senior classes were exclusively British; some Malayan names appear in the lower classes IV and V. Tunku Abdul Rahman appears in class V as assistant registrar, Supreme Court, Ipoh.

The *Rajputana* reached Penang on 29 October. At Halloween, John reported that 'my new country is as wet and grey and almost as cool as summer at home.' An hour out from Penang, *Rajputana* was met by the governor's yacht and Sir Cecil Clementi came aboard to greet his wife. Sir Cecil's private secretary and ADC gave John his programme for the next two years; 'a pretty mixed grill', he called it. As set out at the beginning, it was to consist of one month in Singapore (presumably in the Secretariat), four at Kuala Pilah (Negri Sembilan), said to be a very beautiful 'district', four at Batu Gajah (FMS), four at Alor Star (Kedah), one at the federal secretariat at Kuala Lumpur, one on the east coast, one at Malacca and four in Singapore, 20 months in all. Later, it was to be extended by John's appointment to the secretariat of the Singapore Trade Commission. Immediately on arrival, John and Delavingne were taken to the Residency for a large lunch party given by the resident councillor, the chief government authority there, where John first met Malay leaders, the Sultan of Perak and the Tungku Malkota of Pahang and others who were to take part in the opium conference. After lunch there was a discussion on opium. John was staying at the Runnymede Hotel, 'said to be one of the best in the Far East, which I can well believe'. In the evening, John reported that 'the *Rajputana*'s band played dance music at the hotel and champagne flowed freely — thus confirming a traditional Colonial Office belief.'

Opium was John's main concern at this stage. Delavingne and John were taken by the Penang head of the Monopolies through coconut plantations and padi fields to an opium shop 13 miles out where they watched customers buying opium. They were also taken on a preventive launch to watch searchers at work on a newly arrived steamer. John commented that 'the search is astonishingly thorough, baggage is examined most minutely and even bits of the ship are taken to pieces; but, as it happened, we saw no seizure.'

Delavingne and John travelled to Bangkok by train, a slow journey around the Gulf of Siam. For the conference, Delavingne and John stayed at the British legation, guests of Cecil Dormer, the British minister, and his wife, Lady Mary. Their first morning was spent in going round the palaces of various princes, signing the visitors' book. They had also signed the King's book. John went out in a canoe with Lady Mary along some canals where it was possible to see more of how people lived than from a car. Later there was another canal trip, this time in sampans.

> On Saturday night ... Lady Mary, two of the young consuls and I went for an evening expedition in sampans on the canal behind the legation. It was all rather beautiful by moonlight and interesting to see the people in their riverside houses. One family was busy fishing with a net on poles of Heath Robinson design, another was preparing buffalo

flesh and so on. Hearing sounds of revelry from one of the neighbour's houses (a rich Siamese, incidentally a leading member of the Anti-Betting League here, though he has just won a number in the Irish Sweep), we paddled up and joined the party. They were all squatting on a floor or raft by the water's edge listening to a performance by entertainers on a boat moored a few yards out. As we went ashore, a fish jumped right over my head. One of the performers was dressed as an Englishman, in 'pink' coat and top hat, and kept hectoring his 'boy' in a loud voice in a mixture of English and Siamese. All this was received with roars of laughter by the audience (all Siamese). Just when they had handed us refreshments I saw the dishes being washed up in the filthy canal water beside us.

On the opium trail John reported a visit to a Bangkok opium factory and to a number of smoking-*divan*s. An American with them said he had never seen so much concentrated beastliness, but John wrote that 'it didn't strike me like that at all. The *divan*s are simply a sort of club, in which men have a smoke together after the day's work. One was quite a large place with three storeys and people streaming in, just like a Lyons Corner House.' The opium conference itself met every morning. John did not find its discussion impressive, which was not surprising since little could be done 'so long as there are unlimited supplies of illicit Chinese opium'. The speeches were all in French or English; 'each is immediately translated into English or French as the case may be, an extremely wearisome process and rather absurd as all the delegates except the French speak English.'

The 'side-shows', as John called them, continued in dinners, receptions, visits to the Sacred Mount, to canals, to markets, even a visit to see white elephants at the king's palace.

When the conference ended, John took the train to Penang and then a ship to Singapore, where he was to spend a month.

The head of the office, i.e. the (acting) Colonial Secretary (M. B. Shelley), is, I gather, the man who objected to having me sent out and he hasn't done anything towards making my month in Singapore useful to myself or anyone else. The only work given me is to be secretary of a committee, which isn't going to meet until after I leave.

The reality was not so bad. There was opportunity to see the Secretariat at work and to visit government and other projects in and around Singapore, time to learn Malay, to buy and learn to drive a car, time for riding, golf and hospitality at Government House.

He also saw the liquor control system where he watched tests of *samsu* being made in a government bonded warehouse; the government toddy shops; the chief of police who explained police organization in Singapore; the film censor at work cutting out Manchurian war pictures from a news film; the new naval base, where works were in progress on 'an Egyptian scale'; and the sultan's palace at Johore Bahru. Just before Christmas, John met the head of the medical service in Malaya and saw over the King Edward VII Medical College — its degrees had been recognized by the General Medical Council for 15 years.

It was soon time for the next stage of John's secondment, four months at Kuala Pilah in Negri Sembilan. He drove up with an overnight stay at Malacca. At Kuala Pilah he had his own house, which he adorned with drawings.

> I can't describe to you what a perfect place Kuala Pilah is and am afraid of sounding too ecstatic: the nearer landscape of green padi fields, houses on stilts, coconut palms and small rubber plantations; the distant views of tree-covered hills (specially fine on the road to Seremban, winding up and up through a gorge, with primary jungle on all sides); the polite, finely-formed Malays, their herds of goats and the water-buffaloes as an anticlimax to my rhetoric.

John took to the district officer and formed a lasting friendship with him. 'Macpherson,[1] the DO, is a very congenial person to be put with — Edinburgh and still comparatively young. His English wife too I like.' John was introduced to and joined the local club. The European community was small and consisted of the district officer

---

1. Sir John Macpherson was to become permanent under-secretary in the Colonial Office from 1956 to 1959.

and his wife, a Scottish woman doctor, a Public Works Department engineer and his wife, a schoolmistress, a schoolmaster, a matron, a hospital sister, the police superintendent and a few planters (a much-reduced band with much-reduced income, John reported). John used the club's diminutive nine-hole golf course.

In a letter, written for his mother's sixty-sixth birthday, he made clear the debt he owed to his parents.

> I felt specially on my first Sunday in this country, up at Penang, after the Presbyterian Communion Service there, that amongst all my utterly new surroundings ... that I had several firm anchors and I owed them to you and Father. You haven't solved for me all the theological puzzles and difficulties and I don't share all your opinions (e.g. about prohibition!) — what generation ever shared all its parents' opinions? — but you gave me long ago some principal certainties and standards which are part of myself and for which I'll have reason to be grateful to the end of my days.

The letter also mentioned his happiness in Malaya.

> I can hardly believe in my good luck in having my two years here: it seems almost too ideal. In many ways I'd like very much to be here permanently but from the ambitious point of view I believe it would be a mistake and I don't seriously think of it. It will make all the difference in the world to work in the CO afterwards, though I rather wish I could have a similar tour in Africa.

John gave a short account of his mornings.

> Each morning I go down to Macpherson's room at the office and generally sit and read and watch what is going on. His room is quite open; all sorts of people come in at any time, with all sorts of troubles. I'm beginning to be able to follow what conversations in Malay are about though I'm far from following every word.

He went on to comment on the use of Malay officers.

A Golden Age: Malaya, 1931–34

Today I sat in Court beside the (Malay) magistrate who was
taking minor civil suits. The use of Malay officers is one of
the most interesting things here. In the District Office (with
all its land work and civil and criminal courts) Macpherson
is the only European. There used to be a European Assistant
District Officer, but quite recently he has been replaced by a
Malay. It is very much a Malay district and a large part of
the land (apart from the 40% which is Forest Reserve) is
'Malay Reserve', i.e. it can only be sold to Malays — and it
is mostly 'customary land' — division of estates etc. following the local matriarchal system.

John's syce (a groom and in days of the car, a driver) Mat Nor
was a continual source of interest.

He is getting married as soon as the Fast Month (Ramadan)
is over and is full of the preparations. It means giving him a
week's leave and I am paying an extra month's pay towards
the expenses — $150 for his own absurdly gorgeous wed-
ding garments. He is a nice lad and I find him useful as a
dictionary; it seems to be characteristic of a Malay servant
to talk freely with his Tuan and yet always be extremely
polite and never forget his place.

An early discovery John made was the high infant mortality rate
in the district, especially among Tamils, with Chinese and Malay
rates not far behind. There were only two doctors, a Tamil man
and the Scottish Miss Robertson; there were no dentists and the
first trained midwives had only recently begun to practise. However, through elaborate drainage of the subsoil and other areas, the
district took trouble to keep down malaria-carrying mosquitoes.
The high infant mortality rate in parts of Edinburgh had been a
particular concern of John's mother in her years as a rent collector
and parish councillor.

As a good Scot, John enjoyed a walk. He described a typical one
between tea and sunset.

I took the car out about five miles and leaving the syce to
guard it walked for about three-quarters of an hour out

along a bridle path through padi fields and kampongs. A great many people, all very friendly with smiles and salutes, asked 'where are you going?' on all sides. A man who overtook me got off his bicycle and came with me; we were a party of four by the time I turned back. On the return journey another man, who walked with me for a short distance, asked me in to his house to drink a coconut, an invitation which I gladly accepted. It was a tiny house on stilts, the first I had been inside. I sat on a mat on the verandah and drank from the nut, opened by the man's wife with a large chopper. I offered him a cigarette, forgetting that this was the fast month — a gaffe which caused much merriment. Then on to where another man attached himself to me and explained the poverty of the padi as due to the laziness of Malays and the depredations of rats, while another complained that, the date of planting having been changed by the last DO, all their rice was already eaten five months before harvest — to which I could only say that it was a good thing the fast month was on. Which is all very good for my Malay and for letting me see the life of the 'rayat', which is supposed to be the special purpose of my sojourn in the Kuala Pilah district.

A European coffee-growing couple provided a contrast.

I visited a pair of heroes, who live, I suppose, forty or fifty miles away in a remote place where tigers roar and elephants trumpet at night. The husband has been out over twenty years as manager of rubber estates and now, like so many others here, is out of work. But he has taken up coffee growing, which is very rare now, learning only from a Kenyan book and roasts, grinds and packs and sells about eight hundred tins a month. It isn't yet a paying concern and he and his wife with their two children (two and five) live very simply in a rough native-built bungalow on almost nothing, using up their savings and still hoping for the best as more and more bushes come into bearing and their market develops. The wife helps with the weeding and roasting, cooks, keeps a vegetable garden, breeds hens and never has time to miss the shops and tennis to which she was accustomed. But they both looked fit and so did the children; they seemed thoroughly happy, though anxious about the future.

A visit to a new centralized Dunlop factory showed the new technology in rubber making, a technological improvement that tended to squeeze out the smaller estates. John also experienced one of the satisfactions given to colonial officers in the field. The district officer and John drove out to a village, Johol, where there was 'a complaint that a planter was blocking the villagers' access to a road. By the time we left men were already at work demolishing the obstruction (a small instance of the "seeing results" which must be such a joy in work here, but is so sadly lacking in the CO at home).'

> Yesterday morning I was out with the DO on a sanitary round before breakfast, visiting the market and various coffee-shops, and I was surprised at his strictness, ticking the people off for the least sign of dirt or untidiness and refusing to renew their licences until he is satisfied. There was rather a mess of fruit peel and other rubbish at the Chinese theatre, so ... they could not open for their Saturday matinee unless they had had a thorough clean up and satisfied the inspector. The Chinese must think all this very mad; but they have to have a licence for almost everything and know that these will be taken away if they don't do what they are told.

He attended the wedding ceremony of his syce at Alor Gajah in Malacca territory, staying with the DO there, Cobden Ramsey, who accompanied him. It took place at the bride's house. Some time after 9.00 p.m. the bridegroom arrived; the marriage ceremony proper then began.

> He knelt at one end of the verandah in front of an elder, the bride not being present, and repeated a formula accepting her at the stated price. This formula has to be repeated word perfect and he had to say it several times before the

presiding elder was satisfied. There were then prayers and the bridegroom withdrew, while men and boys kept up a prolonged chant (apparently part of the Koran), some bawling for all they were worth, with their neck-sinews standing out, and almost working themselves into a frenzy. This ended with the reappearance of the bridegroom, arrayed as a warrior-prince in long red robe and richly decorated gilt crown, a silver-handled umbrella held above his head. He was taken out to the road where a procession was formed, boys in front with candles on decorated stands and a band behind, and all marched slowly back to the house to the accompaniment of noisy shouts, strenuous work by the band and deafening crackers. At the house we waited for the bride (aged 16) to make her appearance, no less ornately dressed as a princess, with heavily-powdered expressionless face like a Siamese dancer. The two then sat together on chairs outside and there was a short display of comic shadow-boxing by some of the guests, after which they withdrew into the house and sat on canopied thrones for the sitting-in-state. For this evening they are treated as royalty and five men (including the DO and myself) went and did obeisance to them and sprinkled some sort of liquid and rice on their hands. We then sat in front of them and partook of still more cakes and cold tea. My legs were now breaking with this prolonged squatting (they were quite stiff for two days afterwards) and as soon as we decently could we made excuse and went outside; but there found ourselves expected (though it was now well past midnight) to sit down to curried meats and rice, eaten with the hand.

John's experience was continually broadening. He attended the annual homage of a *lambaga* (tribal chief) and his people. Forest visits followed school visits, Malayan and English. He was given evidence of the growth of communism among the Malays.

On Saturday there was an interesting meeting of minor chiefs from two 'parishes' where a pretty large Malay communist society has been discovered — 400 or 500 members. The detective lectured them about it and there was a dram-

atic moment when, unwittingly, he mentioned to one chief
... [that] on the list of members [was] the name of his own
son. Communism is common enough among the Chinese,
though it is always sat on very hard and those convicted are
usually deported; but among Malays it is very rare. It seems
to be mixed up with religion — I think with the modernist
side of Islam; but I don't know much about it.

He also saw evidence of poverty.

Went with [the] DO for rent collection to a village some
miles off; but owing to the hard-times (a pound of rubber
brings in less than a coconut) there weren't many people
ready to pay. It is pathetic to see people unable to raise such
small sums as one dollar and asking for several months
postponement in which to scrape the amount together.

My syce is a very nice cheerful person, keeps the car
spick-and-span (says he wants to buy it from me eventually), is a champion boxer, keen on soccer, knows quite a
little English. His wife is a merry person, judging by the
noises from the back-quarters. The 'boy' Abu Bakar is older
and apt to look surly, but is always ready to break into a
smile which has been compared to sunrise. His speech is
rather gruff and difficult to follow — he knows little or no
English — and he stutters when nervous. There is a lurid
tale attached to him which I'll tell you some day. He keeps
the house very clean and looks after my clothes, laundry etc.
without any need of supervision. He has recently become
very religious (Muhammadan, of course,) — which is apt
not to improve Malay servants — and rises betimes for
prayer: strange chanting noises can be heard in the evening.
He has a wife but no children. The cook is Lim Heck
Theng, Cantonese. He told me he had no wife: but I believe
he has one in China. Mat Nor told me he thought him half-
mental, which confirmed my own impression; but he cooks
well and seems clean. His range of sounds do not include
several of the commoner consonants. I am not sure whether
his English or his Malay is the more difficult to understand.
When I have bacon he has to wash the plate as Bakar won't

touch the defiling pig. I pay them each the same — $30 a month, from which they provide their own food. This is slightly above the present market rate here in Kuala Pilah, though not more than is paid in bigger towns.

By the beginning of June John had returned to the Land Office in Batu Gajah. He was able to tell the 'lurid tale' after dismissing Abu Bakar at the end of May.

Now that he is gone I can mention the alarming discovery that he had lost his last place for attacking a European with an axe. It was a gross piece of deception on the part of the Bonars ... who sacked him to send him to me with a most glowing testimonial and no mention of this. I discovered it only a few days after engaging him and had visions of an amok; but after all there was nothing worse than harmless quarrels with the laundry in K. Pilah and a cook in Ipoh. I have sent him back to Negri Sembilan, which is as well, for he has sent a silly threatening letter to my syce whom he evidently thinks responsible for his dismissal.

John was in Malaya at a time of economic recession. His letters often refer to it.

Today I went out early to a rubber estate some miles off, where the manager showed me round and explained every-thing — the tapping and the manufacture of sheet rubber. Breakfast afterwards with him and his very nice wife. The news that rubber restriction is definitely off is welcome as the end of months of uncertainty; but the remaining planters are shaking in their shoes and today three of them whom I know here have got news that they're being sacked and the estates closed down.

Meanwhile all day long the office is filled with miserable people who can't pay their rent — often it sounds a ridicu-lously small sum — and come begging for a few months grace. Over a thousand lots are down to be sold by auction tomorrow for non-payment in this district; but Macpherson will withdraw as many as possible. Fortunately the Malays are protected by an enactment which prevents the sale of holdings in any of the large areas proclaimed as 'Malay reservations' to anybody but a Malay.

His family were interested in the religions of Malaya. He supplied this picture.

The Malays are Muhammadans. They were converted by Indian missionaries *c.*13th–15th centuries; but it is a very tolerant form of Islam and they have retained a good deal from their primitive animism and a good deal that is Brahminical in their ceremonies. The British Government is bound by treaty not to interfere in matters of religion, so the imams have quite a lot of power in their own sphere and hold their own courts — e.g. fining people who don't come once a week to mosque and even distributing estates. Women are much freer than in most Muhammadan countries; but of course the peculiar matriarchal system in this state is a pre-Islamic survival. I have never heard of Malay Christians and doubt if there are more than a very few, though there are probably considerable numbers of rather lukewarm Muslims, particularly in the towns. There must be thousands of Chinese, Eurasian and Tamil Christians (mostly RC); but, judging by the number of their temples, most of the Chinese must be Taoists or whatever Chinese are. Most of the Tamils are Hindu and build themselves little images and shrines. I saw the other day a brand-new Hindu temple built by the Dunlop Rubber Co. for the Tamils on one of their estates.

John also wrote about the day celebrating the pilgrimage to Mecca, Hari Raja Haji, the great day for all those who have made the pilgrimage.

Incidentally large numbers go on the pilgrimage (to Mecca) each year; it is quite an industry, organized parties being run by Arab 'sheikhs' with headquarters in Singapore. There is apt to be trouble about people trying to sell tribal (i.e. entailed) land so as to go to Mecca or selling all their private property and coming back penniless. The modernist party in Islam here seem to think that it is a money-making idea of the Arabs and say that, while it is all right for well-to-do people to go to Mecca, there is no need for poorer people to make the pilgrimage.

John's time at Kuala Pilah was drawing to a close. After Easter 1932 he had spent a few days in the mountains with the Macphersons in a bungalow at Fraser's Hill. He went on to attend the three days of ceremonies for the Yam Tuan's birthday.

There aren't many wild flowers, or at least they don't strike the eye, though a few trees, e.g. flame of the forest and the tulip-tree, come out in a blaze of colour. In gardens most of the decoration is done by plants with bright leaves; but big clumps of cannas are common and morning glory flourishes. A few people grow roses but they are not a great success at the lower levels. There are various flowers of the orchid type, some rather like sweet-peas at a distance. There is always lots of rain and lawns are easily kept, though usually of very coarse grass.

I think the stilts on which the houses are built must originally have been meant to raise them above the swamps or rivers by which they stood as much as for defence against beasts. I have seen bamboo stockades which are no doubt for that. The stilts also do something to reduce the danger from insects and snakes (you mustn't whistle in a Malay house for fear of attracting snakes); but on the other hand it makes it easier to be knifed through the floor and there is a special word for stabbing in that way.

Between Kuala Pilah and his next posting he went eastwards to Pekan at the mouth of the Pahang River where the governor met in conference with the sultans and Residents of the Malay states. The posting was northwards to Perak at Batu Gajah near the town of Ipoh with its 50,000 inhabitants, as collector of land revenue in the Land Office. However, this was not to last long. He was soon given other work, which meant a daily drive into Ipoh, 12 miles away. He was to be deputy chairman of the Sanitary Board, in effect deputy mayor of Ipoh. 'The work is the ordinary work of a municipality — town planning schemes, assessments, new buildings and alterations and so on.'

Tin mining was an important industry in Perak. He visited a Chinese opencast mine with one of the inspectors of mines and saw over a dredge and a Chinese opencast mine.

In addition to his social obligations and public events like the King's Birthday celebrations in Ipoh, John had opportunities to see other developments. He visited Tanah Rata, a new hill station in the Cameron Highlands 4700 feet above sea level. Here he found 'wide stretches of highland are being opened up for (mostly European) settlement and tea and other plantations are being started'.

Three contrasting events were all described in one letter. The first was a visit to sports day at the Malay College (the Eton of Malaya), where he enjoyed 'a sumptuous tea of sardine sandwiches and cakes'. The sports 'were not very thrilling — the mile was ridiculously like a slow-motion picture — but I met a good many people and there was an unusual array of big noises — all four Residents and Clementi himself as well as the Sultan of Perak'.

The second was an inquiry into debt.

> Today I set off after 7 o'clock with a Malay settlement officer to Tronoh and picked up the Penghulu there (Malay 'parish' officer) with whom we drove in a lurching rickety old car along the roughest imaginable road to a fair-sized Kampong in a Malay reservation. There we went about from house to house asking the people questions about the amount of debts they owe — for country people suffer as much from official questions here as do the slum-dwellers at home — and when it was all done were entertained with tea, coconut milk and fruit and then rattled back to an assignation with Col. Leslie, the head of the volunteers, and the State adjutant, who were looking for a ground for artillery manoeuvres

The third was a visit to Chinese temples with Dakers, the Protector of Chinese.

> We visited some rather remarkable Chinese temples in cliffs

off the Gopeng road. In the biggest you go in past a pond of lotus and find yourselves in a big cavern, with several (Taoist) shrines, and from this grope along a dark tunnel to another similar grotto beyond from which steps carry up to a series of caverns one above the other, with more shrines, fantastic rock shapes, and views out on to the plain far below. Altogether a weird place, with the screech of bats, faint smell of burnt joss sticks and dim gilt images in their shrines.

A journey by elephant was a test of his riding ability.

I took Meor Ahmad, the Malay Assistant District Officer in the car after breakfast to Pulai, a mining village some miles off, where a lot of elephants were waiting for us. They seem to have expected more people but for various reasons there were only 4 of us — Meor Ahmad and myself with the Penghulu (whose father, a rich Malay, owns the elephants) and Raja Yeop (a Settlement Officer). We went on two elephants, two on each, sitting on a basket saddle, with our legs dangling over the side, a Sakai sitting on the beast's neck to drive it. Servants on a third elephant and men with baskets of goods on a fourth completed the party.

There was quite a little excitement before we started when some extra elephants arrived and one of them (said to be aged 60) was recognized by her daughter (aged 30) who was waiting with us. The daughter rushed up, hitting against my car (and only avoiding wrecking it by the narrowest margin), and there were loud trumpetings and shrieks of joy.

Another animal story came from John's visit to the Parit forest reserve. 'On our walk we passed several animal tracks, including one very fresh tiger's paw. There is an aged lame tiger which is held as the guardian spirit of the forest: whenever a new path is opened up this lame tiger inspects it and leaves its track.'

In July, John handled his first case.

It was a 'banishment enquiry' as to whether 5 Chinese should be banished as gang robbers and dangerous characters. The procedure is simplified for such cases as if the ordinary rules of evidence etc. were applied it would often be impossible to get a conviction against the most obvious rogues. My case was an extraordinary story of abductions and murder, including the imprisonment of an old Chinese woman doctor in a hole in the ground (at a place a few miles from here), a hole 4ft long and 4ft high roofed over with planks covered with sand, where she was left for at least ten days and fed by stuff let down in tins. Banishment is no punishment as Chinese coolies are clamouring to be sent back to China now that most of the mines here are idle. It rather shook me afterwards to discover that until recently banishees were regularly shot on arrival in Canton. (I recommended banishment.)

... The most startling event of the week was the death of the District Officer of the next District. He shot himself the other day, when as it happened I was in the town. Suicides seem to be more common here than at home, partly because the climate and customs are wearing on the nerves and partly because people with a tendency to take to drink have far more opportunity and encouragement. Death is made all the more startling by the suddenness of the burial arrangements. This man shot himself in the afternoon and was buried at 8.30 next morning, when, incidentally, I represented the Governor.

One of John's last experiences at Batu Gajah was a weekend at Taiping, where he visited the prison. 'Taiping Gaol is the Malayan Dartmoor, a big place with a large assortment of prison industries — carpentry, painting, book-binding, mat-making and so on.' This weekend included a seaborne inspection from Port Weld of a mangrove forest in the forest launch, *Elias bin Ahmad*, which was the size of a small cruising yacht.

A visit to the English School at Chenderoh led John to set out the Malayan system of education.

The English School here was interesting — about 350 children and entirely run by Asiatic headmaster and staff. The children, mostly boys, are a most attractive crowd, very bright and interested but better behaved than ours. I don't know if I have ever explained the system of education here. School is compulsory for Malays. The country is covered with most excellent vernacular Malay schools, with very well trained Malay masters. The teaching is entirely in Malay and goes up to (generally) 5th standard. For most boys that is all; but the brighter or more ambitious ones, having had that grounding in the vernacular, then go on to the English Schools, where they are put in special classes and given an intensive course of English so as to catch up with the non-Malays (mostly Chinese) and a few Malays (exceptional) who have started in the primary classes of these schools. The classes then run up to Junior or even (as at Batu Gajah) to Senior Cambridge. Besides these there are various private schools, many getting Govt. grants — Tamil, Chinese, Anglo-Chinese (run by American Methodists) and Catholic.

John's next post was at Alor Star in Kedah, where he was to be secretary to the British adviser, Baker, whom he found a congenial person for whom to work. He described the house he was given as 'thoroughly Ideal Home'. He compared Kedah with the Federated Malay States.

The contrast with the FMS is very interesting. The FMS has been largely Europeanized, whereas Kedah is and remains a Malay country. I think I have mentioned the outward signs of this — the dating of our letters by the Muhammadan calendar (this is the year 1351), the use of Arabic script for all official purposes (except of course between Europeans, but even then there is generally a Malay translation if Malays are to read it) and the fact that we work on Sundays and have Fridays as holidays. The administration is almost entirely in the hands of Malays, with only a few Europeans in key positions. There are historical reasons for all this. Kedah has only belonged to the Empire since 1909.

John took to life in Kedah, though he found it less attractive than his first love, Kuala Pilah.

A Golden Age: Malaya, 1931–34

Life is very quiet and regular. Up every day at 6.30 or there-
abouts. Breakfast at 8. Go to the BA's house at 9 and
usually spend the morning there. Tiffin at 1, followed by a
lazy half-hour on a long chair. Office in town from 2–4,
then tea and change, followed either by golf or by driving
out somewhere and sending the car back a few miles and
walking to it. The roads, as I've said, are too straight for
walks, but that is made up for by the extreme attractiveness
of the landscape. The work in the padi fields is hard while it
lasts, but the little homesteads are ideally picturesque and it
is impossible not to envy the people whose natural life it is
— and will be, as long as Kedah is shielded from too much
'progress'.

There were some out of town expeditions: a week's tour of
forests including travel by raft on rivers, a day on an irrigation
canal and a visit to a large tea estate. He made a private visit to a
Chinese mining village. He commented that 'the one horror on
such walks is meeting buffaloes on the track. They have the most
savage horns and are rather apt to be "fee-foh-fummish" at the
smell of European blood.' Another duty for him at that time of
year was the preparation for Poppy Day and entertaining the aide-
de-camp of a general visiting from Singapore.

Yesterday I drove into Penang to do a little shopping. It is
rather a long way — 70 miles — but mostly very pretty
road. Penang itself (which I hadn't visited since last November) is a thrilling place — the endless variety of craft in the
harbour, from a big Blue Funnel liner down to small two-
oared sampans, and the equal variety of people in the
streets (which, as I think I said last year, are exactly like our
Chinese street of the nursery). From the sea (crossing with
car on a ferry) you have the harbour all spread out in front,
with the town foreshortened behind it and behind that
again the massive bulk of hill, its top lost in cloud. From the
town you look across the sparkling strait to the shores of
Butterworth and the long low line of the Kedah and
Province Wellesley coast, with Kedah Peak and Bukit
Mertijan beyond. After tiffin at the Runnymede (which

must be one of the pleasantest hotels in the world, in its way) I drove a few miles up the island coast and lay on a sandy beach among huge granite rocks, gazing across at the view and watched the little Malay fishing boats bobbing up and down close in shore.

A visit to the Langkawi islands revealed the enterprise of two ex-planters there, 'starting,' he wrote, 'a new industry, canning the tuna, or tunny, which they say exists in great quantities out in deep water. I am putting them in touch with the Empire Marketing Board, so perhaps you may have a substitute soon for cold salmon for Sunday supper.'

John's next posting was to Kuala Lumpur where he was due to stay until the end of February. His time now was to be divided between the Selangor state secretariat and the federal secretariat.

A visit to a leper colony impressed him strongly.

Morning out in the country at Sungei Buloh Decrepit Home and Leper Settlement, shown round by the Medical Supt., a youngish Edinburgh doctor called Ryne. (There is also another Scotch doctor, Badenoch.) The decrepit home is a much more cheerful place than the only workhouse I have seen in England. The inhabitants (the halt, the lame and the blind) are a pathetic crowd but those who were not so old as to have no feelings at all seemed wonderfully contented, sitting about, making baskets or gathered in a group round one who would read the newspaper aloud. They are all Chinese, I think.

The leper settlement is, of course, a sad place, with its thousand odd patients, including eighty children for whom in the ordinary way there is no chance of ever seeing the outside world. One expects horrors too and horrors there are. And yet the whole atmosphere is also wonderfully cheerful and I didn't see a single case of complete depression or hopelessness. One reason is that the surroundings are also model. There are hospital wards for the cases that need hospital treatment, but most of the people live in well-built little houses of their own — complete with gardens, kitchens and modern sanitation. There are clubs, markets, shops, games grounds, school, though, except for a new Plymouth Brethren Chapel, there are no temples, mosques or churches. The place is almost entirely run by the lepers themselves. The nurses are lepers, so are the men in charge of the wards and even the little police force which turned out a guard of honour on our arrival, broke the flag and blew a bugle salute. But another reason for cheerfulness is that there have been some cures. There seems to have been great excitement about a year ago when for the first time, patients were discharged and there have been more since. Dr Ryne seems to have hit on a cure and, though it is still at the experimental stage, some of the results seem very promising. It involves injection of a sort of dye ('fluorescent'?), an idea which he hit on from the fact that these dyes are fatal to TB bugs which are very similar to the bacillus in leprosy. They have a very nice English matron, who volunteered for the job: she deserves a medal if ever anyone did. It is all rather a nightmare to look back on, one of the things that break any theory of the problem of evil.

Later in February, John was appointed assistant secretary of a commission that had just been appointed to report on the trade of Singapore. By this time he was in Malacca.

No other place in Malaya has such monuments of its past — Portuguese fortifications and churches, Dutch buildings (my office is in what is still called the Stadt House) and picturesque Chinese streets. Portuguese and Dutch names are common, though the blood is mixed, and while Dutch speech has vanished the earlier Portuguese has survived and is still spoken.

I think Malacca was included in my programme just to let me see the interesting place. There is very little work for me to do or see and my energies are chiefly employed in the struggle to keep awake. I sit in the Land Office and see something of the incredible confusion of the land system here. I have also visited the High School, a fine new place complete with science labs, and the vast new hospital which is being built near my house. The hospital is a ludicrous product of boom time mentality and now in less spacious days seems likely to be quite a white elephant. It is an immense place, with huge five-storey blocks of wards, so immense that one would suppose it could hold the entire population of Malacca. Who is to pay for the doctors and the army of dressers and nurses, nobody knows. In the school I saw a ridiculous sight — boys learning to typewrite to music. There are special gramophone records for this, which play stirring martial tunes at a regulated pace [at] which the boys have to tap their keys in time with the music.

From Malacca he moved to Singapore, and plunged into the Singapore Trade Commission's work.

Nobody has any idea how long our Royal Commission will take. Its purpose is to enquire into the trade of the Colony, the directions in which it has gained and lost and why and the possibilities of future expansion: but the special purpose is to go into the question of shipping 'conferences' or rings, which are a subject of perennial complaint by some of the local merchants. The members are partly officials and partly unofficials (European, Chinese and Indian). The President is one Gibson, the retiring Legal Adviser (= Attorney-General) of the FMS, who was on the boat on which I came down from Hong Kong, and the Secretary is Innis Miller, Registrar-General of Statistics.

The commission's headquarters were to be in the Department of Statistics.

I've got thoroughly accustomed to the climate and to sitting at a desk all day, but I'm still very homesick for the Malay States — the scenery, the people and the jungle noises. Today is a holiday, the great day of the year for the Malays who have been to Mecca, and up-country you would see them all going about in their best silks; but here there are only the shut offices. When I can afford it I mean to spend most of my weekends in Johore.

A Golden Age: Malaya, 1931–34

Until leaving Singapore in June 1934, John's life was dominated by the commission, apart from a break of a few weeks in Kelantan. His letters have much to say about it, its activities and travels.

> This has been a busy week, with the Commission examining a witness on three days. The Chinese members are apt to be tiresome, or two of them are, always scenting deception where none exists and labouring small points. I think one inevitably acquires more and more of the white-man superiority complex out here. The Europeans are by no means all picked specimens and they are rather apt to be animals in the matter of food and drink and on the other hand the Chinese beat them hollow in industriousness and often in sharpness, but in what you might call average mental character the Chinese seem to be different (as somebody said — their minds are triangular while ours are square so we never meet along more than one line at a time) and not only different but inferior. The defects are of course most obvious in the coolie class, many of whom are quite animal-like, and much must be forgiven to Europeans who retire from the East with frayed tempers. The stupidity of my boy is more exasperating than I can say at times.

John's awareness of acquiring a white man's superiority complex was a good mark for his own self-examination. After moving among the top stratum of Malayan administration and society for a year and a half, he was determined not to let his head be turned, but could see why he had developed the complex. As his letters show, there was a well-marked social and racial pecking order in Malaya, with the British at the top, followed by Malayan, Chinese, then Indian, with various subdivisions down the line.

'His' commission enlightened him a little about shipping. 'All the jargon about bills of lading and manifests and so on is a little less obscure.' He found it 'interesting to see to what an extent the centre of power is in London. All the people who are big men in Singapore take their orders from London and little can be done without referring home.'

The commission swamped its members with paper. 'My Commission is in danger of suffocating itself in papers and it now meets three days a week, so that there is no lack of work. I have a Chinese clerk who is a perpetual source of irritation. He doesn't understand English properly, is stupid to begin with and — most exasperating of all — begins every sentence with 'Yes, sir.'

By this time, a proprietorial note enters his reports opened by 'My Commission'. It was becoming clear that the commission's work was to be a long haul. 'My Commission now has a full draft programme reaching to past the middle of October so its labours are not likely to be finished before the end of the year.' From time to time John commented on witnesses. 'This week's witnesses so far have been the head of the Public Works Dept (a very Aiden-burgh man called Sturrock) and the head of the Municipality.' He allowed himself a remark on his secretary. 'Innis Miller is a most depressed looking person, with a face all hanging down like the face of some dogs and a most anxious expression, but I think he is happy though his sense of humour is not conspicuously great.' In the same letter, he spoke of the week's witnesses as 'representative manufacturers — out to make Singapore an industrial city. One difficulty of traders here is the way in which trade marks are initiated. An amusing instance mentioned was that of a Japanese firm who sold motor accessories as Rucas, well knowing that the ordinary Chinese pronounces R as L.' This led into a sleight of hand on his own part.

I have been the cause of upsetting one apple cart. The Nestlé milk people have put forward a proposal for a duty on milk — 5 cents a pound on foreign milk and only one cent on British milk. The result of this would be to put most of the milk trade in their hands and there has been a good deal of excitement among the other importers — a public meeting and a committee. The Nestlé man was twice before the Commission. It then struck me that the Anglo–Dutch treaty of 1824 had something to say about all this and so it has — the duties proposed are impossible. All rather an absurd situation and a sad blow for the Nestlé company.

This topic, which has a modern ring, continued to keep the commission busy.

This week's subject for the Commission has been further discussion of a duty on milk. All the importers of foreign milk are up in arms and there are great arguments about coffee-shop prices, monopolies and so on. I was surprised to discover that my syce gets for his baby (the first stage of weaning her) Milkmaid (condensed) milk, the most expensive brand on the market. She takes a tin every 2 days and a tin costs 31 cents. However he seems to have Truby King standards and will only use the best — 'the brand they always give in hospitals' he says.

The flood of documentation, he thought, was far more than the commission's members could hope to digest. It was exhausting his own department's stationery, as well as the central office supply. He remarked that Innis Miller had added to the stress by going sick for several days. However, a break was at hand for John.

All my excitement is about the prospect of getting away to Kelantan for six weeks. The Assistant Adviser has had to go home in a hurry to avoid a breakdown and there is a hiatus before his relief arrives from home leave. Gibson and Miller at first both refused to let me go, when I broke the news to them today, but after discussion agree. It is very noble of Miller on whom a lot of extra work will fall.

At Kota Bharu in Kelantan, John stayed first at the residency with the British adviser, Baker, but then moved into the quarters of J. A. Craig, the head of the agricultural department, who had been a contemporary at the Edinburgh Academy.

My chief occupation so far seems to have been collecting rents. The British Adviser sent me out with no explanations or instructions and nothing but a Malay orderly. However all went well and we brought home about a thousand dollars a day for three days running. The collecting is done in the houses of the local Malay headmen (that sounds better than parish clerks) and a crowd of *ryot*s (peasants) sits round staring. The language is rather a difficulty as the Kelantan variety takes a little getting used to.

He was very taken with Kelantan, 'the most Malay Malay state I've been in — much more even than Kedah and completely unspoilt.' He found that 'the European gets much more deference than elsewhere. I got quite shy of walking outside the Residency, because there wasn't merely one sentry but the entire guard turns out, slopes arms and salutes. They are a sort of military police and extremely smart.'

He took an opportunity to go to Trengganu, which meant that he had visited every Malay state in the peninsula. A week was taken up with celebrations of the Sultan of Kelantan's birthday. He had his only tiger hunt in Malaya, but the tiger failed to turn up. He visited gold mines. On a long expedition with the British adviser, he visited Pulai:

> a unique place, almost unknown until the opening of the railway at Gua Musang a few years ago, an island of Chinese in a Malay country. The original people must have come from China hundreds of years ago, no one knows when. They intermarried with Sakai and Siamese women, but they have kept up their Hakka dialect and their Chinese ways. The little earth-work houses and shops, with red charms above the doors, the temple of the goddess of Mercy, the paved streets, the tiered padi fields are all just what you might find, I imagine, in any village in China. The original settlers were gold miners, but as the mines became exhausted they took to padi-growing and now the long valley is covered with rice-fields. Here and there rises a high lumpy lime-stone hill, while on all sides the island of cultivation is surrounded by jungle, to the horizon.

He was back in Singapore by 21 August, sailing down the east coast from Kuala Trengganu, a two-day voyage, in a Danish ship.

> The new house is miles above all expectations. Till a year or so ago it was a convalescent bungalow and so it is naturally very airily built and has one of the healthiest possible sites. It is at a place called Labrador, a high promontory over-looking the main entrance to the harbour and a fine land-scape of sea and islands. Every morning I sit out on a seat in

the garden drinking it all in with my early tea and in the evening you could gaze down for hours at the changing colours, the lights of the fishing boats and on the islands and right out to the Raffles Light, the extreme point of British territory.

He reported later that this house has 'the distinction of being the southernmost house on the mainland of Asia (including Singapore in the mainland as it is joined on by a causeway)'. He shared the house with a changing company of cadets and other young professionals.

One morning the Trade Commission went out in a launch to look at the shipping in the roads. The number of steamers of all sorts and sizes is astonishing. ... There is something very exhilarating about the harbour on a fine day. There is always a coolish breeze and the light, of course, is extremely bright and brings out colours very clearly. Incidentally, fog is unknown in Singapore.

We had an unusually interesting witness before the Commission this week in Sansom, Commercial Counsellor at the Tokyo Embassy, who is on his way to some trade discussions in India. According to him, a large part of the Japanese success is due to the depreciation of their exchange. A given number of gold dollars now exchanges for twice as many Yen as a few years ago, while Yen prices in Japan and wages remain much as they were.

He returned to the pleasure of the views from his new dwelling.

My letters must tend to repeat themselves about our views, but they are as endlessly fascinating as the loch [Lochearn] from Fox Knowe. The main harbour is in water sheltered by islands and the entrance from the west is between an island and the promontory on which our house stands. We are near enough to hear the engines as the big steamers pass in and out: besides them there are all sorts of smaller craft down to the junks, with their high sterns and big ribbed sails, and the brown sailed fishing boats. At night Bukum, the island where the Asiatic Petroleum Company have their tanks, is a blaze of lights, like a big steamer lying at anchor, while two light-houses blink in the distance and the flares of the Malay fishermen blaze by their stake traps close inshore.

Yet the Commission was a source of irritation.

I became very Bolshie about my work early in the week and had difficulty in being civil to Innis Miller, but have got over that now. It is annoying to see the Commission being run as I think in such a sprawling, stupid way. It goes on and on and on and nothing is considered irrelevant. I do think we do some of these things better at home, but 'don't repeat that!'

A little later he could say that something had been achieved. 'The Commission has at last paused for reflection and produced three interim reports, so that something at last has been achieved and done. In spite of all my complaints, I quite realize that it is a most instructive experience. The only doubt is whether the expenditure of so large a chunk of my young life is justified.'

The same letter reported a row over the Governor's statement of educational policy.

HE has aroused a new storm by announcing with character-istic definiteness the Government's educational policy, which is to provide everybody with free elementary educa-tion *in Malay* and secondary education in English only (apart from scholarships) on payment of increased fees. The refusal to provide education in Chinese for the Chinese (and actually the Colonial Secretary's invitation to their parents to send them to China if they want Chinese education) or alternatively to give them elementary education in English is, in my humble opinion, monstrous in such a predomin-antly Chinese city as Singapore. Nobody pretends that the Chinese will send their children to the Government's Malay schools. It is all part of the excessively pro-Malay bias which is now the fashion in high quarters. Needless to say there have been strong protests from the Chinese and one Chinese member broke down in tears in the Council and walked out — for good. Meanwhile the Chinese and Indians in the FMS are up in arms against an import duty on rice intended to help the Malay (who alone are allowed most of the rice lands).

As a sideshow to the commission, he had visited the Ford Motor Company's assembly works.

Cars for Malaya, Siam and the Dutch East Indies are imported here in pieces — the engines from England and the other parts from Canada and assembled in Singapore by native workmen. This is presumably much cheaper than sending out whole cars. Their trade seems to be looking up a little, but it is only a small fraction of what it was a few years ago.

The Commission has been dealing with some contentious legal questions. More evidence of the continued spread of Japanese commercial penetration was heard. An impressive list of their prices was read out — all sorts of articles and the Japanese price always about half the British, with quality much the same. The result is that whole lines of trade that were British a very few years ago are now handled by Japan. 80 per cent of the cloth exported from the Colony to neighbouring countries is now Japanese.

In December the Commission paid a visit to Malacca.

The Trade Commission's Malacca visit was quite a successful interlude, though I seem to have met death in the pot on the way there. (I think one's inside is slowly rotted by the miserable products of Chinese cooks.) We went up by a fast steamer, leaving Singapore in the morning and arriving in time for dinner. Lady Clementi and her daughters were on board. It felt quite like the *Rajputana*; 'Now, Mr Martin, come and talk to me' and I was led downstairs to a sofa where we discussed many things.

At the New Year, 1934, John saw four months of hard work on the commission ahead:

hearing the last witnesses (there have been 150 already and 100 meetings, by tomorrow), writing the report and seeing a stupendous amount of material through the printer. The printer can scarcely cope with the amount of the material. I was at the printing office the other day (the Government printing office), a spacious new place with lots of modern equipment and, I should think, about as good as any place of the same size at home.

The commission's visits continued.

The Trade Commission took to visiting the industries and port of Singapore, starting each morning at an early hour, for five consecutive days. We visited a biscuit factory, oil mills, a soap factory, a foundry and engineering workshops, a sugar refinery, ship yards, two rubber factories, a produce godown (warehouse), wharves, docks, etc. and also spent several hours travelling about in a launch. The launch trip was very 'British'. Our intention was to travel up a certain tidal river which it is proposed to develop as an industrial area: but we found our launch waiting for us *below* a bridge at the river-mouth which it could not pass

The various factories, besides being smelly and rather hot, were extremely interesting. Generally working conditions are not at all bad and as far as light and air go things seemed better than in old-fashioned places at home. Labour being very cheap isn't replaced by machinery as much as it might be, for instance one of the rubber factories employs 4000 people (and when trade was better had 6000). There was no sign of anything that could be called 'sweaty', though a good many children were working in the Chinese places — but at light work and probably as happy as if they had been left at home. The women all astonishingly well-dressed and quite prosperous-looking. The Chinese-run places are much less orderly than where there are Europeans. This was particularly so in the big rubber factory, where the processes seemed to be spread about in the most haphazard way and mixed up with quite dissimilar processes. There was almost no sign of supervision but the crowds of employees were all working away each on his or her own, so that the whole concern seemed like some huge living organism with each cell performing its function without conscious direction from the centre. I imagine Castle Mills could hardly equal the variety of products of this factory — not only the ordinary rubber goods (shoes, goloshes, wellington boots retailed at about a shilling a pair, balls, balloons, gloves, hoses, tyres, and so on), but also biscuits, toffee, peppermints and other sweets, and even a daily newspaper.

The Commission has been the subject of many gibes for having reached its 100th Meeting. It now seems likely to last till May; but I shall be more definite about the date of my return in a week or a fortnight

In February, after the commission had visited Penang, he could say 'we have practically finished the examination of witnesses and now it is a matter of pressing on with the printing of minutes of evidence etc. and drafting the report. My part in all this will be very mechanized and dull, but it has to be done by somebody.' He had worries about winding up the affairs of the commission in a reasonable space of time: 'there are moments I quail at the amount still to be done and the amount of inertia to be overcome. I shall certainly know a great deal better how such commissions should be run if I ever have one again,' which was a prophetic remark in the light of his later experience.

By the end of April, the work of winding up the commission was becoming oppressive.

The mass of work to be done grows every day and I can't pretend it is fun. The Commission have collected such an absurd mass of evidence that it seems almost beyond human powers of digestion to reduce it into a report. Gibson, the President, is most impressive in the way in which he turns out chapters with the relentlessness of a sausage machine: but he is spared all the miseries of dealing with the printer.

John concluded the letter: 'this must be a short letter, unless I tell you how many cranes the Harbour Board owns or how the trade in sago flour is going: my brain is so steeped in that, I can't think of anything else.'

At the end of May, it was

> a race against time to get the Report finally ready for signature next week (when several members go on leave) and the printing completed before the 18th of June. It is all made more difficult here by the absence of reliable clerks: nothing can be left to be checked by anybody else. There has been time for almost nothing else. .... On Friday night I was at the printing works till 2 a.m. and up again at 6.30 a.m. We have used 20 tons of type metal and the printing alone has cost over $10,000. I wish I could think that all this was going to do some good; but I'm afraid I don't.

On 13 June, he could report the end.

> I am living in a mazed state, what with the stress of trying to finish an impossible amount of detailed work in a short time, various goodbye celebrations, the general excitement of going home and the real heartbreak of leaving this country, to all appearances for ever. It is like knowing the date of one's own death.
>
> On Thursday our Report was at last printed and I went about the town getting it signed, seeing several picturesque streets I had never visited before. That night was Gibson, our President's, last night in Malaya (after thirty-five years). The Millers threw a dinner-party, followed by cinema.
>
> Next morning we saw him off on the P & O. 'Seeing off' the P & O is a regular fortnightly function, to which hundreds of people troop down, though I hadn't been before. Mobs of people, baskets of flowers in stacks, much shaking of hands and raising of elbows and general heartiness. The heartiness in Penang (where the steamer leaves on Saturday night) used to be so boisterous that the time of sailing had to be advanced to a more temperate time of day.

In Singapore, to be fresh for commission work, John had tried to keep his Sundays free to drive out to the sea or countryside, though he found Johore, the neighbouring state, the least interesting of the Malay states. In the evening, he would attend church, though was somewhat disappointed with both the Anglican and Presbyterian churches in Malaya. There were public events, dinners, parades and receptions. He and the commission members attended the inauguration of Imperial Airways' Singapore–London service on 31 December 1933 and went up in one of RMA *Athena*'s flights giving a good view of Singapore island. There was golf, tennis and a little riding.

Towards the end, he had to wind up his own affairs and dispose of his possessions. He found a good new appointment for his syce, Mat Nor, of whom he wrote to his mother: 'He has been an excellent servant and a real friend and adviser in all my travels and my various houses ... it was a lucky day when I chose him: very long ago it seems.' Being entitled to longer than four months leave, he secured the permission of the Colonial Office to return eastwards with extended stops in the Dutch East Indies and Fiji, with shorter ones in Sydney, Auckland and Honolulu.

The coda to John's Malayan tour was a month in Java and Bali, under Dutch administration, and a month in Fiji, a British territory. A programme to see how the Dutch administration worked had been arranged for him in Java. The economy was in recession, more severely, he thought, than in Malaya. Sugar growing was particularly depressed. The incursion of Japanese trading was strong.

> The Japanese invasion is even more obvious here than in Malaya. Everywhere cheap Japanese goods are on sale, shops crammed with them, and not merely cheap but ludicrously, incredibly cheap — silk ties for the equivalent of twopence and the like. It is possible to clothe yourself quite respectably — coat, trousers, shirt, tie, shoes, socks for 2.50 florins or say seven shillings.

He found Java even more beautiful than Malaya. The culture was predominantly Muslim but with traces of Buddhism and Hinduism. When he saw a crowd of Javanese waiting outside a church as the bell tolled, he remarked, 'an unheard of thing in Malaya where practising Mohammedan religion is part of the definition of a Malay'.

A Scottish Life

A stop in Fiji enabled John to see government and church agencies at work, industries, occupations and something of Fijian culture. Once again, the impact of economic recession was to be seen, notably in the copra slump. An overland journey with the district officer, Peck, a former naval officer, had its moments:

> It would be difficult to give any impression of the peacefulness of the view of these villages as you first come on it over the brow of a hill — an island of green grass dotted with little houses, a river and on all sides miles of bush. We were again in the chief's house, but were taken to the church for the Yangona ceremony. I made a short speech of thanks in which I apologized for travelling on Sunday (an apology suggested by Peck, which seemed to be appreciated). I said I should go to the service, so they delayed it to enable me first to visit the school in daylight. The service (Wesleyan) was conducted by the local Fijian pastor and was of course all in Fijian. He preached very eloquently on the Fijian motto 'Fear God and honour the King' (apparently we represented the King!). The singing was very fine.

On the following day they travelled by water.

> A punt with prisoners had been sent up the river to meet us and we spent an idle afternoon going downstream to Nakorosuli, a fairly large village. The school children were drawn up in front of the school and greeted us with God Save the King in English. The headmaster then took us to his house (the usual thatch), where we spent the night, surrounded by sitting hens. For the first time I saw the full yangona ceremony, with a choir of boys dressed in leaves and musical honours, the cup bearer doing an elaborate dance before me, all without spilling the cup. Also presentation of whale's tooth. We then sat outside and saw a club dance by the boys, followed by a presentation of food. After supper (including delicious river prawns) they entertained us with a long and noisy school concert, songs, dancing and plays by all ages of children, sometimes in English and sometimes in Fijian. At the end I made a short speech,

A Golden Age: Malaya, 1931–34

interpreted sentence by sentence, and asked them to sing their beautiful Goodbye song Isa Lei.

By the end of September, John's tour of colonial administrations, British and Dutch, was over.

On his return to the Colonial Office, John would have to report on his experiences. His letters reveal how and how much he was learning. His approach was one of interest and appreciation. The ways in which people in different cultures managed or mismanaged continually fascinated him. He was aware of the bonding power of religion in any society. He saw this in a harmonious form in the Malay states and in Bali. The more aggressive communalism, which surfaced in India from time to time, was not apparent in Malaya in the years John spent on his secondment. He learned of the racial, religious and other conflicts within the country. He was aware also of the impact of economic forces. These were the years of world economic slump bearing hard upon the rubber producers of Malaya and copra producers of Fiji. His experience with the Singapore Trade Commission taught him much about trade and shipping, about the actions of other countries, especially the Japanese, and about running commissions, which was to serve him well later. The opium conference showed that some problems are insoluble and that their effects have to be contained.

His love of the British Empire was apparent, as was his admiration for those who administered and served it on the ground. He was impressed by the quality of work of the district officers and other officials he met, and with whom he travelled and stayed. He was made aware of the pressures of climate, distance, and sometimes loneliness and depression, which bore upon them; he learned also that, for a few, the demands of their position were too much. The three years in Malaya were happy ones for him and he continually looked back on them with pleasure. They revealed to him the entertaining and instructive comedy of human life.

To Carstairs, in 1969, John said: 'It made me tremendously keen on the British colonial task. I really was bitten by this bug.' What he had seen in Malaya and Singapore had revealed the great opportunities given to the British for constructive work in their overseas territories.

I in many ways hated coming back to London. I was very very homesick for these territories as soon as I left them and always hoped in those days that an opportunity would come to work there again before too long. I must say this was very much the same feeling as that I heard expressed by most of the young men from the Colonial Office sent to serve overseas. They found the routine of office life in London and the general way of life in London desperately depressing and dull after the much more colourful existence they had had overseas.

For a short period before the war, he joined the Far Eastern Department. Later, after the war, he became head of the department, so Malaya and Singapore were never far from his thoughts and concern. The 'Golden Age' was soon to come to an end. The Japanese invasion of Malaya and the fall of Singapore in 1941 and 1942 brought much suffering and anxiety. The postwar years saw conflict and warfare before a new settlement was reached and the independent Federation of Malaya was created along with an independent Singapore. John returned to Malaya in 1954 during the emergency and again in 1962, when he also visited the other countries involved in the negotiations for the creation of Malaysia.

5

The Palestine Royal
Commission, 1936–37

Palestine must have been a word to dread in the Colonial
Office of the 1930s. John Martin recalled it as 'one of the
most awkward responsibilities of the Colonial Secretary in
those days', as the cause of 'an enormous number of parliamentary questions', as many as 20 in a single day, all needing replies, as
well as 'endless drafting of memoranda for Cabinet Committees
and so on'.

The British government had administered Palestine, formerly
under Turkish rule, since 1918, first as an occupying power after
the victorious Allenby campaign, then since 1923 under a League
of Nations mandate. Two conflicting undertakings made during
the First World War complicated the administration of Palestine.
First, in 1915, to encourage the Arab revolt against Turkish rule,
Sir Henry McMahon, high commissioner in Egypt, gave an undertaking that Britain would recognize the independence of all
Arabian territories in the Middle East then under Turkish rule.
This was understood by many Arabs to include Palestine. It was
known as the McMahon pledge. Second, in 1917, to encourage
worldwide Jewish support in the war, Secretary of State for
Foreign Affairs, A. J. Balfour, issued what was to be known as the
Balfour Declaration. It appeared in a letter to Lord Rothschild as a
'declaration of sympathy with Jewish Zionist aspirations',
approved by the Cabinet. It stated:

> His Majesty's Government view with favour the establish-
> ment in Palestine of a National Home for the Jewish people,

and will use their best endeavours to facilitate the achievement of this object, it being clearly understood that nothing
shall be done which may prejudice the civil and religious
rights of existing non-Jewish communities in Palestine, or
the rights and political status enjoyed by Jews in any other
country.

The Mandate had come into force in 1923. Its preamble had
these words:

the Mandatory should be responsible for putting into effect
the declaration originally made on November 2nd, 1917, by
the Government of His Britannic Majesty, and adopted by
the (Principal Allied) Powers, in favour of the Establishment
in Palestine of a national home for the Jewish people, it
being clearly understood that nothing should be done which
might prejudice the civil and religious rights of existing non-
Jewish communities in Palestine.

The proportion of Jews in Palestine continued to grow by immigration, particularly in the 1930s with the flight of Jews from
Hitler's Germany. The immigrants' energy and industry, their
purchase of Arab lands, the wealth they brought and the international backing they had in the creation of Tel Aviv, seemed
increasing threats to the Palestinian Arabs.

Tension between Arabs and Jews had led to disturbances in
1920, 1921, 1923, 1929 and 1936. Riots in Jaffa in April 1936
prompted the British government to set up a Royal Commission.
In 1936, Arabs cut down 150,000 Jewish-owned fruit trees and
more than 60,000 forest trees planted by Jewish settlers. In that
year, 200 Arabs and 81 Jews were killed, as were 21 British
soldiers. The British garrison of 20,000 had great difficulty keeping the peace.

The commission received its royal warrant from Edward VIII in
August 1936, which George VI confirmed in December 1936, a
month after its work had started. Its terms of reference were:

to ascertain the underlying causes of the disturbances which
broke out in Palestine in the middle of April; to inquire into

the manner in which the Mandate for Palestine is being implemented in relation to the obligations of the Mandatory towards the Arabs and the Jews respectively; and to ascertain whether, upon a proper construction of the terms of the Mandate, either the Arabs or the Jews have any legitimate grievances on account of the way in which the Mandate has been, or is being implemented; and if the Commission is satisfied that any such grievances are well founded, to make recommendations for their removal and for the prevention of their recurrence.

The British government wanted the commission to be authoritative and its members were chosen to command respect, 'men of prestige whose names will carry weight', as the colonial secretary (W. G. A. Ormsby-Gore, later Lord Harlech) put it. Lord Peel was to chair the commission and Sir Horace Rumbold would be the vice-chairman. The other four commissioners were Sir Laurie Hammond, Sir Morris Carter, Sir Harold Morris and Reginald Coupland.

To serve these 'men of prestige', the colonial secretary, Orsmby-Gore, had to find a secretary of known ability. He would need a first-class brain, combined with unshakeable courtesy, and a capacity for immensely hard work. John may have been surprised to be chosen, but his few years in colonial service had shown his potential. He had had the experience of the Singapore Trade Commission.

John himself commented that, for him, teaching at home, school and church had diffused a greater familiarity with the holy land's geography and ancient history than with those of almost any other foreign country.

I remember how, as a boy in Scotland, I often looked at a relief map of Palestine hanging in my father's study. Indeed I have a photograph of it brought out into the garden on an easel for instruction, when it was accompanied by such audio-visual aids, as they would now be described, as a ram's horn trumpet, a model of a Palestine village house and a bottle of rather dirty water said to have come from the river Jordan. Features of geography like Ebal and Gerizim, the Sea of Galilee and the Dead Sea were as familiar to us in Scotland as the mountains and lakes of England.

On 6 November, the commission left London for Palestine. At a talk at the Hebrew University in Jerusalem in 1978, John gave portraits of the commissioners. He said that:

the government's decision to appoint a Royal Commission ... was received with general approval and relief. The importance and difficulty of their task was reflected in the great care taken in selection of the members of the commission — hailed ... as a strong and well balanced team.

The chairman, Lord Peel, had an inherited instinct for statecraft, ... himself had long experience of government ... and had held high Cabinet offices. ... In public life he had earned a reputation for calm, geniality and good judgement, a clear head and great powers of conciliation. ... I remember him for his industry in mastering the huge mass of briefs and evidence submitted to the commission, for his conscientiousness and for his strong sense of public duty. ... In listening to witnesses he was alert (though his closed eyes did not always give that impression) and fair. In the end, it was only after mental struggle and painstaking and judicial consideration that he reached the conclusion that only partition offered a solution of the problem. Weizmann, recalling his own appearance before the commission, paid tribute to Peel's 'innate courtesy, ... patience and kindliness'. He died soon after presentation of the report and was a sick man in the final stages of the enquiry; but he never allowed that to interfere with full participation in its work.

The deputy chairman, Sir Horace Rumbold, was an outstanding diplomat of his generation. Harold Nicholson, who had served under him and knew his quality, dedicated a book on diplomacy to him as 'an ideal diplomatist'. He had a long and distinguished career, culminating in the embassy in Berlin, where he was one of the first to recognize and give warning of the Nazi menace. His bland and impassive face gave the unwary almost an impression of stupidity. Indeed, it was said that his dossier at the Quai d'Orsay began '*malgré son air idiot* ...' That story led me into embarrassment when, going to our first meeting with Lord Peel, I shared a lift with a man whose appearance of stupidity left me in no doubt of his identity, so that I addressed him as 'Sir Horace', whereat he asked 'How did you know me? I don't think we have met.' But the deceptive mask, perhaps a diplomatic asset, concealed a keen and discerning mind. Having seen him in action in Jerusalem, I recognize the justice of Harold Nicolson's description — 'He would listen unimpressed and unresponsive ... and some brilliant conversationalist would pause in his discourse, wondering whether the Ambassador had really understood. Sir Horace always understood' — continues Harold Nicolson — 'He understood not merely what was being said, and why it was being said, but what relation even the most gifted sentence bore to reality.' In Jerusalem, Rumbold occasionally reacted with irritation to witnesses whom he found unreasonable; but when it came to weighing the evidence, he was scrupulous and fair-minded and the hard argument with himself that persuaded him finally to subscribe to such a revolutionary recommendation as partition give all the greater value to his ultimate acceptance of the report, which he afterwards loyally supported.

Of the other members, Sir Laurie Hammond had long administrative experience in the Indian Civil Service, in which he had been a successful provincial governor; Sir Morris Carter had been a chief justice in East Africa and chairman of the land commissions of Rhodesia and Kenya and was a recognized authority on land problems; Sir Harold Morris was chosen in the first instance as a first-class barrister at a time when it was understood that both Arabs and Jews were briefing counsel to appear before the commission. In fact, counsel were excluded; but Morris also contributed expertise in conciliation gained as for ten years president of the industrial court. Finally, there was Reginald Coupland, Professor of Colonial History at Oxford since 1920 and known as editor of the influential *Round Table* and author of several brilliant historical and biographical studies. At Oxford, he was an inspirer of young men interested in imperial questions and was a fellow of All Souls, in those days so near the centre of authority in church and state. He had been adviser to the Burma round table conference and had previous experience on a Royal Commission — that on the superior services in India. He brought to the commission an exceptionally clear and able mind, familiarity with the problems of plural societies, particularly in India and Canada, great powers of exposition and persuasion, and skill in draftmanship, recognized in the taut style and lucid presentation of fact and argument which marked the commission's report.

Weizmann was later to describe the commission in his autobiography as 'by far the most distinguished and ablest of the investigatory bodies ever sent out to Palestine'.

While the commissioners were on the way, the Arabs announced that they would boycott the hearings. Arriving in Jerusalem on 11 November, the commissioners first attended the armistice ceremony and on the following day the opening meeting of the commission was held at Government House.

As soon as our luggage had been got up we changed into morning coats, unpacked our top hats and drove off to the Armistice service at the British War Cemetery on Mount Scopus. It was all very impressive — a large number of troops with pipers and military band, Jewish war veterans, various ecclesiastical dignitaries and a great crowd of onlookers. In the afternoon we had our opening meeting at Government House, again a top hat affair, driving up in great state with an escort of mounted police. There was a crowd of local notables, though only one Arab seems to have accepted the invitation. The Italian Consul-General on finding himself next to a chair marked as reserved for the Ethiopian Consul marched out. God Save The King. A speech of welcome by the HC. The Commission read out Lord Peel's speech. Everything had to be done in three languages, so the proceedings were quite drawn out. Afterwards we had tea with HE. Returned to GH again for an official dinner.

The Palestine Royal Commission, 1936–37

After an extended tour on the next two days, 13 and 14 November, the commissioners opened their hearings in Jerusalem. Though they were eager for as many as possible to be in public, some were held in secret. On 19 November, they visited northern Palestine for the weekend. The public hearings began on 24 November, with British officials being questioned about land policy. Dr Chaim Weizmann, the Zionist leader, was heard over the next two days, followed by the director of education on 27 November and then, on the following days, by members of the Jewish Agency. There was a break at Christmas with sessions resuming on 28 December with the last public session on 7 January with David Ben-Gurion. By this time, the Arabs had abandoned their boycott and five days later their representatives, led by the Mufti of Jerusalem, appeared. Their evidence lasted for five days.

The commissioners and their staff were staying at the King David Hotel with an office nearby, made by converting a ballroom, with 'nice new furniture and central heating. Besides the staff brought out from England I have an English "Office Assistant", three stenographers, two clerks and several messengers.' A typical day for John was to go to the office at about 8.30 a.m. to work in his own room until the commission met at 10.30. After lunch, he would return to the office for two hours or so, followed by a lengthy discussion in the chairman's room at the hotel until it was time to dress for dinner. He pointed out that he had few opportunities to emulate H. V. Morton, the travel writer. 'The Secretary of a Royal Commission', he said, 'is not a holiday tourist and there has been very little time for anything but the work of the Commission.'

From 19 to 22 November, the commissioners were based in Tiberias and the journey there gave them an interesting drive past many familiar biblical place names.

> We stopped at Nablus ... and talked to the district officials and also at a Jewish agricultural college, full of KOSBs [King's Own Scottish Borderers], near Mount Tabor. These were the KOSBs to whom the Arabs complained that they only played soccer with the Jews: a complaint which was soon remedied. There are still a great many troops in the Nablus–Jenin area, but all is now peaceful and it is difficult

to realize that we could only have driven along these roads a month ago at the risk of our lives. ... The country is everywhere utterly dried up, but it looks less hopelessly barren as you go north.

It was dark when we reached Tiberias, but the early sunrise this morning woke us up to a quite startlingly beautiful landscape. I needn't repeat what all the books say about the contrast between the harsh hills of Judea and the coloured beauty of Galilee: but it is very striking.

The commissioners visited the Sea of Galilee where the water had reached its lowest allowed level. The sea had now become a reservoir for an electric power station. That day, John was caught in a cloudburst.

Even in Malaya I have never seen heavier rain. This was the breaking of the rains and for the next few days there were torrential downpours. On Sunday, however, we managed to drive up to Lake Huleh (the Waters of Merom), where there are plans for a big irrigation scheme, and on to the Syrian frontier. ... On Monday we tried to drive along the lake to the power station at the south end, but floods across the road turned us back and we drove straight back to Jerusalem, stopping for a long talk with the Arab district officer at Jenin on the way.

On December 5th we took a day off and drove down to Jaffa, visiting a survey camp on the way. The change in the country in the few days since we came here is almost miraculous. The barren lands that looked as if by no stretch of the imagination could they support life are now taking on a coat of green and even the thirsty olive trees look brighter and fresher. As we swung round the shoulders of the hills each new view seemed more beautiful than the last: I have seldom felt so much sheer elation at the goodness of the world!

... At an interesting dinner one evening to meet three Arabs, where I heard plenty of the Arab case. All the Arabs we meet seem to realize that the boycott is a mistake, but there is no sign yet of the leaders calling it off.

This was the time of the abdication crisis; John commented:

You will know more about the King by the time this arrives; but abdication seems now almost inevitable. (The Arabs, who (like the Jews) import their politics into everything here, say that Mrs Simpson is a Jewess!) Dereliction of duty on such a tremendous scale can share few parallels. As somebody here said, Dante's Grand Refusal was as nothing compared with it.

By mid-December the weather was turning colder. Into John's commission work, diplomatic dinners and an outing to Jericho were inserted.

It can't be much colder in Edinburgh than it has been here for the last few days, with a piercing East wind whistling at the windows. The central heating is defeated in this unequal struggle, but it is an improvement on the charcoal brazier at which I have shivered twice in Arab houses. By day, how-ever, there is bright sunshine, with scarcely a cloud in the sky, and the houses and walls and even the rocky hillsides sparkle in the most dazzling way.

Dined that evening (a small party) at Government House and every night since I have dined out until yesterday — Monday with 'Nebi' Samuel, Sir Herbert's son, who has married a local Jewess and is in the Government service here; Tuesday with the new Director of Education, Farrell; Wednesday with the Treasurer, Johnson — a large party of the usual type of Government people — in a large house built by a tax collector under the Turkish régime whose salary was £70 a month; Thursday with George Antonius, a Syrian Christian and one of the most remarkable figures in Jerusalem, rich, extremely cultured and good company, with an entertaining wife; Friday, in the less opulent home of an Arab who runs the Arab music in the local broadcasting service — where we were entertained by a gypsy playing a playing a sort of mandoleen [*sic*]. Naturally there was a great deal of interesting talk at all these; but I can't attempt to tell you about it.

By this stage in the proceedings, Lord Peel was driving the commission hard. 'We have increased our tempo and hear witnesses three afternoons a week as well as in the mornings — a great mistake from the point of view of digestion of evidence, but our Chairman is determined to get back to England as soon as he can.'
The Bishop, Dr Graham Brown, took John on Sunday 21 December to a confirmation at Es-Salt in Trans-Jordan.

(After the service) ... we walked through the town to the house of one of the leading merchants (Arab of course) for lunch, being joined by the Italian Roman Catholic priest, who seemed to be on the best of terms with the Anglicans. The lunch was an overpowering meal of soup, rice in various forms, with much tough mutton (from a sheep boiled whole), stuffed cabbage, ½ sweet ½ savoury made out of cheese and oranges.

Christmas brought some relief to the commission. 'A memorable cheer; a rather exhausting one.' John, with some of the commissioners, drove to Bethlehem on Christmas Eve:

a perfect night of clear stars and bright moonlight. Entering the Church of the Nativity by the little low door at which even the greatest visitors must stoop we stumbled through it in almost complete darkness and up some steps to a court-yard beneath the bell tower. ... Halfway through this little service the bells broke out overhead — most thrilling. I need not trouble you with the emotions of the place and the occasion; but it was an evening I shan't forget.

Work resumed and John optimistically mentioned 24 December or possibly 17 January as days for sailing from Port Said, 'so you can see how things are being rushed'.
The future was still uncertain. 'We have been kept', John wrote, 'in a state of complete uncertainty by the Arabs, who may be

going to give evidence after all and if they do we shall stay in Jerusalem a little longer.' The work had continued. 'We have had a strenuous week of taking evidence, far more than it is possible to digest now; but we have it all on paper and the process of digestion must wait.'

The chief event of the week after Christmas was the Toscanini concert on 30 December.

A wonderful Palestine Orchestra has been started, recruited from among the leading artists in the world — mostly men who lost their jobs in Germany — and Toscanini came especially from America without fee to conduct its opening season. Heathcoat Amery and I were taken by Dr Weizmann, the Zionist leader, and had excellent seats. It was a most memorable concert. I have never known one more inspired or thrilling. It was, of course, a great occasion in the history of the 'Jewish National Home'.

A bizarre incident occurred during the New Year celebrations in the hotel. The hotel had arranged a dance for 500 Jews. John said he heard nothing, 'unlike one of our more dignified members, whose room was invaded in the small hours by a young woman carrying a trumpet who said he was the ugliest member of the Commission, and told him other home truths while he cowered helpless beneath his counterpane'. The victim was Sir Horace Rumbold who, irritated by pressure from the Jews, had referred to them as an 'alien race'. He had mentioned the duty of the mandatory to 'develop the country with regard to the unique experiment, the injection of an alien race into the body politic of this native race'. At the next public session, Rumbold took the opportunity to say that what he had meant was 'a race having different characteristics from the Arab race. It seems to me quite the obvious explanation.'

On New Year's Day he visited Tel Aviv where he saw 'the new jetty and other works by the Jews who are trying to create their own port' and so cut out (Arab) Jaffa. 'Tel Aviv is an astonishing place: 25 years ago there were only sand-dunes, now there is a population of 150,000, with miles of streets. It is all very cheap and jerry-built and it is a nightmare thought how all those

150,000 people are going to support themselves when the immigration boom ends.' Early in January the Arabs ended their boycott. John took part in a weekend diplomatic expedition to Trans-Jordan.

The expedition was a pleasant break in our work and interesting in itself. Only Peel, Rumbold, Coupland, Amery and I went, accompanied, after much changing of plans, by the ladies. We drove to Amman on Saturday morning ... down in to the Jordan valley, then up and up into the highlands on the eastern side. The country is very empty and undeveloped compared with Palestine, with few villages and scattered bedouin encampments. There is beginning to be more and more greenery, though as we got nearer Amman the scene became wintery and there were occasional deep patches of snow by the road side.

Amman has kept its name since it was the city of the Ammonites, but in its present form it has largely grown up since the end of the war, when it was made the capital of the Amir Abdullah and an RAF headquarters.

We first drove to the Residency, where we were received by the British Resident, Colonel Cox, and then went on to the Palace for lunch. Abdullah met us on the doorstep and was most friendly and hospitable. He is a jolly little round man, in long black robes, with white head cloth – plump little hands and a short pointed beard. The conversation was through an interpreter and was not very exciting.

We had a western style lunch, along with the Prime Minister, the Court Chamberlain, the Court doctor, the Chief Minister's secretary and Naif, the Amir's younger son, rather an uncertain quantity to me, but I should say wild and pleasant.

Coupland and I then went for a short walk, returning in time for a tea-party at the Residency – a great many Arab Officials and Ministers and most of the few British, including ... Major Glubb, of the Arab Legion, who quite outshines Lawrence nowadays in these parts, a curiously insignificant, chinless-looking little man.

At 6 o'clock we returned to the Palace for an interesting

and important political interview with the Amir. He spoke with great frankness and made a favourable impression.

Amery and I dined at the RAF Officers' mess. The cold at night was intense and even with an oil-stove my bedroom in the little hotel was almost intolerable.

By this time the public hearing of Jewish evidence was completed. The Arab evidence was beginning, but was not expected to take long. The Mufti of Jerusalem was the first to be called and George Antonius the last on 18 January.

John commented at the time that the Arab witnesses 'state their case extraordinarily badly; but the Commission (I think) quite understand it'. He said in his Jerusalem address that among the Arab witnesses they were impressed by

> an eloquent appeal by the last Arab witness, George Antonius, who declared that it was not anti-semitism but a desire for national independence that motivated Arab refusal to compromise with the Jews. But the belated appearance of Arab witnesses did not really affect the Commission's understanding, to which they had already come, of the nature and causes of Arab opposition to the growth of the National Home. Any unprejudiced reader must agree that the Report gives a fair account of Arab fears and frustrations and of the reasons for them.

John and the commission found Dr Weizmann's evidence the most impressive. He described it in his Jerusalem address.

> I remember feeling something of the tension of those days when his car drove up at speed and on stopping was protectively screened by another car on the outside. 'Aware', as he wrote afterwards, 'of a crushing sense of responsibility', he gave a lengthy and often deeply moving exposition of the Zionist case. Describing the Jewish problem as 'a problem of the homelessness of a people', he spoke of the plight of six million (a prophetic figure) in places where they were not wanted 'and for whom the world is divided into places where they cannot live and places where they cannot enter',

'a minority everywhere', 'the disembodied ghost of a race'. 'There should be one place in God's wide world', he exclaimed, 'where we can live and express ourselves in accordance with our character, and make our contribution to the world in our own way and through our own channels'. He went on to speak of the steadfast preservation throughout the ages of the Jewish people's memory of Palestine, which 'they carried in their hearts and heads wherever they went' and of the long British connection with the idea of the return to Palestine. The Balfour Declaration was a well considered act in accordance with a long tradition. The reference to a National Home meant that the Jews shall 'be able to live like a nation in Palestine' — a Home 'in contradistinction to being on sufferance everywhere else'. He claimed that 'in intention, consciously, nothing has been done to injure the position of the non-Jewish inhabitants' and went on to describe the achievements of Zionism in Palestine. He then turned to various practical problems — immigration, land, labour, self-government. In a final passage he declared that 'deep down in the heart of every Jew there is gratitude that there is at least one nation in the world that has given us a chance. ... But we cannot close our minds to many omissions, a great many things that could have been done. ... I do not think that the Government has done enough for the Arabs.' He hoped that the Commission would formulate conditions under which self-governing institutions might be initiated.

I have described this evidence at disproportionate length because Weizmann was certainly the most impressive witness to appear before the Commission. The Zionists were lucky to have a spokesman of such calibre. One of the outstanding statesmen of his day, in the small category which includes Churchill, Roosevelt and Smuts, he was able, with magnetic and dominating force like that of the conductor of a great orchestra, to maintain rapport with the representatives of such a wide range of experience and opinion as the separate Jewish communities in the countries of Western and Eastern Europe and in the United States; the Zionists and the Non-Zionists; the British and American Governments. While he was an inspiring idealist, the cast of his mind was scientific, making him also a realist, though never sacrificing the long view to immediate expediency. He was quick in acceptance of the merits of the principle of partition when that opportunity was offered by the Commission and remained consistent in support of it in spite of many difficulties and much opposition. In personal contacts with him one always realized that one was in the presence of a truly great man in whom the power of a scientific intellect of the first order was compatible with a deep and generous emotional inspiration.

The commissioners had decided to withdraw from Palestine for private consideration at Helouan near Cairo of what they had heard and seen. They had suspected, correctly, that the Jewish Agency had placed a listening device in their conference room in Jerusalem. (The Jewish Agency was and is a powerful body for the defence and welfare of worldwide Jewry. By 1936, its branch in Palestine had almost become a parallel government for the Jews.) The commissioners arrived at Helouan, a few miles south of Cairo.

It is a delightful climate and a quiet, old-fashioned hotel, most suitable for the Commission's deliberations. We meet in the morning and spend the afternoon sightseeing ... the astonishing Tutankhamun treasures in the museum ... the pyramids and the sphinx — such a strange cat-like creature, with that inscrutable face now sadly weatherworn, but still the face that old Herodotus saw when he came as a tourist in his day. We told the car driver in Cairo to drive us 'To the Sphinx'. He looked completely blank for a minute, then a smile of comprehension broke over his face and he drove us through a great many back streets, landing us eventually triumphantly at the office of a weekly newspaper, '*The Sphinx*'.

On returning to London in January, the commissioners had more work, more papers and documents to consider and more witnesses to hear. On 11 February, Lloyd-George was questioned about his thoughts at the time of the Balfour Declaration and, on

12 March, Winston Churchill, colonial secretary in 1922 and responsible at the beginning of the mandate, was asked about the government's intentions towards Palestine at the time. He said that creating a national home for the Jews was 'the prime and dominating pledge upon which Britain must act'. It was John's first meeting with Churchill.

Immediately on his return from Helouan, John Martin began to prepare an outline of the report. In the discussions at Helouan, Reginald Coupland had come to form a firm view that the only solution to an otherwise insoluble problem was partition. As time went on he carried his colleagues with him and was anxious to draft the sections of the report that put this policy forward. On 2 February, he wrote to John to this effect, having marked the sections he wanted to draft. In the result, the writing of the report was largely his. It is a well-written, thorough and clear report. It ends (on p. 397) with a warm appreciation of John's work.

> Finally we wish to place on record our very warm appreciation of the ability and industry of Mr J. M. Martin, our Secretary, whose services were placed at our disposal by the Colonial Office. An exceptionally heavy burden was placed upon his shoulders, and we gratefully recognize the manner in which he dealt single-handed with the large volume of correspondence and the mass of literature, produced by an enquiry extending in detail to all the Departments of the Palestine Government. In our own relations with him we have observed the same unfailing courtesy which he displayed in the arrangements for our sessions and innumerable personal interviews.

The report, which all the commissioners signed, was published in July 1937. It was in three parts: the 'problem', the 'operation of the mandate' and the 'possibility of a lasting settlement', along with appendices and maps. They painted a picture of an intolerable situation for all parties, the mandatory, the Jews and the Arabs. The conflict between Jew and Arab was fundamentally 'a conflict of right with right' (p 2). Their historical analysis of events from the First World War, when undertakings were given under pressure of war, through to the mandatory's attempts to satisfy the two contending parties and to maintain peace and prosperity during a series of disturbances, was judicious and fair. They considered the administration's difficulties over land, immigration and education — all sources of conflict. These included the power of Jews to buy land, the number of immigrants and the education of children in separate schools, which bred division. They paid particular attention to public security, recommending a firmer line: 'should disorder break out again there should be no hesitation in enforcing martial law throughout the country under undivided military control.' They called the recommendations they had made to deal with the various grievances put to them by Jews and Arabs mere palliatives that would neither remove grievances nor prevent their recurrence — 'the only hope of a cure lies in a surgical operation' (p. 368).

The surgical operation was partition. The commissioners put forward a tentative plan for partition, which they recommended should be explored by another working party in more detail than was possible to them. In their conclusion (p. 394), they argued the case for the principle of partition:

'Half a loaf is better than no bread' is a peculiarly English proverb: and, considering the attitude which both the Arab and the Jewish representatives adopted in giving evidence before us, we think it improbable that either party will be satisfied at first sight with the proposals we have submitted for the adjustment of their rival claims. For Partition means that neither will get all it wants. It means that the Arabs must acquiesce in the exclusion from their sovereignty of a piece of territory, long occupied and once ruled by them. It means that the Jews must be content with less than the Land of Israel they once ruled and have hoped to rule again. But it seems to us possible that on reflection both parties will come to realize that the drawbacks of Partition are outweighed by its advantages. For, if it offers neither party all it wants, it offers each what it wants most, namely freedom and security.

The report outlined these advantages. The Arabs would obtain national independence and would no longer fear being swamped by Jews. The holy places would never come under Jewish control. For loss of territory, the Arab state would receive a subvention from the Jewish state and a grant from the British government.

For the Jews, partition would establish the Jewish national home. To both Arabs and Jews, the commissioners thought partition offered the prospect of obtaining 'the inestimable boon of peace'.

John Martin's own copy of the report is marked with pencil underlinings and strokes in the margins. He used points and phrases that particularly struck him in talks and addresses he was to give on the commission. For him, the commission opened up lasting friendships, notably with Coupland and among the Jews, many of whom later became prominent in the Israeli state created in 1948.

In his later thoughts about the commission's recommendations, John was interested in two questions: how did the idea of partition arise and was the commission right to sketch in a possible scheme for partition? He spoke on each of these in his Jerusalem address.

[P]artition was ... first put forward in a very tentative way after a discussion of Cantonization at a meeting with Dr Weizmann in camera just before Christmas. The idea was put to him that, instead of having a bunch of cantons, there could be two big areas offering the possibility of self-government. Weizmann replied that he did not really understand the proposal, but that, if there were a more definite suggestion, he would do his best to consider it. A more definite suggestion put to him at his last meeting with the Commission on 8 January 1937 envisaged termination of the Mandate and the splitting of Palestine into an independent Jewish state ('as independent as Belgium') and an Arab state, with a British enclave. Weizmann declined to give a definite answer then but said that perhaps he might be given an opportunity to come back to it.

There is more than one version of the sequel; but I shall give it as it was told to me by Coupland himself some years afterwards after checking with the journal he kept at the time. Some days after the last meeting with Weizmann the Commission heard that he was leaving Jerusalem for Haifa, to spend a few days there before returning to England. ... There was just time for Weizmann to meet Coupland at

Nahalal ... their interview lasted less than an hour and apart from explaining that the suggestion implied the possibility of a small Jewish sovereign state, [Coupland] entered into no details. In fact the Commission had not at that stage gone beyond considering the principle of partition and it was not until some time afterwards that they began considering various forms which it might take. Finally, Coupland told me, Weizmann said that personally and provisionally, and provided that the frontiers were drawn to his satisfaction, he favoured the idea of partition.

It was inevitable that on publication much criticism would fasten on the details of the plan of partition. Were the Commission wise to put forward such a revolutionary proposal and even recommend frontiers without closer examination of the practical implications? This question occurred to the Commission themselves. They realized that in proposing termination of the Mandate they might be going outside their terms of reference, as these were understood when they were appointed. But they had come to their belief in partition at a late stage in their enquiry and they did not think that HMG would expect them 'to embark on the further inquiry which would be necessary for working out a scheme of partition in full detail'. ... With the information at their command ... they submitted (a proposal) which they believed was practicable and just, recommending that a frontier commission should be appointed to draw a more precise line.

With hindsight it is possible to doubt if the Commission were well advised to map even a rough frontier without a more profound study of the economic and demographical factors and some consultation with the people who would be affected. Alternatively, and this is what Coupland at one time proposed, the Commission might have limited themselves to recommending the principle and then been replaced by a body composed of a few of their members, with one or two co-opted from Palestine, to work out the details. Statistics available to the Commission were defective; e.g. there had been no census since 1931, and considerable work was necessary to collect more adequate data for the Woodhouse Commission, whose launching was indeed delayed for that purpose.[1]

Consultation might conceivably have led to reconsideration of some features of the plan which even Zionists who, under Weizmann's leadership were not unfavourable to the principle of partition, found most difficult to accept, such as the complete separation of Jerusalem from the Jewish state and the allocation of the Negeb to the Arabs. ... While the Arabs, at least in their public statements, were unwilling to consider partition in any form, consultation might, for example, have enabled the Commission to form a more reliable estimate of reactions in Galilee. ... Whether even so the recommendations would have been implemented by the British Government must remain doubtful. ... Meanwhile the war clouds were continually gathering over Europe and a Report delayed until, say, the summer of 1938 would have reached British ministers at a time when ... they would have found it more difficult than it seemed a year before to accept the implications — financial, military and political.

The report came out on 7 July 1937. On 8 July, the permanent under-secretary, Sir Cosmo Parkinson, wrote to John.

I am writing to you at the request of Mr Ormsby-Gore to tell you that he is placing on record his appreciation of your work as Secretary of the Palestine Royal Commission. ... It is a matter of great personal satisfaction to him that you have earned credit not only for yourself but also for the Colonial Office by the wholly admirable way in which you have carried out your very laborious and responsible duties; and he congratulates you with all sincerity.

The Times (8 July 1937) described the report as a 'State document of the highest importance'. It said 'the Royal Commission has set forth with unanswerable cogency (and, it may be added, with rare felicity of language) the whole case for the revision of the

---

1. Later D. G. Harris, an official in Palestine and one of the collectors of information for the Woodhouse Commission, was to express doubts to John on this point.

British Mandate and the partition of the Mandatory Territory.' It stressed that 'the hope ... of a Judaeo–Arabic nation must be abandoned'.

In Palestine, the first reactions of Jews and Arabs were cool and unfavourable. Neither, as the commission had shown, were getting all they wanted. The *Daily Herald* (9 July 1937) published two comments on the report, by David Ben-Gurion from a Jewish point of view and by H. St John Philby from an Arab one. Ben-Gurion was disappointed, the partition proposals fell far short of a national home, while Philby thought that the report would be acceptable to the Arabs.

The British government welcomed publication of the report and undertook to put its recommendations into effect, but this was not to happen. John attended debates in both houses of Parliament:

> the debate in the Lords was a comparatively dull affair, the House by no means full, though the limited space for distinguished strangers and the public was crowded. Lord Peel spoke well in support of the Report and Samuel was an effective critic on the other side. The Archbishop was almost inaudible except by the use of earphones.
>
> However, in the Commons ... after much coming and going between Churchill, Lloyd-George and other leaders, the Government accepted an amendment, the effect of which was that they could take the scheme to the League for consideration but that the House was not yet committed to approval even of the principle of partition.
>
> It was an unfortunate result as it leaves things very vague and opens up unpleasant prospects of delay and political manoeuvres. On the other hand the question has been saved for the moment from becoming a party matter, as seemed likely at one point. Many people don't like partition (with its obvious difficulties) and hope that, faced with this alternative, the Arabs and Jews will come to terms. I see little or no chance of such a result, but there is no harm in giving them a last opportunity.

An inquiry into the possible frontiers of partition, recommended by the Royal Commission, was undertaken by a working party, the Palestine Partition Commission, chaired by Sir John Wood-house with S. E. V. Luke, John's correspondent in 1936, as secretary. Its members could neither accept the Royal Commission's proposals nor agree on alternatives. In December 1937, the government, after increasing hostility to the partition proposal, said that it was not bound by the commission's report, a decision that angered Sir Horace Rumbold.

Outrages in Palestine continued. On Monday 27 September, on returning from a weekend with his sister in Hampshire, John read of the murder by Arab gunmen of Lewis Andrews, district officer of the Galilee district, who had been shot the previous evening as he came out of church in Nazareth. His obituary in *The Times* (28 September 1937) described him as the strong man of district administration. He had been a great help to the Royal Commission. The report had spoken of his 'constant attendance on the Commission, ... on him was placed the responsibility for the arrangements of our tour and our visits to the districts. This he discharged with conspicuous success. His wide local knowledge and long acquaintance with the country were invaluable'.

Andrew's murder was a great shock to John.

> All that day I was filled with a helpless rage and sorrow. We had worked closely together every day of the visit and I came to have a real affection for him. He was a remarkable man (an Australian, a bit of a rough diamond) and his death is a cruel blow to the Palestine administration. ... I spent a family Christmas with him in Jerusalem.

On 10 October John wrote.

> To my great relief it was finally decided to take firm action. ... The Mufti of Jerusalem, who has been the villain of the piece, has been stripped of the offices which gave him his great power. He took refuge in the Haram [the Mosque of Omar area] and it has not been possible to arrest him; but his committee has been outlawed and the only members who have been caught have been shipped off to the Seychelles.
>
> Now I have come down for a weekend with Coupland and we have had long discussions about Palestine and what

is to be done. There are great difficulties ahead; but at the moment the first steps of the way are becoming clearer.

Earlier in the summer, Lord Peel had died, 'unexpected at the time', John wrote, 'but not altogether surprising, as he had aged visibly since our return and looked worn and shrunk in the summer. It seems that the trouble was cancer after all. He had his 70th birthday at Jerusalem, but he was annoyed when the fact was mentioned and we had no celebration.'

In October, John attended the memorial service for Lord Peel. All five surviving members of the Royal Commission with John and Sir Arthur Wauchope sat in one pew at St Margaret's.

John's work for Palestine was not over. After the war he was to take part in new negotiations on the future of the country.

He concluded his 1978 address in Jerusalem with remarks on the long-term effect of the report.

> One comment may be made in the light of the history of the last forty years. The recommendations of the Royal Commission may in the end have been shelved, so that in Weizmann's prescient phrase, the Mandate had been discredited, 'but there was nothing to take its place'; but we need not share the views of Rumbold, in a bitter comment, that, in the light of what had happened, he had to admit that 'all of us wasted 10 months of our time'. The Report, with its painstaking analysis of the problem of Palestine and its revolutionary proposals itself changed the situation and introduced a new chapter of History. For better or worse, the Peel Commission bequeathed to the future two legacies. First, there was the concept of partition, which, in one shape or another continued to find supporters and was of course an essential feature of the plan accepted by the United Nations in 1947. Second, although the Commission were not creators of the idea of a Judenstaat, they brought to the forefront with emphasis and authority the concept of the National Home as an independent, sovereign state. It was not without reason that Weizmann, so we are told, after the meeting with Coupland at Nahalal exclaimed 'Today we have laid the foundations of the Jewish State'.

6

War Service: With Churchill, 1940–45

Until May 1940, John Martin continued at the Colonial Office, though with a move from the personnel division to the Far Eastern Department, which reunited him with his much-loved Malaya. In May 1940, he was called to the Prime Minister's private office to join the team of private secretaries; in May 1941 he was appointed principal private secretary and served there until the end of June 1945. John Martin found these five years in the private office, his war service, unexpected, strange, disruptive and exhilarating, as war service was for many millions. They were unexpected because he had foreseen a straightforward career in the Colonial Office; strange in the remarkable shape of work under Churchill; disruptive because he felt the Colonial Office to be his true vocation; and exhilarating because they brought him close to the heart of government in the dangerous wartime years. He regarded the private office as a deviation he had to accept because of the demands of the war.

Much has been written about these years and the inevitable historical revisions and reassessments of Winston Churchill have been made. Yet, Churchill remains the saviour of his country in 1940 and a great war leader.

John Martin himself, though reluctant to enter the public domain, made two published contributions. The first was an essay in *Action This Day: Working with Churchill* (Macmillan, 1968, pp. 139–57). This publication was an attempt to counteract a book by Churchill's doctor, Lord Moran, called *Winston Churchill: The Struggle for Survival*, which many of those who worked closely with Churchill thought to be improper in revealing professional confidences and misleading in the opinions expressed. The second, *Downing Street: The War Years* (Bloomsbury, 1991), appeared at the time of John's death, though the material had been assembled some years before. It contained extracts from his brief personal diary, a skeleton diary listing dates and facts, and from his letters to his mother and wife, along with month-by-month summaries of the main events of the war. After the war, and later in his retirement, historians often consulted John, which is evident from the number of references to him in the works that followed.

In correspondence, John referred to Churchill as 'my master'. 'Our finest hour and our greatest moment came from our work with him,' said Harold Macmillan on Churchill's death. These words expressed the feelings of almost all who were close to Churchill in the war years, especially in the first year of his premiership. It was a daunting prospect for John to join the private office.

He was introduced to Churchill in his room at the House of Commons on 23 May. 'See,' he said, looking John up and down with a searching gaze, 'I understand you are going to be one of my secretaries.'

Four days before, as battle raged in France and Flanders, Churchill had made his first broadcast as prime minister. He looked ahead to the time when 'the bulk of that hideous apparatus of aggression which gashed Holland into ruin and slavery in a few days will be turned upon us'. John noted how he ended his words: 'Today is Trinity Sunday. Centuries ago words were written to be a call and a spur to the faithful servants of truth and justice: "Arm yourselves, and be ye men of valour".' John fastened onto these words, and later quoted them (pp. 155–6).

'Today is Trinity Sunday.' It was as if a great bell tolled. This sudden and unexpected reminder of our Faith and its most mysterious doctrine had a strangely moving effect. The dark scene in Europe ... was shot through and illumined as by a great flash of lightning. ... Our eyes were opened to a vision like that of the prophet's servant, who 'saw; and, behold, the mountain was full of horses and chariots of fire round about Elisha'.

The crisis of 1940 could be understood in many ways, but the cause was a great one, best interpreted in terms of the country's Christian faith. If John could find this in his master he could serve him with devotion and total commitment.

The difficulties of working with Churchill are well documented. His speech was hard to understand at first and his daily routine exhausted those who worked for him. At first, 10 Downing Street was the base, but on 16 October 1940, John wrote to his mother:

> I shall remember this birthday [15 October] by the evening before it when we had, as it seemed, the worst night of air raids since that first weekend in September. A high explosive bomb fell just a few yards from the house (No. 10). I was upstairs when it came down and dashed down to the shelter as I heard it fall to the accompaniments of the most terrific explosion. It was difficult to remember afterwards exactly what happened, but I seemed to fly down with a rush of 'blast', the air full of dust and the crash and clatter of glass breaking behind. There was a rush of several of us into the shelter and we tumbled in on top of one another in a good deal of confusion ... by the light of torches we were able to survey the damage. The mess in the house was indescribable — windows smashed in all directions, everything covered with grime, doors off hinges, curtains, furniture etc. tossed about in a confused mess. Fortunately the PM has been using the basement and was dining down there at the time at the opposite side of the house, so was none the worse.

John, who briefly continued to sleep at No. 10, commented: 'It is extraordinary how little attention is paid to the occasional daytime raids. People mostly go about in the streets as if nothing was happening.' The next letter, of 3 November 1940, told that 'I no longer "sleep" at No. 10 (quotation marks because of several interruptions last night) but underneath our new office in a neighbouring, more modern building.' It was difficult running an office between three sites. This came to an end when Storey's Gate was established and No. 10 repaired and strengthened to be brought back into use in 1943.

He commented in a letter to George Abell: 'I never thought of myself as a Londoner till now when it has become a real honour to boast of, for I don't suppose there has ever been anything more magnificent than the cheerfulness and sheer guts of the people of London in [the] face of this horrible experience.'

Churchill was both prime minister and minister of defence. Thus, the whole range of military and civil affairs came under his hand in the direction of the war. Documents, messages and information of all kinds passed through the Annexe as well as persons bearing various responsibilities in government and in the execution of the war. Up to the entry of the Americans, as a result of the Japanese attack on Pearl Harbor in December 1941, there was no certainty of victory. The entry of the Russians in June 1941 had hardly turned the tide, for the Germans made deep inroads into the USSR. Faith and high morale amid many disasters had kept British hopes alive, along with discreet support from President Roosevelt. Churchill managed his affairs in his distinctive way, almost as a family affair, with a circle of trusted friends to assist him. The private office had a key place in this circle.

'The Private Office' was a term Churchill brought with him from the Admiralty in May 1940. The staff he brought were Eric Seal, his principal private secretary, John Peck (KCMG 1971, diplomatic service after the war, ambassador to Irish Republic 1970–73), who was to remain in the private office until the end of the war, and Mrs Hill. He inherited from his predecessor's office Anthony Bevir and Jock Colville, along with Miss Watson who dealt with parliamentary questions and with letters from the public. It was into this company that John Martin was recruited. Certain changes were brought about. Seal thought Colville would be better in dealing with Churchill, which may well have been true, and asked Bevir to take on ecclesiastical patronage of the Crown and Crown academic appointments, a decision that was to service church and state well.

Churchill had high expectations of his private secretaries. He required them to be available, at hand when he wanted them. This often meant waiting about for long periods at awkward times. He required them to understand his ways of doing things, to interpret his words and personal slang or terms. He required discretion. In the family atmosphere, Churchill liked to talk freely in the office, over dinner, or at other times when his mind was turning over problems, to try out ideas and possibilities. He wished to be entirely confident in knowing that those with whom he talked would take matters no further. Churchill's secret circle entirely respected his confidence and nothing got out during the war, though afterwards diaries and narratives of all kinds appeared.

John Martin was entirely in tune with this. His own diary, as *Downing Street* reveals, is the barest skeleton of headings. His letters to his mother and wife reveal nothing about confidential discussions or policy and only refer to national events that had already been or were about to be made public. His references to discussions and policy making are always in terms of forgetting. Discretion required forgetting so that he cultivated an art of forgetting. 'My memory is like a sieve,' he would say in later years. Yet, when he was then asked for evidence in defence of Churchill's reputation, his disciplined memory could call up the necessary case, action or word needed. One criticism of Lord Moran by those who wrote *Action This Day* was that he claimed inside knowledge of decisions about which he could not have known because he was not present when they were made. Colville put the criticism, as he wrote in *The Fringes of Power* (p. 759), 'unkindly but truthfully. Lord Moran was never present when history was made, though he was often invited to luncheon afterwards.'

Churchill required the people around him to be of robust character. His own regime was a punishing one. The war itself, so disastrously begun, could be won only by superhuman efforts and exertions. His staff should set an example. At the same time, he wanted those around him to be good humoured, agreeable persons who could relate to him and enjoy the experience of working for him, hard though it might be. In his private secretaries, Churchill looked for men of intelligence with the power to think and to discern. When, in May 1941, Sir Eric Seal, the principal private secretary, left to join the Admiralty, John Martin was appointed to succeed him. John had his doubts. On 11 May 1941, he wrote to his mother:

> The job is one which ought to be held by someone with much bigger guns than I possess (or in fact at my age could be expected to possess). Ought I in the public interest to fight

the proposal? On the other hand it would be a quixotic thing to do and if the PM is satisfied who am I to question it? ... Then I don't want to be too long divorced from the CO, which is my real home. It is all rather wearing and I wish the point could be settled soon. It is an alarming prospect.

John's appointment was settled on 14 May. 'The PM told me when I put him to bed on Sunday night (or rather Monday morning *circa* 2.00 a.m.).'

The four years during which John held the appointment tell the story of a happy and efficient private office. The main quality Churchill sought in a PPS was intelligence, for he needed someone with the ability to decide which items from among all the material entering the office needed Churchill's attention and which could be handled by somebody else. The same sort of discrimination had to be exercised over the many people who wished to gain access to the Prime Minister. Jock Colville, a colleague at No. 10, described John Martin as 'a first-class product of the Edinburgh Academy and Corpus Christi, Oxford'. He had 'a shy and retiring disposition combined with a ready wit, a delectable sense of humour and a conscientious devotion to the public service'.

In *The Churchillians*, Colville wrote: 'under Martin's leadership ... the Private Office was both cheerful and effective. It was so well attuned to Churchill's personal predilections and his unusual methods of work that none of its members succumbed, though they may occasionally have wilted, beneath the stresses and anxieties of war.' While preparing *The Churchillians*, Colville asked John Martin to comment on his draft of the chapter on the private office, in which he suggested that John tended to be 'alarmed by Churchill' and that Churchill 'failed to understand' him. John was not prepared to have this. His reply was robust.

I wonder if you know what inhibitions a naturally reserved and shy Scot has to overcome in such a relationship; but I doubt if Winston 'failed to understand' if indeed he ever took the trouble to think about it. After all he accepted me as PPS after a full year's experience of me as a PS and at least tolerated me for the next four years.

John drafted a few sentences, which he saw as more fitting the facts. Colville made use of them.

It is worth noting that John Martin recruited Leslie Rowan — he knew the kind of man Churchill would like to have working for him — and that Jock Colville left the private office for periods in the war for honourable reasons. From October 1941 to December 1943, it was to train in the RAF as a fighter pilot and to make his first operational raids; and, for eight weeks 'fighting leave' in 1944, it was to take part in air strikes over Normandy. Above all, Churchill required in those around him a total devotion to the great cause he represented and symbolized. In his own way, John could make this plain to those who worked for and with him.

As a war leader, Churchill used the spoken word with power and effect. From his early days in public life, he had learned to take great trouble over his speeches and would spend hours, even weeks, preparing them. The private office contributed very little to his wartime speeches. The PM occasionally asked for factual information, or to have a literary or other quotation checked. The private secretaries would also read the texts of speeches for accuracy. More generally, the topics the PM tackled in his speeches would come up in the work of the office or be introduced over dinner at No. 10, Storey's Gate or Chequers. Churchill might try out an idea with a colleague in government or with a private secretary. The PPS's main contribution was to keep the office running effectively so that the atmosphere was relaxed and conducive to intelligent and stimulating conversation.

In his restrained way, John Martin did not see himself as an adviser to the PM, so felt no need to suggest topics or ideas for speeches. This was probably why his predecessor, Eric Seal, was moved to the Admiralty. Seal thought that advising was among his duties. John's very usefulness to Churchill was that he did not give advice. For this reason, if on a rare occasion John chose to intervene on the grounds that he thought that the PM was wrong, Churchill would listen to him, as Eden recounts (*The Eden Memoirs: The Reckoning*, p. 367) of an instance in 1943.

On the evening of February 24th the Prime Minister's chief Private Secretary, Mr John Martin, rang me up to say that he thought I ought to see a telegram which Mr Churchill was despatching to our Minister Resident in Algiers. I sent for the telegram and saw that the Prime Minister was urging that every opportunity should be taken to press for the admission of M. Pierre-Étienne Flandin into the French North African administration. I did not think this a wise move or likely to be welcome to the French.

In due course, Churchill tore up the document and a variant was agreed between Eden and the PM.

Though John had great respect and regard for Churchill, he was not uncritical of him. He was against Churchill's dangerous but successful expedition to Athens at Christmas 1944. As he wrote in his diary for 24 December, 'Glad I am not going on an expedition of which I disapprove, the prize not being worth the risks.'

Among the women in the private office, apart from Miss Watson, who belonged to the 'scheme of things', there were many secretaries. These were particularly important because of Churchill's method of dictating straight to a secretary and silent typewriter, which was exhausting work for the secretary. One, Elizabeth Nel, wrote a warm assessment of John's leadership of the private office and of his relationship with the PM.

> John set a very high standard for himself and his staff — loyalty, efficiency, reliability, absolute confidentiality and devotion to duty being 'musts' for us all. At the same time he was very human and pleasant with all of the staff. His dry humour was ever-present, he always looked for a restrained laugh. ... Regarding the other Private Secretaries, so far as I recall under John's restraining hand there was peace in the Private Office. Everyone was far too busy and dedicated to be resentful of office discipline. John was always pleasant and cheerful to us of the Personal Staff. Mrs Hill and I would go in turns to Chequers for the weekend, and as Personal Secretary would usually travel with the duty Private Secretary — which was perhaps the time when one got to know them at a more relaxed level.

Private secretaries had general and particular duties. General ones were shared on a rota basis, but two particular duties fell to

John. The first was to prepare the twice-yearly honours lists, New Year and Birthday, which, as he often hinted in his letters, was not a task he enjoyed. The other was to accompany Churchill on his many journeys. This was altogether different, full of interest, surprises and drama.

Churchill's personal advisers were also part of the secret circle, but outside his private office. These included Desmond Morton, Churchill's link with secret service work, the Free French and other governments in exile; Professor Lindemann, his scientific adviser; Beaverbrook and Brendan Bracken. The secret circle was like a family, an extended family with a powerful and often unpredictable head, yet a family with a strong common purpose. Mrs Churchill was a significant figure within it and its members knew her and consulted her. John saw a good deal of her in London, at Chequers and on journeys when she accompanied her husband. The Churchill children and their spouses were well known to some members of the secret circle and their names appear in diaries. Daughters sometimes travelled with the PM, particularly the youngest, Mary. From time to time in his letters or diary, John referred to her agreeable and charming presence. It was a privileged yet very hard-working family.

A private secretary's first task was to be there, and to wait constructively for people to come and go, for decisions to be made and passed on, and for interviews and meetings to happen and to end. How else did Jock Colville find time to write his voluminous diary, kept under lock and key in the office? (Though frowned on then — his colleagues once tried to unsettle Colville by writing a memo from the PM asking to see his diary, but eased off under the impact of his terror — it has been a delight to readers in later years.) How else did John Peck have time to write his agreeable light verse? And, how else did Colville and, to a lesser extent, Leslie Rowan manage to dine so frequently in clubs and mingle with the aristocracy and *haute bourgeoisie* of London and the country? John himself found time for courtship and marriage. In all this, he was the coordinator, making sure that his colleagues provided the services his master required.

This might suggest that, in the war years, the private office was run like a gentleman's club of a certain social standing with literary tastes and interests. It was more than that; it was an effective and well-run organization to carry out what the PM required in continually changing circumstances. John joined the private office at a time of extreme crisis, with the impending fall of France and loss of continental Europe. The success of the Battle of Britain, 'the finest hour', justified the decision to fight on in 1940, but, though a German invasion of Britain had been delayed if not averted, there was no certainty of ultimate victory. (It would be dishonourable not to mention the gathering in Britain of the Free French under General de Gaulle's leadership, or the forces from Poland and other European countries being overrun by Germans.) When John was appointed PPS in May 1941, the picture was no brighter. Britain and the Commonwealth were still alone. In June, however, when a devastating German assault plunged deep into the Soviet Union, Britain gained a new ally. The hoped-for entry of the United States into the war occurred in December when the Japanese attacked Pearl Harbor and the Germans declared war on the USA. Even so, victory on all fronts was to take another three and a half years. From fighting alone with the Commonwealth, Britain entered into an alliance with what were to become the two postwar superpowers. The task of cementing the alliance changed the work of the private office, for the PM was no longer the sole leader but one of a triumvirate of Roosevelt, Stalin and Churchill. As the years went on, the US and Soviet contributions to the armed struggle exceeded that of Britain. Churchill once remarked that it had been easier to get things done on one's own. Diplomacy became of key importance and the PM's journeys overseas became longer and more frequent.

The private office needed to be informed of what was happening, of what the pressures were and from where they were coming. Their main informant was the PM himself, partly through his own work and partly because he enjoyed discussing his ideas, anxieties and hopes with people he trusted. The private office was also informed by the continuous stream of people coming in and out, documents, messages, correspondence and telephone calls. The simple objective was victory, but there were numerous roads to it.

Among John's papers is an account by an American journalist, Marquis Childs of Madison, Wisconsin, who saw Churchill in June 1943 at Downing Street.

There are two police at the entrance to the short street. ...
At No 10 ... Mr Martin, the PM's secretary [who] shows
you to a small reception room on the side of the house. ...
Mr Martin is friendly, knowledgeable about America. He
talks about the *New Yorker* which he reads when he has
time, asking whether profiles are fairly good portraits. He
talks about the PM in the blitz; how difficult it was to make
him observe any caution. ... Martin says, yes, the PM is
without personal fear. He, Martin, has accompanied him on
all but one of his journeys ... from a door apparently giving
off the cabinet room Sir Stafford Cripps pops out and asks
Martin if he knows 'where the Captain is'. Martin goes off.
... From somewhere comes a booming voice that might be
that of the PM. ... The voice goes on. It is nearly quarter to
four; the appointment was for three fifteen. ... It is four
o'clock when Martin comes in to say, 'He's ready now.' He
leads the way, opens the double doors and calls out my name.

This passage reveals one side of a private secretary's work, the
care of a visitor who could be helpful to the Allied cause and the
discrimination that lets some in and excludes others. On this
occasion, John's duty was to keep the visitor pleasantly entertained during a fairly lengthy wait.

Family links became precious to those who had endured the
London Blitz, so, when he could, John would take a holiday in
Scotland. His mother in Edinburgh was becoming frail and his sister Peggy had returned from medical mission work in India to be
with her. His brother William was running a medical practice in
Peebles, but the nearest place for him to relax and escape the dangers and pressures of London was his sister's home near Andover.

He still had strong Oxford links. Reginald Coupland's home on
Boar's Hill was a frequent refuge; after John's marriage to the
daughter of the provost, Sir David Ross, Oriel became his second
base.

One of John Martin's main duties was to accompany the PM on
his overseas journeys. These journeys had two main purposes. The
first was consultation, planning and decision-making at significant
points in the war with political and military leaders. The second
was to see what was happening on the ground. There was some

overlap in that longer absences from home included each of these purposes. Sometimes John did not go himself, but arranged for another private secretary to take his place.

John's letters to his family, mainly to his mother and later, after his engagement and marriage, to his wife, describe some of the scenes and drama of these journeys. His engagement and marriage brought a new dimension to John's writing. Long absences at critical times before and after his marriage and during the later stages of his wife's pregnancy created anxieties. His heart and mind belonged in two places, the task in hand and the distant home, as it did for so many in their war service.

John's first overseas journey with Churchill was to the Atlantic Charter meeting with President Roosevelt in August 1941, at Placentia Bay, Newfoundland. In a letter to his sister, Detta, he wrote:

I can't attempt to give an adequate account of the Atlantic affair and haven't even written a proper diary of it for record purposes as I ought to have done. I wonder how soon you guessed where we were. One of the London dailies said it was the best-kept secret of the war; but another (the same day) said it was the worst. Anyhow it was all arranged in a very short time — just over a week. My master was as excited as a boy, planning all the details of his entertainment of the other fellow — ordering grouse, ordering turtle, ordering a band. With Chief of Staff, Staff Officers, clerks, extra marines etc. we were quite a little party and went north in a big special train as long as an express, crossed in a destroyer and found ourselves in remarkably spacious and comfortable quarters on the *Prince of Wales*. We had a little mess of our own — the PM, the 3 Chiefs of Staff, Harry Hopkins, Cadogan (of the FO), Cherwell, Tommy Thompson (the ADC) and myself — and I have never enjoyed a fortnight's meals so much. (And incidentally in all the rest of my life I have never eaten so much caviar, for HH had brought ample supplies from Moscow.)

The first day out was rather rough and I couldn't take breakfast. ('*Tout au contraire*' alas). The PM most tenderly dosed me with Mothersill, which he finds an unfailing remedy — but my self-respect was restored on the last day of our homeward voyage, when it was again stormy and it was *he* who had to take the Mothersill. ... We arrived at our destination in the early morning and came slowly into quite a Hebridean bay. ... As we passed the President's flagship (the USS *Augusta*) our band played the Star-spangled Banner, while every one on the deck stood at attention and the Marines presented arms. Then across the water came the National Anthem from the other ship.

As soon as the usual naval courtesies were over the PM took us over to greet the President, who received us supported by one of his sons on an upper deck. We stood about there for a little, the PM handing over a letter from the King which I had carried in my pocket and then, while President and PM went off alone, we were taken down to a cabin and talked to the American Officers and (their Navy being dry) were regaled with tomato juice, followed by a fork lunch. After that official conversations went on for the rest of the visit.

The President, being such a cripple, visited our ship only once — on Sunday, when the PM had planned a big joint service on the quarter deck. You would be surprised if you knew how much thought he gave to this, choosing the hymns himself and vetting the prayers (which I had to read aloud to him for the purpose while he dried after his bath). It really was a great occasion — hundreds of men from both fleets, all mixed together. One rough British sailor sharing his hymnbook with one rough American ditto. You would have to have been pretty hard-boiled not to be moved by it all and I felt it was a sort of marriage service between our two peoples. After it the President stayed on to a big lunch party in the ward room (when we ate some of the grouse!). You have no doubt seen the picture of the PM watching him go off in his destroyer when it was all over. He was very genial and asked me if I'd like to go ashore with him. We were a small party and were pulled ashore in a whaler. It was queer to wander about like the first discoverers, with not a human soul to meet us.

That night I dined at the President's table, only a few

people and not at all formal. I will show you the menu, which he signed. Two of his sons were there. I particularly liked young Franklin, a big good-looking fellow, serving as an Ensign in their Navy.

This was when John first met Harry Hopkins, the personal liaison officer Roosevelt used in his discussions with Churchill. Hopkins became an admirer of Churchill, committed to the British cause and proved himself a friend not only to the country as a whole but to those who worked for Churchill, including John. Hopkins was generous with presents. One came to John on 11 August with a charming note well adjusted to John's sensibilities.

Harry Hopkins sent me large cartons of canned fruit, hams, candies etc. (worth their weight in gold in rationed Britain), accompanied by the following note:

My dear Martin:
  If your conscience will permit, these are to be taken to London. If the niceties of the war would disturb, I suggest you give them to some other member of the party whose will to live well may be greater than yours.
  Ever so cordially,

  Harry Hopkins

The wartime journeys were to promote many such friendships.
  The first Washington conference, codenamed Arcadia, came soon after Pearl Harbor. A meeting with Roosevelt and his colleagues was clearly necessary in the new situation of the USA becoming an ally and fellow combatant. When the USA was brought into the war in December, John noted in his diary of 11 December 1941, 'the stars in their courses [are] fighting for us.' The PM's party was away from 12 December to 17 January, John staying with the PM at the White House. 'We are a big party, the principals, besides the PM, being Lord Beaverbrook, 3 Chiefs of Staff and the American Lease-Lend man, Averell Harriman. These have with them staff officers from the 3 services and a few civil servants. The PM also brought his doctor, Sir Charles Wilson.' He

reported that the profusion of things in the shops seemed 'like a dream after the rigours of our besieged island. ... Washington's millions of lights as seen from the air the night we arrived was one of the most beautiful sights I have ever seen.'

On 11 January, he wrote from a train on the way back from a few days' break in Florida.

> The high-up conversations were necessarily suspended for a few days while the Chiefs of Staff on both sides cleared up a mass of detailed business and the PM took advantage of this to escape to the south and the sunshine ... but we by no means escaped from the daily conduct of the war, for we were of course connected with Washington by telephone and a courier once and sometimes twice a day brought down a pouch to us by aeroplane. ... We were closely guarded by secret service men and, though the Press soon scented our presence, we were not molested in any way. The story was put about that a Mr Lobb, an invalid requiring quiet, was staying in the house and, to explain my un-transatlantic accents when answering the phone, I was 'his English butler'.

Early months in 1942 brought a series of military disasters in the Far East and setbacks in the Mediterranean, but Arcadia had placed a priority on defeating Germany and Italy and expressed the intention to liberate Europe in 1943. Arcadia also brought into use the term 'United Nations', 26 nations headed by Britain, the USA, the USSR and China having signed an agreement to put their full resources into defeating Germany, Italy, Japan and their allies.

The second Washington conference was between 18 and 27 June 1942. This time they had two nights at Hyde Park, the president's country estate north of New York before returning to Washington. 'On arrival we went to our old quarters at the White House, where Mrs Roosevelt was waiting to receive us. Everyone gave us a most kind welcome and we felt as if we were coming home.'

On his return, he commented: 'What a rich, spacious country America seems after our little, rationed, strenuous island. Whatever Tobruk may mean [news of the fall of Tobruk had reached Washington on 21 June], it is impossible not to feel that the tide is setting strong and irresistible on our side. . . . I hope this is not my last visit to the western hemisphere.'

The main matters the conference considered were preparations for the liberation of Europe and reversal of the deteriorating situation in North Africa by reinforcing Auchinleck and a US landing in French North Africa. The conference also considered strengthening convoy defences. News of the fall of Tobruk had cast a cloud of disappointment, with US papers predicting the fall of the British government. Churchill came home to a vote of censure. 'Now for England, home, and — a beautiful row,' he said to Harry Hopkins as he left Baltimore (*Road to Victory*, p. 134). The debate on the motion of censure took place on 1 and 2 July. John's diary for 1 July notes, 'up late in connection with preparation of PM's speech'. The motion was defeated by 475 votes to 25.

John did not attend the first Moscow conference when Churchill had to tell Stalin that there would be no second front in 1942, 'a somewhat raw job,' he called it 'like carrying a large lump of ice to the North Pole.' John went in his special train with Mrs Churchill to meet him at an aerodrome 'somewhere in the south of England. We had become quite friends during Winston's absence, for I used to go and see her most mornings to take the latest news of the travellers. So on the train we had a long heart to heart talk.'

John's world changed forever with his courtship, engagement and, on 1 May 1943, marriage to Rosalind, third daughter of Sir David Ross, Provost of Oriel and Vice-Chancellor of Oxford University. Wartime travels were to bring frequent separations during their courtship, engagement and marriage, so letters were frequent. Hunting for and equipping their house were managed in small fragments of time snatched from work.

Their home, 25 Pelham Place in South Kensington, was purchased on a ground lease. Furniture was acquired. Rosalind was sent 'the form of application for Utility Furniture and the Catalogue. I'm just back from a wild-goose chase to Peter Jones for — of all things — an ironing board,' John wrote on 23 March. 'You may be relieved to hear that none was to be had, the one of which I had been told having evidently gone.' A doubt about the timing of the wedding service entered John's mind on 17 March 1943. 'On second thoughts I was a little sorry about the 2.00 p.m. decision as we must obviously invite the august person (however embarrassing his presence) and it may seem unkind to have chosen what is quite the worst time for him.'

On 1 May, John and Rosalind were married at the University Church in Oxford. Photographs show a radiantly lovely bride triumphing over wartime austerity; traffic on the High Street was held up for the procession back to Oriel of many of the great and the good of the day, Mrs Churchill among them, the 'august person' himself being unable to attend. John's mother had made the journey from Edinburgh, frail but immensely happy and proud, to walk out of church on the arm of Sir David Ross, not Just Vice-Chancellor but a Scot and a Presbyterian.

The honeymoon was spent in Scotland. The CVO (awarded in the Birthday honours) was a pleasant surprise. On 3 June 1943, John wrote: 'Awards in this Order are a personal affair of the King's, not made on the Prime Minister's recommendation, and so do not come through our machinery. I only learnt on receiving a letter from the King's Private Secretary on Saturday. The award was nicely timed: I wonder if it was meant as a wedding present.'

Churchill had returned from a tour to Washington and Algiers and his presence increased the tempo of work in the private office. On 10 June, John commented to his mother: 'Now that the PM is back I am realizing more and more (what I knew beforehand) how ill the duties of a PS and those of married life go together.'

The office continued to make demands. On 1 August 1943, he complained that 'there was a midnight Cabinet one day, when I didn't get to bed till 4.20 a.m.' Absence for a newly married husband, especially when his wife is approaching childbirth, can be painful. It was a wise ordinance of ancient Israel that a newly married man should not be called up for war service for three years after his wedding. The exigencies of his appointment did not allow John that kindness.

Four substantial conference journeys took place in this period. John did not attend his master at the third Washington conference in May/June 1943, held soon after his marriage, but was present at the Casablanca one in January/February 1943, the first Quebec one in August/September 1943 and the Cairo and Teheran ones in November 1943 and January 1944.

There were storms during the sea passage to North Africa, which brought seasickness to John and others.

Somehow lunch was faced and surmounted — though the noble lord fled suddenly from table with a face the colour of parchment — and a change of course in the afternoon brought much improvement. Since then all has been well and we have enjoyed a pleasant week-end of occasional work, a fair amount of sunshine, much fresh air, plenty of food and more than the usual ration of sleep, all with a seasoning of Trollope.

... At Valletta the PM visited the naval dockyard where he received a tumultuous welcome from hundreds — or thousands — of Maltese. We drove from there up to the Governor's (town) palace, where Winston appeared like Mussolini on the balcony and beamed upon a large cheering crowd in the square below.

In early December, John was still hoping to return home for Christmas. On 13 December he mentions Churchill's illness and a letter of 16 December says: 'Here's a how-d'you-do and for various reasons I must be careful what I say. First, the illness is serious. Secondly, the doctors' latest indications are that we shall probably be here (the place from which I wrote last — Tunis) a fortnight and possibly for convalescence as much as four weeks.' John thought that when Churchill's convalescence began he might be able to get John Peck out to take his place, but this did not prove possible. He was worried also about Rosalind staying at Pelham Place at a time when 'the intermittent Blitz' still continued. To his mother, he wrote on 19 December 1943:

Whatever happens I shall certainly arrange to be back with her (R) at the end of January, already near; but just at the moment and until the PM is out of the wood I cannot leave my post here. Jock Colville (who has returned to No. 10 from the RAF) flew out with Mrs C and he and Francis can perfectly well hold the fort together during the period of convalescence.

He emphasized his undertaking to Rosalind to be back before the end of January. In fact, he stayed to the end, arriving with the full party on 18 January.

However, news was better at Christmas.

It was quite a cheerful Christmas, though I couldn't help thinking all the time how much better it might have been at home. Those who went to early Service, in a sort of shed, reported a most dramatic end when the bells of the cathedral near by began to peal loudly and at the same moment a dove flew in at a window and alighted in front of the altar — taken by everyone as an excellent omen. Later in the morning I went with Mrs C and others to an open air parade Service for the troops guarding us. Meanwhile the house was filled with generals, admirals and air marshals and their hangers on for a big military pow-wow.

The day after his return, John and Rosalind attended Leslie Rowan's wedding at Holy Trinity, Brompton. Then, during a blitz two days later on 21 January, their son David Ross was born at Westminster Hospital, some days earlier than the forecasted 29 January. Unfortunately, a severe streptococcal infection delayed Rosalind's return home until 16 February. Lady Ross, Rosalind's mother, made plain her indignation at the enormity of an infection caught at the hospital. Rosalind, weak after almost four weeks in hospital and with the ever-present threat of the blitz, needed somewhere safer than the Pelham Place house. If the long nightly blitzes were to continue, John told his mother on 23 February 1944, it would be impossible to maintain their home there, 'but it will be hateful if we have to separate'. By the end of the month the decision had been made. Rosalind and David went to Oxford, to Oriel, for a stay that was to last for over a year. John stayed at the office and 25 Pelham Place was shut up. John visited the house from time to time and spent weekends when he could at Oxford. Later, in March, Lady Ross was taken ill, which made Rosalind's presence there very valuable. The infant David was christened on Easter Day at St Columba's, Oxford.

By mid-1944, V-1s (also known as doodlebugs or flying bombs) were targeting London and, later in the year, the V-2 rocket-propelled bombs joined the attack. John's new home suffered.

Alas, a flying bomb burst on top of a block of flats near

Pelham Place on Monday night and blew in all our front windows, besides some of the glass at the back. ... Windows, with frames and shutters, are badly smashed and part of the ceiling in our bedroom had collapsed. I organized a party of cleaners in the afternoon and once the glass, plaster and soot had been swept up the house didn't look so bad. Fortunately the furniture had been covered and I didn't find any real damage to the contents of the house beyond one lamp shade twisted and our bedroom carpet filthy. The main structure of the house is undamaged. I got in touch with a builder at once and he has promised to start emergency repairs as soon as possible. When I called today I found a slater examining the roof, but otherwise no progress has yet been made. The whole street is looking rather derelict. Yesterday it was roped off, with a police-man on patrol.

The long-awaited D-Day for the Normandy landings came on 6 June 1944. Less than a week later, on 12 June, John accompanied Churchill and others for a day on the Normandy beachhead.

Luckily we had a perfect day on Monday, with not a cloud in the sky until evening, for our expedition to France.

We had spent Sunday night in the train (with the three American Chiefs of Staff — General Marshall, Admiral King and General Arnold) and embarked on a destroyer after early breakfast for the Channel crossing. This took about 3¾ hours, in almost perfect conditions. I was on the bridge all the time and there was always something to watch — shipping passing or being overtaken and aircraft high overhead, swarms of Fortresses, Liberators and others. There was a little excitement at one moment as ack-ack fire was sighted ahead, but this turned out simply to be a ship practising its guns.

We went ashore in a duck (a swimming tank), landing on the beach at Courseulles, the town next to Bernières. Monty was waiting with two or three jeeps, into which we crowded. I shared one with an admiral, three other naval officers, Smuts'[s] son and the driver, a very tight fit. Thus we drove off through the town and out into the country. The houses on the sea-front have been badly damaged by bombardment, but inland we were astonished by the general peaceful aspect of the countryside. Here and there buildings had been knocked about or there was a crashed plane or burnt-out car, while German signs with 'Minen' and skull and crossbones showed where there were minefields (possibly bogus); but generally speaking the landscape was little changed. Crops were ripening for harvest: I even saw fat cows munching contentedly and the people on the roads, friendly and happy, showed no obvious marks of privation.

The PM with the CIGS and Smuts had a conference and lunch with Monty at his HQ. Meanwhile with the rest of the party I hurried through some sandwiches and then went for a stroll in the near-by village. It was full of military patrols, but some of the inhabitants were also going about or looking out of their windows. ... From this HQ we drove to another one and, while there, saw a German bomber come over. There was a burst of ack ack fire ('quite like London') and we heard that the plane had been brought down. Meanwhile the louder barks of the bigger guns (chiefly naval) had been going on all the time.

On returning to the beach the PM was mobbed by the troops and there was some difficulty in clearing a way to his launch. We then cruised along the shore, watching the ships disembarking troops, lorries, tanks etc. in great quantities. As far as the eye could see the water seemed to be covered with a stupendous mass of craft of all sizes for miles to the horizon on both sides. There can never have been such a sight in the history of the world and I doubt if there ever will be again.

Eventually we rejoined the destroyer and passed back along the beach to the end of the British line (the end near Caen), where the smoke of battle could be seen ashore. Before turning away we fired three or four rounds at the enemy's position. We weren't back in England till 10 o'clock at night after one of the most memorable days I have ever spent. It was a thrilling tour and everyone was immensely impressed.

John went with Churchill to France again from 20 to 23 July.

> On Thursday we went to Cherbourg and drove round the
> port, seeing the German demolitions and the great progress
> already made in restoring the place for Allied use. Away
> from the port the town is not too badly damaged and there
> were a great many people about, some of whom recognized
> the PM as we drove past. It was wonderful to see how their
> faces lit up with pleasure and the enthusiasm of the crowd
> at one place where we stopped.
> A few miles out of the town we visited one of the flying-
> bomb sites — an elaborate erection of concrete only 60%
> complete and apparently intended for landing bombs in the
> direction of Bristol.
> Then from one of the American beaches we went out in a
> duck to a motor torpedo-boat in which we travelled along
> to the British area. It was very rough and the voyage took
> 2½ hours (which gives you some idea of the size of the area
> liberated in Normandy). The PM went below and took
> Mothersill, but I remained on the bridge and just managed
> to survive.
> Friday, Saturday and Sunday were spent in the British
> area, where we drove about a lot and saw a great deal,
> visiting Monty and some other headquarters. ... Bayeux
> fortunately has survived with little damage, but Caen,
> which I saw yesterday, is very badly knocked about. We
> went on beyond Caen towards Bourguebus, where we were
> among our guns shelling the Germans, whose front line was
> only about 4000 yards away.

In November, John went to France with Churchill again for the
Armistice Day commemoration in Paris and for visits to Allied
headquarters.

> We flew over on Friday afternoon and returned by air
> yesterday. At Paris we stayed at the Quai d'Orsay in the
> rooms prepared for the King and Queen when they visited
> France before the war. ... You will have read in the *Scots-
> man* about the scenes on Armistice Day. I was with Mrs C

and Mary in a stand on the Champs Elysées, where we watched the long march-past and saw the PM and de Gaulle drive along in an open car. There were immense crowds, kept back by the Police with the greatest difficulty, and wild enthusiasm; of all the troops none were given a louder cheer than a Highland pipe band in kilts.

We were entertained at various formal meals, with the most delicious food.

Earlier in the autumn came two significant conference journeys: in September the second Quebec conference and in October the second Moscow conference. On 12 September 1944, John reported the first as successful. 'We are back in the familiar surroundings, everyone very kind and welcoming. ... I am very fit in spite of much over-eating.'

On 14 September, he went on to say:

There have been so many of these conferences now that the machinery has been made more or less perfect and the people concerned, having changed remarkably little in these last four years, know one another very well. ... We couldn't have better hosts. ... At past conferences some of my worst troubles have been about the press; but this time Brendan has given us Cruikshank, head of the American division of the Ministry of Information and formerly editor of the *Star* and there could not be a better man for the job.

Otherwise much the party as before — Pug and the three Chiefs of Staff (the latter almost inseparable even at the cinema), the Prof, Lord Leathers and Jock, as the other PS. We have as usual attracted various visitors — Dick Law on his way to the UNRRA meeting at Montreal, Cadogan from Dumbarton Oaks, Anthony Eden and others from England. We live as before in the Citadel, shared between the President and Mrs R and the PM and Mrs C and their personal staffs. The PM and the President have their meals together and can have constant conversations without any fuss about arranging meetings. We also have a cads' party downstairs, with the most delicious food.

Recovering from the disagreement in June over Anvil — the landing in the south of France Churchill and the British chiefs of staff opposed as a 'major strategic and political error', but which Eisenhower and the US chiefs of staff advocated — the conference members met in good heart. Much of the conference was devoted to the Pacific war, the Greek and Balkan operations and the post-war handling of Germany. A joint declaration on Italy was agreed.

John thought that 'Tolstoy', the second Moscow conference, was one of the most important his master had undertaken. As he wrote on 7 October 1944: 'It may make all the difference to the peace of the world in which David [his son] will grow up.' Issues tackled were postwar influence of the great powers in the Balkans, the future of Germany, the eventual peace treaty and Poland. On 16 October, he wrote:

[The] event of the day was Stalin's luncheon party — in an ornate house (once owned by a rich sugar merchant) used à la Lancaster House for official receptions. The party began at 2.30 and lasted till after 6.00. First a string of hors d'œuvres — caviare, smoked salmon, various forms of other fish and meat, including delicious sucking-pig, and then, just when you thought the meal was over, soup — and you know that fish, meat, pudding and dessert etc. are to follow. ... About five o'clock we adjourned from the lunch table to another room, where we sat down again and continued with coffee, liqueurs, chocolates, cakes and fruit. At length it was all over and, after a short visit to the Embassy, we drove out in the dark to our country house. How we faced dinner that night (menu as above) I can't think.

One evening at the Bolshoi theatre there was a show especially arranged for the PM, who sat with Stalin, Molotov and co. in the central box. The first half of the programme was part of *Giselle*, superbly done. At the interval everyone turned to the central box and cheered. Stalin had drawn back out of sight when the lights went up, so as to leave the PM to receive the applause, but Winston got him to come back and there was a greater burst of cheering than ever, which kept on for some minutes with obviously genuine cordiality.

The last of the big conferences John attended was the Yalta one, 'Cricket', with its preliminary in Malta in January and February 1945. On 7 February, John described their accommodation at Yalta.

> We are in a large house overlooking the sea, with high rocky mountains rising behind. ... The public rooms are large and imposing, but bedroom and lavatory accommodation is more limited. Leslie and I share a small bedroom, completely lacking in pegs, shelves or wardrobes, and there is much competition for the single tap; but we are much better off than many of the delegates, for instance the sixteen American colonels who share a single bedroom.

In a letter of 18 January 1993, Elizabeth Nel (née Layton), remembered their difficulty over access to the tap:

> When we went to Yalta in January 1945 I was lucky enough to stay with the important members of our delegation, including the PM himself, in the Vorontsov Palace. There was only one small bathroom for the staffs, so that in the morning one queued with Cabinet Ministers and Service Chiefs for a quick wash in a very little water ... and I noted that poor John Martin, with his neat and reserved Scottish soul, hated to be seen tousled and unshaven, in a dressing-gown, by others of his staff.

On 12 February 1945, John wrote of their abrupt departure.

> The conference ended successfully yesterday. We had planned to leave today and I was sitting at the villa, snoozing off the effects of a lunch that had almost been too much for me, when suddenly the PM burst in like a whirlwind and said we must be off in half an hour. There was a mad rush to pack, very inadequate goodbyes to all the kind Russian staff who had looked after us so well and then off to the port where this ship had been anchored during the conference. ... It was a great joy to get aboard the ship and find everything clean and bright and welcoming, with familiar stewards from the Q[ueen] M[ary] and an excellent English dinner.

126

In *Downing Street* (p. 183), he added this comment: 'in the light of subsequent events it will be seen that this optimism [over Yalta] was unjustified owing to the failure of Moscow to carry out the terms of the agreement reached at Yalta.'

7
Return to the Colonial Office: Palestine and the New UNO, 1945–47

The long-awaited VE Day came on 8 May 1945. By June, John's war service was nearing its end. 'R and David are back at last,' he was able to say on 7 June. 'Here I am at Chequers for the last time as PS,' he wrote ten days later, 'and fortunately it is a bright sunny weekend with the familiar country-side looking its best. I shall be very sorry when the time comes to say goodbye to a place where I have spent so many interesting and pleasant days.' Some 20 years later, he and Rosalind found their retirement home in Watlington, not many miles from Chequers lying under the Chiltern hills.

By now John's time at No. 10 was drawing to a close. The coalition government came to an end and, on 23 May, Churchill was asked to form a caretaker government for the lead-up to the general election. The PM had agreed to John's return at the end of June to the Colonial Office as an assistant under-secretary. John had already turned down the post of Colonial Office representative at the British embassy in Washington in succession to Jock Macpherson, formerly of Malaya. Early in his married life he wished to work from London. He left Churchill's services with a CB in the resignation honours of August 1945. In these honours Patrick Kinna became an MBE and Marian Holmes, Elizabeth Layton, Nina Sturdee and Frank Sawyers, Churchill's valet, were the first to receive the new defence medal for accompanying the PM into operational areas.

On John's departure from No. 10, many felt that they owed much to him and wrote to thank him. Chief among these letters is one of 30 June 1945 from Alan Lascelles, the King's private secretary, with whom John had had many dealings:

> For your sake, I am glad that you are moving on; four years of that kind of life, with that kind of master, is as much as anybody should be asked to do at a stretch. You go at a good moment — the obvious end of an epoch — and with the satisfaction of knowing that, in the most critical period of her history hitherto, you have done as much to help your country as any man alive. But, from the personal point of view, I shall greatly miss you and shall always regret that it is not you at the end of our well-worn telephone.
>
> We have had some very remarkable conversations, and correspondences; still more remarkable is that we have never had a serious difference of opinion — a rare thing in secretarial inter-relationships. I need not tell you again how grateful I am for the help you have always given me.

He returned after a month's leave as assistant under-secretary in charge of the Middle East and Mediterranean departments. His diary entries show a certain revival of social life, of continuing friendships from the war years and of a cultivation of the artistic and cultural life of London.

He was able to get back to his biblical studies, made almost impossible in the pattern of service in wartime No. 10. He resumed study of Acts, he noted on 5 August 1945. He left five large notebooks of his studies of the four gospels and of the Acts of the Apostles. His method was to work on the New Testament Greek texts comparing them with the classical Greek he had learned in his school and university days. He made use of the commentaries available at the time of his studies. While he was able to give more time to these in retirement, the practice of New Testament study was a feature of his working life.

At the end of September, John's mother died. She, like his father, had been a great figure in his life, an influence for good and a source of encouragement, to whom John and other members of the family turned.

In Rosalind Martin, there is a largely unsung heroine in the pages that follow. Though a woman capable of an active public life, as her first and essential duty she chose to establish a welcoming and hospitable home in support of her husband. This was clearly right, for if the war years had been demanding, for John the next 20 years in colonial administration were even more so. John was under continual pressure, travelling widely, often in dangerous circumstances, and caught up in complicated negotiations. Their home in Pelham Place was not only a refuge for John, it was a delightful place for overseas visitors and family members. In John's absences, Rosalind became the chief recipient of his personal letters and the one person to whom he could write frankly. That he was able to survive the next 20 years and then a lengthy and profitable retirement, was largely due to Rosalind.

After the war, the Colonial Office still had a great empire to administer, but the war had changed the perspective. It had weakened the British economy, thus reducing the financial resources available for nurturing an empire. The general election at the end of the war had produced a Labour government that was not only prepared to meet its obligations to colonial territories, but was also open to anti-colonial thought. Further, the war had brought the two superpowers, the USA and USSR, to the fore. For a mixture of reasons, both were anti-colonial yet dominant in the new forum of international debate, the United Nations Organization. While before the war the British government could adopt a long-term programme of preparing colonies for self-government and independence within or outside the Commonwealth, after the war the time frame shortened. Instead of thinking in terms of generations, it now had to think in terms of a few years. Given the strong anti-colonial climate of opinion at the time, the Conservative administrations that succeeded Labour in 1951 were also eager to promote colonial independence as quickly as possible. However, the consultations and negotiations required before territories could achieve independence were demanding, especially for senior members of the Colonial Office. Yet, only 20 years after the end of the war, though some residual duties were incorporated into the Foreign and Commonwealth Office, there was no longer a Colonial Office. It had completed its decolonization programme and had become part of history. These 20 years were ones in which John played a considerable part before taking on a final two-year diplomatic post as high commissioner in Malta.

The year 1956 marked a turning point in this comparatively short period. The Suez affair caused grave offence, especially to the USA, and worldwide hostility. Postwar presidents Truman and Eisenhower were strongly anti-colonial. Before Suez, the Colonial Office understanding of the US attitude to the British Empire was that Americans wished it to end, but, provided the British were proceeding towards the independence of their colonies, they could do so at their own pace. Suez changed this. Eisenhower was shocked by the whole Suez operation, by the collusion between Britain, France and Israel and the secrecy with which it was planned. Suez fuelled his anti-colonialism. He felt that Eden, the prime minister, had betrayed a wartime friendship and had deceived him. From then on, the Americans called for more rapid decolonization and, within the United Nations, there was increased hostility to the British Empire. The Suez operation had seriously weakened Britain's standing in the world, particularly in the Mediterranean and Middle East, leading to a revision of global military commitments and hastening the ending of empire.

John Martin was discreet about his views on the Suez affair, but those close to him said that the event that precipitated the crisis, Nasser nationalizing the Suez Canal, had appalled him. Yet, the British and French response to the situation, and their collusion with the Israelis, appalled him even more. He, like the great majority in the civil service, had known nothing of the plans a small group of ministers and military leaders had been making.

John's diaries and letters reveal much of the hopes and frustrations of the postwar and post-Suez years. The hopes often proved to be gambles, while the frustrations were compounded by a sense of haste and of being rushed. The normal pursuit of colonial business had to go on, often amid lengthy negotiations over a territory's future.

The terms and concepts of decolonization in the postwar period are of some interest. The starting point of the journey to independence was paramountcy, in which the colonial power ruled the colony. Paramountcy could re-emerge in independence when in the former colony one racial or ethnic group dominated or ruled the rest of the population. The second stage of the journey was trusteeship, in which the colonial power held the colony or designated territory in trust on a double assumption. At the time of being placed under trust the territory was assumed not to be ready for independence yet the power holding the trusteeship was assumed to have the duty to prepare that country for eventual independence.

A third, more open-ended term, which covered both the journey and relations within the newly independent country, was partnership. By the nature of things, partnership had a weakness. Partners were rarely equal, be they colonial power and colony or, in independent countries, one social group and another. Strength and power lay on one side or the other.

Strong forces were pushing colonial power and colonies along the road to independence. The first was nationalism, that sense of belonging to a common tradition and identity, which aroused in the people a desire to run their own affairs. This came about in many parts of the British Empire through the success of the Christian missions. It was not a matter of the churches promoting an anti-colonial policy but of the missions' educational work, largely through their schools and also in the daily life of parish and congregation, which taught self-worth and responsibility. The success of the missions also provoked a certain revival of other religions, notably Islam, but also native religions, which strengthened this desire for independence.

In addition, anti-colonialism was a strong element in world opinion, which John Martin was to meet in the new United Nations Organization, orchestrated by the two superpowers emerging from the war, the USA and the USSR. It was hard for Great Britain to resist, had it so desired. The practical difficulties in maintaining empire, especially the economic ones, became increasingly apparent.

Self-government did not necessarily mean independence because, in some cases, the colonial power could retain reserved powers. A form of parliamentary democracy, by which a majority party ruled, was the preferred solution to the question of how a colony should govern itself. There were difficulties, such as the protection of minorities. Partition was adopted, though only after bloodshed in India and Palestine and, after the colonial days, in Cyprus. Against world opinion, apartheid was enforced in South Africa to protect the dominant, white minority from the black majority. Another difficulty was that parliamentary democracy, which had matured in Western conditions, was not necessarily right for the very different conditions of many parts of the empire.

There were also questions of how colonies on the way to independence should relate to one another. Closer association was a general term applied to colonies that retained self-government yet developed ways of helping one another through common services. Even the smallest colonies largely resisted amalgamation because nationalism had a strong hold everywhere. Confederation, or self-governing institutions with treaty arrangements for cooperation, is mentioned in some documents. Federation, which became popular in the postwar world, was put into practice, but with less success than its sponsors had hoped. Here, self-governing territories managed their own internal affairs, but an overarching federal authority was responsible for their external affairs and some internal affairs such as taxation. John Martin was to deal with various plans for federation in the next few years.

In the early years after the war, John was associated with one swift and painless move to self-government, Trans-Jordan as it was then known, and one territory whose future the British government could not resolve and consequently put in the hands of the United Nations, namely Palestine. After his work before the war in the Royal Commission, Palestine was particularly close to his heart, yet it continued to present almost insoluble problems.

In 1920, four years after the successful Arab revolt against the Turks, Trans-Jordan was placed under a British mandate. In 1923, the administration was handed to the Hashemite Emir Abdullah and, in the same year, Glubb Pasha was appointed leader of the Arab League, a position he held until 1956. In the Second World War, the Arab Legion fought with the Allies.

In early 1946, the Colonial and Foreign Offices were actively trying to promote a settlement with the Arab rulers of Trans-Jordan. On 22 February, John records Emir Abdullah's arrival in London with his prime minister, Ibrahim Pasha Hashim, for discussions about the treaty. Negotiations continued in February and March. On 21 March, the government gave a lunch in honour of Emir Abdullah at Lancaster House and, the following day, the treaty was signed in Bevin's room in the Foreign Office. As a consequence of the treaty, Great Britain relinquished its mandate on 25 May and the Hashemite Kingdom of Jordan was created, with the emir becoming King Abdullah. In the conflict over the future of Palestine, in 1949 King Abdullah annexed the West Bank and East Jerusalem, but some years later his son abandoned his claim to these territories.

The British government had rejected the 1937 Royal Commission's proposal of partition for Palestine and the 1938 Woodhouse Commission had failed to agree on any alternatives. In 1939, the British government outlined plans to establish an independent Palestine state within ten years in which Arabs and Jews would share government in such a way as to ensure the essential interests of each community. In the meanwhile, the British government would retain responsibility. At the end of five years, an appropriate body would review how the arrangement was working and make recommendations for the constitution of an independent Palestine state. Over the next five years, 75,000 immigrants were to be admitted subject to the territory's economic absorption capacity. Thereafter, no further immigrants were to be admitted unless the Arabs were prepared to acquiesce. Land transfers were to be regulated.

During the war, both Jews and Arabs supported the Allied cause, with 27,000 Jews and 12,000 Arabs recruited to the British services. The Jewish Brigade was formed in 1944. Terrorism was halted at the beginning of the war, but resumed in 1942. The (Jewish) Stern Gang carried out political murders and robberies in the Tel Aviv area, while in 1944 the Irgun Zwei Leumi destroyed much government property. Jewish leaders condemned these outrages. In 1946, Hagana continued to attack communications throughout Palestine and members of the Jewish Agency who were implicated in these attacks were arrested.

Jewish immigration slowed down during the war and the 75,000 places reserved for them in the government's 1939 White Paper were not filled until the end of 1945. The problem of illegal immigration became acute in 1946 when, in the summer of that year, illegal immigrants who could no longer be contained in camps in Palestine were taken in British ships to Cyprus. The flood of immigrants was not surprising. European Jews had suffered grievously in the war. Six million were killed in the Holocaust, the Nazi regime's systematic attempt to destroy all European Jewry. Their wartime suffering and military contribution to the war strengthened their case for a national home in Palestine. As paragraph 126 of the memorandum the British government prepared for the UN Special Committee on Palestine (UNSCOP) stated (p. 34): 'the tragic fate of the Jewish people in Europe had created a demand that the Palestine problem should be examined again in relation to the needs of the survivors of racial persecution.'

Since much of this pressure came from the USA, Britain sought its help. In April 1946, the Anglo-American Committee of Inquiry reported. Its members recommended the immediate admission of 100,000 Jewish immigrants, which President Truman had already asked for in August 1945. They also felt that there should be no Arab or Jewish state and that until hostility between Arab and Jew ceased, government should be continued under the mandate, pending the execution of a trusteeship agreement. They also called for more Jewish immigration and for land transfer regulations to be rescinded. They were thinking in terms of a bi-national state.

A US delegation came to London in summer 1946. In July, the Morrison–Grady plan for provincial autonomy was put forward. Palestine was to be divided into four areas, Arab, Jewish, Jerusalem and Negeb. The central government would have exclusive authority for defence, foreign relations, customs, and law and order; there would be immediate admission of 100,000 immigrants. Thereafter, entry would be on the basis of recommendations by provincial governments, subject to economic absorption capacity. Land transfer regulations would be repealed. The plan would leave the way open for development towards either partition or federal unity. The British government supported the plan but Truman did not.

The Jewish Agency proposed a scheme of partition that would create a viable Jewish state in an adequate area of Palestine. Truman endorsed it, again calling for the admission of 100,000. Britain then invited the Jews and Arabs to a conference in London. Bevin put forward the scheme for a five-year trusteeship with autonomous cantons. By this time, Arab and Jewish positions had hardened. The Arabs required a unitary Arab state for Palestine, the Jews a Jewish commonwealth (within if not the whole of Palestine). Both parties rejected the British proposals.

In February 1947, the foreign secretary announced that it had been decided to refer the whole question to the United Nations. A special session of the United Nations Assembly was held in April at which the UN Special Committee on Palestine was appointed, reporting in the autumn. The majority report proposed partition into Jewish and Arab states in an economic union; the minority report proposed an independent federal state. At this time in the General Assembly, the USA was backing political, anti-colonial struggles and was exerting pressure behind the scenes; the USSR supported this policy. On 29 November 1947, the Marshall Plan, recommending partition, was approved in the UN by 33 to 13 votes with 19 abstentions, including the UK. In committee, only a minority supported the plan, but US arm-twisting caused enough to switch in plenary session.

US policy, of which John was from time to time critical, was coloured by the anti-imperialism President Truman inherited from Roosevelt. As commander-in-chief in foreign and military affairs, Truman was particularly concerned about the relief of displaced Jews in Europe. However, though pro-Jewish, he advocated minimal involvement in Palestine. He disliked being thought to be in the pocket of the New York Jews and was angered by the charge that Jews called the tune in US foreign policy. His first secretary of state, Byrnes, backed the Morrison–Grady solution of provincial autonomy, but lost interest when it failed. His second, General Marshall, secured the decision in favour of partition on 29 November 1947. Acheson, who served both Byrnes and Marshall, had favoured partition and encouraged a British resolution of the matter rather than a referral to the UN, where he knew that the USA would be required to lead. Henderson, the British ambassador in Washington, worked cordially with senior US officials.

The UN Palestine Commission, set up by the November resolution, reported that an international police force would be needed to implement partition; such a force was not forthcoming. In March 1948, the USA announced its withdrawal of support for partition to the Security Council, having concluded that it could not be carried out peacefully. It urged that Palestine be put under UN trusteeship.

Having passed the Palestine problem to the UN, which then adopted the policy of partition, there was no more the British government could do. The appropriate legislation to end the British mandate went through Parliament in 1948, coming into effect at midnight on 14/15 May.

On 14 May 1948, the British high commissioner sailed from Palestine. Jewish leaders in Tel Aviv immediately proclaimed the state of Israel, which Truman recognized within minutes, despite the US decision in March to withdraw its support of partition. Arab forces advanced and engaged the Jews; Arab refugees left. The UN Security Council ordered a cease-fire. Count Bernadotte secured this for a time in June, but fighting resumed in July. In 1949, Dr Bunche of the UN negotiated armistice agreements.

Later years brought more Arab–Israeli wars. In 1956, Israel joined the attack on the Suez Canal. In June 1967, Israel occupied East Jerusalem, the Golan Heights, the West Bank and the Gaza Strip. In 1972 an Arab assault on Israel failed.

John's diary for the years 1945 to 1948 records the comings and goings of the main actors in a drama that was moving to a climax through a series of meetings, consultations and conferences. He had a clear view of what was happening, for he was dealing with appointments in Palestine and reacting to events there amid consultations with interested parties. He was also given other duties. From 1 January 1946 he was made responsible for the Colonial Office Public Relations Department, Palestine. Being prominent in the eyes of the world, it presented a difficult PR problem.

In July 1946, there was a distressing bomb outrage at the King David Hotel in Jerusalem. News of it reached John on 22 July when he was in conference at the Colonial Office with the high commissioner, Sir Alan Cunningham, who decided to return at once to Palestine. A hotel wing, containing government secretariat offices and part of the military headquarters, had been blown up with heavy loss of life. Some 86 public servants, Arab, Jewish and British, and five members of the public were killed. John had stayed at the King David during his work with the Royal Commission.

On Saturday 27 July he went to Chequers with Secretary of State G. H. (later Viscount) Hall for a short conference with Prime Minister Attlee. On the next day, he accompanied Hall to Paris where the PM was in interview with US Secretary of State Byrnes. He was present at a meeting of ministers on Truman's attitude on

Palestinian policy and prepared a statement to be delivered to Parliament by Lord President Herbert Morrison. John attended the debates in the House of Commons.

The increasing difficulty of negotiation was shown by John's diary note for 10 September that year. 'Opening of Palestine Conference at Lancaster House. (It was attended only by the Arab States and Secretary General of the Arab League. The Jewish Agency, Palestinian Jews and Arabs, though invited, did not attend.)'

There was a significant entry on 15 January 1947: 'FO bombshell with paper on Palestine circulated without consultation with us.' It revealed a problem of which John was very conscious at the time and on which he commented in his later reflections. It was the difference in perspective on Palestine between the Foreign and Colonial Offices and also a difference in power between the two departments of state, with the Foreign Office holding more.

By February 1947, Palestinian affairs at the London end were drawing to a close. At the Palestine conference in early February, the Arabs and Jews met separately. John's diary for 7 February noted that new proposals for Palestine were sent to the Arabs and Jews. These were to be the final ones put forward by Britain as Mandatory, meeting final rejection by Arab and Jew. On 18 February, the government issued its statement of policy on Palestine to refer to the UNO. It was approved in the House of Commons on 25 February, with Bevin opening the debate and Creech Jones, now secretary of state, winding up.

John's later reflections on the 1945–47 negotiations and the decision to refer Palestine to the UNO, were given to Carstairs in 1969. The following extract was held back for some years at his request because of his criticism of the government.

> The new Labour government was immediately faced by the Palestine problem with all its hideous difficulty. ... The Zionists, I believe, thought that I was one person in the Colonial Office who was sympathetic to their view. I would like to think I was sympathetic in the sense that I was understanding without being partial either to them or against them. One thing ... was the extreme pressure under which they had been put by the horrible experiences of the

Jewish communities in Germany. This had resulted in a tremendous increase in would-be immigrants to Palestine. ... [Nonetheless,] the incompatibility [remained] of the obligations which the British Government had accepted under the Mandate towards the Jews and towards the Arabs. We had undertaken to provide the establishment of a national home for the Jews without prejudicing the position of the original Arab inhabitants in the country. ... On the one hand the British Government was under intense pressure from the Arab States ... not to be favourable to the Zionists and the British Government attached great importance to the friendship of the Arab States at that time. On the other hand we were under repeated pressure, particularly from the United States, to be favourable to the Zionists. This always seemed to relate to the Jewish vote in some election in the United States. ... [Elsewhere John called this the vexatious effects of US politics.]

The situation was made more difficult in its handling by the fact that it fell between two Departments. There was the Colonial Office responsible for handling the administration of Palestine. It was the Colonial Office's duty to bring its problems to the Cabinet if necessary. On the other hand the Foreign Office was concerned with arranging relations with the United States and with the Arab States, and with handling the business in the United Nations, where the question became one of the great contentious issues. ... The Foreign Office was inevitably the more powerful Department ... [and] would in any event have been the leading Department in a conflict, or an argument or discussion, between the two on Palestine. But for a time it was made even more so when Creech Jones was the Colonial Secretary and Bevin was Foreign Secretary. Their past relationship with one another was such that Creech Jones looked up to Bevin as his superior and was not surprised if he was knocked over by Bevin in a discussion in the Cabinet.

Carstairs remarked that 'One gets the impression that the Zionists, for some reason, had omitted to cultivate Bevin as they had successfully cultivated a number of others?' John replied that 'they had tried but certainly they hadn't succeeded. The result, of course, was that in the end the ... British Government had to throw in their hand. It was a very humiliating and unhappy end of a long and difficult chapter of history.'

Once the government had made its resolve, the scene of negotiation and decision moved from London to New York, the seat of the newly formed United Nations Organization, the successor of the League of Nations. Papers had to be prepared. The government of Palestine prepared a *Memorandum on the Administration of Palestine under the Mandate* (Jerusalem, June 1947) and the British government a memorandum for the United Nations Special Committee on Palestine entitled *The Political History of Palestine Under British Administration* (London, July 1947). John himself was to travel to New York in the British team to help the UNO seek the solution the British government had failed to find.

John Martin had a considerable part to play in the New York negotiations. The meetings there in April and May 1947 were to set up the United Nations Special Committee on Palestine (UNSCOP), which was to visit the country and report. The meetings in the autumn were to consider the UNSCOP report, which, in four volumes, presented a choice between a federal state and partition. The UN chose partition and John's subcommittee dealt with the partition boundaries.

The UK delegation office was in the Empire State building and the conference at Flushing Meadow. On 29 April 1947, he wrote:

> The assembly meets in a large hall, with the UK delegation (because it begins with U) at the back — which was a long walk up to the rostrum from which all speeches are made. I sincerely hope that Alec Cadogan doesn't fall ill, so that I (as his 'alternate') don't have to face that ordeal.
>
> Today's proceedings (in committee) were quite interesting. Some rather wild speeches by the Arabs, an excellent one by the United States Delegate and a characteristically unhelpful intervention by Gromyko. The atmosphere of the crowded room in which we met was much more exhausting than the speeches.

On 2 May John wrote:

The sessions at Flushing Meadow vary in interest. Sometimes they are dull and boring and the process of translation (from English into French or vice versa or from Russian or Spanish into both) is a weariness to the flesh; but in general the processes of this world parliament are interesting to watch. They seem much more complicated than those of Westminster and there is a good deal of light relief, particularly when [one] delegate makes speeches — a pretentious ass and complete figure of fun. One of his better phrases was 'an arcana of complications.'

The Russian (Gromyko) sits through most of the debates with a completely expressionless face and only seems to intervene occasionally to add to the difficulties.

Part of the business took place at Lake Success. John reported on 7 May that: 'The proceedings at Lake Success are going much more rapidly than those at Flushing as we have the simultaneous interpretation system, with earphones which you can switch to English, French, Russian, Spanish or Chinese. It is amusing to see the Spanish interpreter inside his glass-fronted box gesticulating to the microphone.'

On 16 May, John mentioned that the Assembly had wound up the day before with unexpected rapidity. A fact-finding committee had been set up to meet in New York and then visit Palestine. By this time John was hoping to return on 24 May by the *Queen Elizabeth*.

On the whole the Assembly has not been unsatisfactory, though the composition of the Committee is not perfect — for which we have to blame the Americans (but that lamentable story is too long to tell now). Prince Feisal of Saudi Arabia gave an evening party at the Waldorf-Astoria on the last day — a most lavish affair, with much champagne, foie gras, lobster pilaff and the like. Alas I had supped beforehand and was able to cope with little except the champagne.

On 19 May he wrote that he had gone to Lake Success for a talk with one of the secretaries of the Palestine Committee. 'It is rather a shock to find that the principal secretary is to be a Chinese and his deputy a Mexican. UNO has been thoroughly infected with American lavishness and it seems that the travelling circus to be taken to Jerusalem will number little under 100. I don't suppose our total party for the Peel Commission exceeded about 15.' John was in New York again from late September to early December.

> An ad hoc committee of the Assembly has been set up to deal with the Palestine question under an obviously efficient chairman, Evatt of Australia, and the SofS has fired off his shot. The statement has gone down well generally, though both Arabs and Jews express doubts about the sincerity of the references to withdrawal and the Americans (now firmly placed on the spot) are puzzled to know what line they should take. The *Herald-Tribune* describes the British decision 'as wise as it is honorable'. In the lobbies everyone is very friendly and there are many familiar faces, as we are mostly veterans of the long Palestinian wrangle.

On 30 September, he commented:

> Paradoxically one of the most striking features of the US — and one of the most irritating — is the general slowness of tempo. We are suffering from that in connection with UNO at the moment: having heard the Arab statement on Monday (all the old stuff) we are now kicking our heels till Thursday when it will be the Jews' turn. Meanwhile no progress is made, the Americans have not disclosed their hand and I feel extremely gloomy about the remoter outlook.

His letter of 3 October reported little change of tempo. 'We have made very slow progress, as our Committee was held up while the Assembly spent two days in plenary session in an unsuccessful attempt to settle the elections to the Security Council. Yesterday we were able to meet again and heard the Jewish Agency statement — jeers at the Arabs, criticism of us and acceptance of partition.'
Further letters documented the progress of debate.

At Lake Success we have had a week of speeches, mostly very boring as there has been so much repetition of arguments we have all heard many times before. The outstanding speaker has been Safrullah Khan of Pakistan, who held the attention of the committee for an hour and a half in a masterly presentation of the Arab case. The Americans at last declared themselves this morning — for partition, though the extent to which they are ready to help in enforcement is still far from clear. I feel a little more hopeful of the outcome.

Our debates have taken a more interesting turn with American and Soviet statements, but the future remains as obscure as ever. There is clearly a general feeling in favour of partition (apart of course from the Arabs and their few supporters) but no one has come to grips with the vital question of enforcement. The Americans seem blandly to expect that we shall continue to hold the baby, but we are going to make it quite clear that we have no such intention. I see endless discussions ahead.

Our long general debate ends today. Next week we shall get down to considering resolutions; but the way ahead and its length are still by no means clear. The SofS is planning to go home at the end of next week, if the PM approves, leaving me with Beeley and MacGillivray to hold the fort — though fortunately there are other Ministers here on the UK Delegation — Hector McNeil, Hartley Shawcross and Norman Younger.

Our general debate ended yesterday with speeches by Weizmann (read with painful slowness owing to his feeble eyesight) and by Jamali of the Arab Higher Committee. In the evening I dined at the Waldorf with another member of the Arab Committee (from Jerusalem) and his wife, both Christians. The wife was missing very badly her young children left behind in Palestine, so we exchanged sympathy with one another — like so many Palestine wives she is of Lebanese origin, with that chic which the Lebanese women seem to have caught from the French.

On 22 October, subcommittees were appointed. 'Today we agreed on the appointment of sub-committees, the most important of which (which incidentally I shall attend, though the UK won't formally be a member) will try to work out an improved partition scheme.' On 29 October, he went on:

> My sub-committee has been active, but there is still not very much to show for its work. I have had to speak a certain amount (as the SofS has left me to this) and have to walk very delicately to avoid offence to Jews or Arabs. The SofS has decided to return to London at the end of the week. He is curiously irresponsible about the whole business and seems quite content that things should take their course in whatever direction the tide carries them. MacGillivray is a tower of strength and I very much enjoy working with him.
>
> We are at a tricky stage of our work. The FO didn't like my reply to an American statement; but I am myself convinced that it was right (except on one detail) and in any case it was on lines agreed with the SofS (who really ought to have delivered it himself, but he seems to shirk this sort of responsibility). He left the next day.
>
> Last night I went as guest of the Chairman to a Balfour Day Dinner of the Zionist Organization of America at the Waldorf. I felt like walking into the lions' den, but it turned out to be a very pleasant and interesting evening. I sat among the 'honoured guests' at the high table, next to Governor Lehman, and when presented to the assembly of several hundred (to whom I had to bow, covered with confusion) I received an astonishingly warm welcome. Friendly references to Britain in the Chairman's speech were also received with cheers (but so, I must add, were some criticisms of past policy).
>
> We are having a very difficult time over Palestine, here and with London. It is hard to see how this chapter can be brought to a reasonable end and I have to keep tight hold of myself not to worry about it all the time. There are suggestions that the discussions on Palestine should continue here even after the Assembly is finished, but we are all against that. ...

1. ABOVE LEFT. John Martin's parents, Edith and John

2. ABOVE RIGHT. Sunday morning at the Manse, August 1909. Map of Palestine on the easel. John at the front; from the back, Edith Martin, William, Detta, Peggy

3. RIGHT. Schooldays: John with bagpipes

4. ABOVE. Corpus Christi College, Oxford, June 1924. John Martin standing, far left, second row from the back

5. BELOW. International Opium Conference, Sahadaya Suragom Hall, Grand Palace, Bangkok, November 1932. John Martin behind left table

6. RIGHT. Mat Nor, John's syce in Malaya, Labrador, 1934

7. BELOW. Palestine Royal Commission, 1936. Left to right: John Martin, Hammond Rumbold, Coupland (with Carter Behind), Peel

8. ABOVE. Palestine Royal Commission in session, 1936. Left to right: the two liaison officers, Carter, Rumbold, Peel. Hammond, Morris, Coupland, John Martin, Heathcoat – Amory

9. LEFT. Churchill's Private Office, 10 Downing Street, September 1941. Left to right: Jack Colville, Leslie Rowan, P.M., John Peck, John Martin, Miss Watson, Cmdr Thompson, Andrew Bevir, Barker

10. RIGHT. Wedding of John Martin with Rosalind Ross. On the left: Mrs Martin with Sir David Ross

11. BELOW. Meeting of CCTA at Brussels, *c.* 1950. John Martin second left, front row

12. ABOVE. Conference of Heads of Colonial Medical Departments, Oxford, July 1952.
John Martin, Seated seventh from left

13. BELOW. John Martin with Malayan group, near Kuala Pilah, 1955

14. RIGHT. John Martin with Alan Lennox-Boyd, Government House, Nicosia, February 1956

15. BELOW. Remembrance Day, Valletta, November 13, 1966. Left to right: Dr Dazzi, Italian Ambassador, John Martin, Dr Wollenweber, M. Desmensers, Mr Hassine

16. Sir John and Lady Martin arriving for reception for the Diplomatic Corps at San Anton, Malta, February 8, 1966

We met at Lake Success yesterday morning, afternoon and evening and didn't adjourn until nearly midnight, so it was one o'clock before I got to bed. A nine a.m. meeting this morning and now again we are at Lake Success for a long day. We are waiting for instructions from London on the attitude we are to take about the latest Soviet–American proposals here; but meanwhile my sub-committee continues discussion of boundaries etc.

On 12 November 1947, he wrote:

The sub-committee is entirely composed of supporters of partition and the Jewish Agency are making the most of their opportunity to press for improved boundaries for their state, with no one to state the Arab case or expose the inaccuracies or suppressions in the Jewish presentation. It is all rather sickening to watch — it is simply theft on a large scale — and I can't help thinking all the time of the unfortunate Arab villagers thousands of miles away, ignorant of the way in which this partial and ill-informed jury is deciding their fate. But perhaps it is not deciding, for the main problem, for which there is yet no solution, is how any decisions reached here are to be implemented.

In a letter written on 23 November 1947, he said:

The UK has been under heavy fire these last few days at Lake Success and, as Cadogan had gone off to Toronto to receive a degree, the burden of the defence fell on me — which I must admit I have thoroughly enjoyed. On Friday most of the discussions were in private session of a sub-committee; yesterday — morning, afternoon and evening — in public. The Americans have behaved pretty shamelessly — accusing us of contributing nothing, of not cooperating enough. They thought their latest plan was a way of getting the UK to enforce partition alone and now that they find we aren't falling for it they are showing signs of a rather nasty temper. I have hit back fairly hard and have been encouraged by various congratulations and signs of sympathetic approval from other delegations. A woman in the Canadian delegation said she 'purred every time Mr Martin spoke'. The most ludicrous attack was from the Guatamalan, who had to be called to order by the chairman, when he referred to Britain as 'behaving like a scornful child'. But I can't help feeling a bit nervous when I speak in these public meetings, a form of activity in which we have no practice in the Civil Service. It has all been rather wearing, particularly as it has generally been well after midnight before I get to bed for the last week or two.

On 27 November, he continued:

Meanwhile the last stages of the Assembly are exciting, with great uncertainty whether the partition plan will get the necessary two-thirds majority. It is a matter of one or two votes: in fact, it was said yesterday that the fate of Palestine now depends on the vote of Liberia, which is still uncertain. There are all sorts of stories of pressure and intimidation, in which I'm afraid there is some truth. The Liberian (a woman) is even said to have asked for Police protection.

On Wednesday night I went to a huge birthday party in honour of Weizmann at the Waldorf. The Boston Symphony Orchestra played (as a tribute), conducted by Koussevitsky – including the Eroica – superb playing such as I don't remember since Toscanini's last visit to London before the war. Then there was a speech or two and afterwards supper. All very lavish, and the ballroom packed. ... I was taken to shake hands with Weizmann who, to my embarrassment, flung his arms round me and kissed my cheek. I don't know if he expected me to kiss him back, but I was too stunned to do more than grasp his arms and pump them up and down.

It is all over at last and I can scarcely believe it. For several days, up to the very end, the issue remained in suspense and as late as Friday it looked as though our discussions might be prolonged indefinitely. The decision is not one on which anyone will be able to look back with pride, though at the moment the Jews are elated. The pressure (to say no more) by which the votes of small countries were obtained (even after their representatives had spoken in the opposite sense) was worthy of the more corrupt political systems and has set a sad precedent for the future of UNO, and the form of partition endorsed is one which is most unfair to the Arabs and likely to provoke violent reaction from them, while (as we were at pains to point out) the 'plan' is accompanied by no means of enforcement. The UK delegation were throughout in a very difficult position, but I think we can flatter ourselves that we made the most of it. The High Commissioner has sent me from Jerusalem a very kind telegram of appreciation.

The Assembly finished late on Saturday afternoon, after which I went with three others to spend the weekend with the Cadogans in their very pleasant house at Oyster Bay (Long Island).

John's part in Palestinian affairs was almost at an end. His diary in early 1948 mentions the UN Commission seeking to persuade the Palestinians of the merits of partition. The Jews needed little persuading, the Arabs much. On 23 February he recorded that he was 'much fussed about a private notice question (in the Commons) about the Ben Yehuda Street explosion in Jerusalem'.

Meanwhile, the government was passing the Palestine Bill through the House of Commons. On 15 May, John wrote 'Palestine Mandate ended (just after midnight 14/15),' and on 18 June: 'My work is now much reduced. Table clear in afternoon.'

John could see through the folly, pretentiousness, time-wasting and emerging corruption of many of those in action at the UNO. His sense of the ridiculous enabled him to appreciate the funny side of the proceedings and his good humour won him many friends. He was not afraid of straight talking and of defending his or his country's position. The latter was not an easy position to defend, being based as it was on Britain's contradictory promises to the Jews and Arabs in the Balfour and MacMahon treaties. That Britain had handed over an unsolved problem it itself had created after years of holding the mandate somewhat weakened its own voice. It gave John some satisfaction that the UN advocated partition, as the Royal Commission had done in 1937, yet it was a was a matter of regret that no plan of enforcement was adopted. Although held by the Jews as a friend of their cause, John was critical of their conduct in the partition subcommittee in seeking to rob the Arabs of territory. 'It was a very humiliating and unhappy end of a long and difficult chapter of history,' John said to Carstairs on the surrender of the mandate, certainly of British history and of world history. The chapters to follow in Palestine have been no easier.

John's letters to his wife have a different character from those to his mother. To his mother they showed a certain restraint and a selection of items he thought would interest her. To his wife he can say more. He can express his criticism freely, his agreements and disagreements, his pleasure at exposing folly and pretension. It was clear he much enjoyed his defence of British policy. He was also prepared to reveal the actions and words of others as contemptible. Integrity was always a guiding principle for him. In the UN negotiations over Palestine he found little of it.

8

Colonial Power and the
United Nations, 1949–52

I n autumn 1949, John Martin returned to New York as
Colonial Office adviser to the United Kingdom delegation at
the United Nations General Assembly. His work was mainly in
the fourth committee, appointed to deal with trusteeship and non-
self-governing territories. Trusteeship entailed taking over the
work of the League of Nations' former mandate committee; the
non-self-governing territories part of the work meant keeping a
check on the colonial powers. This was a controversial matter, as
John explained from time to time. His fullest statement of the
controversy was in an address he gave to the colonial service
weekend conference at Cambridge in April 1950.

> The United Nations Charter devotes three of its nineteen
> chapters to 'non-self-governing territories', Chapters XI to
> XIII. It provides for two distinct categories of non-self-
> governing territories — those which are and those which are
> not placed under the trusteeship system. The essential differ-
> ence between the two is that, while Chapters XII and XIII
> specifically provide for United Nations supervision over the
> trust territories, Chapter XI does not confer any such right
> or function on the United Nations in relation to the other
> non-self-governing territories.
> When the Charter was drafted at the San Francisco Con-
> ference it was the United Kingdom Delegation which
> suggested the inclusion of a declaration regarding non-self-
> governing territories and the United Kingdom and Australia

took a leading part in framing Chapter XI, which in fact expresses the principles and purposes which have long governed our own Colonial policy. For example ... 'to ensure, with due respect for the culture of the peoples concerned, their political, economic, social and educational advancement'; 'to assist them in the progressive development of their free political institutions'.

Nearly fifty years later, one wonders exactly what was meant by 'advancement' and 'progressive development'. From John's account, there seem to have been considerable differences of opinion among various UN representatives. The strong anti-colonial lobby at the UN, which John goes on to depict, thought that such things could hardly be looked for under colonial rule. It was certainly John's view, and that of the British government, that such objectives were being achieved in the British Empire. The chief problem he and the British representatives had to face at the fourth committee was interference from the UN, not warranted by the terms of Chapter XI. He went on to show that Chapter XI did impose one new responsibility on the colonial powers, namely

to transmit regularly to the Secretary-General, for information purposes, subject to such limitation as security and constitutional considerations may require, statistical and other information of a technical nature relating to economic, social, and educational conditions in the territories for which they are respectively responsible (other than trust territories). ... The obligation has in fact been faithfully honoured by HMG; each year Colonial Secretariats have poured out sweat and tears in the preparation of the Annual Reports required for transmission to Lake Success.

However ... the issue is that of 'international accountability'. Has the UN a right and duty of supervision over fulfilment by the Colonial Powers of their obligations to the peoples of the non-self-governing territories? Are the Colonial Powers, for their part, bound to submit their policies and actions to this international supervision?

Our view has always been that the declaration in Chapter XI and, in particular, the limited obligation under Article

73(e) imply no degree of 'accountability' towards the United Nations on the part of the Colonial Powers. The information transmitted to the Secretary-General is expressly stated to be 'for information purposes' ... responsibility lies exclusively with the Colonial Powers. ... Chapter XI contains no provision for any supervisory organ of the UN in respect of territories not under trusteeship.

There have been continuous efforts by strong forces in the General Assembly of the UN to ... set up machinery for supervision parallel to the Trusteeship Council. ... At its first session, in December 1946, the Assembly instructed (the Secretary General) to summarise, analyse and classify this information and appointed an ad hoc committee to examine his summaries. This ad hoc committee was composed of the eight Member States transmitting information and eight other Members. A similar committee was appointed again in 1947, but called a 'Special Committee' and there was added to its terms of reference an invitation to make 'such substantive recommendations as may seem desirable relating to functional fields generally but not with respect to individual territories'; i.e. the committee could, for example, make a recommendation on educational policy in general, but not on policy in any particular territory. This 'Special Committee' was re-appointed by the Assembly in 1948 and again by last autumn's Assembly, but on the latter occasion appointment was for a three-years term.

We were prepared to agree that, at the beginning, there was some justification for appointing such committees to settle procedural questions. ... But much energy at their meetings has been devoted to efforts to induce the Colonial Powers to transmit political information, information on the development of self-governing institutions ... to discussion of the question which are the territories for which information must be supplied; to consideration of the future of the Committee and, at the last session, to making recommendations regarding policy in non-self-governing territories on a number of subjects.

As regards the future of the Committee, there have been strenuous efforts, notably by India and the USSR, to perpetuate it as a permanent organ of the United Nations for the supervision and control of the administration of non-self-governing territories. An Indian draft Resolution defeated only by a narrow margin in the 1947 Assembly would have set up a permanent committee with power 'to examine the information submitted under Article 73(e) of the Charter and to submit reports thereon for the consideration of the General Assembly with such recommendations as it may deem appropriate.' It would in fact have been a substitute Trusteeship Council for all non-self-governing territories.

John was in New York from the end of September to mid-November. He addressed the committee on 3 October, a 'general defence of the administering powers', and particularly of his government's policies in the trust territories.

Administrative unions had greatly benefited the British-administered Trust Territories. Such an arrangement was, moreover, a specific requirement of the Trusteeship Agreements, for compelling geographic and other reasons.

Mr Martin replied at length to what he called the familiar charges about 'oppressed peoples', and 'colonial exploitation' used by several delegates during the debate. 'The peoples of the Trust Territories', he said, 'had been oppressed in the past — oppressed under the sombre tyranny of diseases they could not understand, of inter-tribal warfare, of the slave trade, of recurring famine, of fear in many and often horrible shapes. It had been the task of the Administering Authorities to end that dark chapter. ... Enlightened critics recognized that Administering Authorities had secured a large measure of freedom from want and fear for the peoples of the Trust Territories, but the critics were often not satisfied with the pace of the advance, particularly in the field of political development. The Administering Powers themselves would never be fully satisfied until their task was complete but the possibilities were limited by factors which were not entirely within their control.'

Mr Martin emphasized that the British system of democratic government in the Trust Territories was not necessarily the best for the indigenous peoples, and it was considered preferable that they should develop democratic institutions in their own way rather than having a fixed pattern thrust upon them. . . .

In conclusion, Mr Martin said that all concerned in the work of the Trusteeship Council must have noticed during its last session a real improvement in the spirit of co-operation amongst its members. He recalled the words of Mr Noriega, of Mexico, who had contributed much to the Council's work — when he referred to the mission of the members as a 'supreme moral obligation' to put aside all considerations of international politics in order to secure the welfare of the indigenous populations as provided by the Charter.

A problem John encountered at Lake Success was that speeches were being reported inaccurately. Draft reports of his speeches were marked by his own corrections. John described the business at Lake Success in a letter of 7 October.

The Committee meets at Lake Success morning or afternoon (alternating each week) and there is a certain amount of reading and preparation to be done at the office. As usual here much time is wasted in waiting for cars or on the long journey to and from Lake Success. I have made two prepared speeches, besides one or two shorter interventions.

I sit next to the Soviet delegate (called Soldatov), who is always quite affable, with the American (usually one Gerig of the State Dept.) on my right. Usually we lunch with other delegates or members of the Secretariat (and have established much more friendly relations than at one time existed!).

John found much of the proceedings very irritating. On 10 October 1949 he refers to 'Another fruitless debate at Lake Success on a Philippino proposal that the United Nations flag should be flown over all Trust Territories — just the sort of idea that goes down big at Lake Success. The comic relief was supplied by the Liberian delegate who talks very entertaining gibberish.' Later that month he allowed himself an uncharacteristically xenophobic outburst to release pent-up exasperation.

We are in a hopeless position in our committee, the few delegations who know what they are talking about completely outnumbered by the Latin Americans, Arabs, Slavs etc. The United States can never be relied on and even those few civilized countries that might be expected to support us, such as Holland, Sweden and Norway, give us no help at all. Our one friend is the Greek! Today, for instance, there was a resolution that corporal punishment should *immediately* be abolished in the trust territories. Needless to say this was warmly supported by the Soviet delegate, who expressed horror at the survival of such a barbarous practice in our Colonies. Among other reasons we had to vote against it because it hasn't even been abolished (for certain prison offences) in the UK. Only South Africa voted with us.

By 23 October, John was feeling it all 'a most frightful waste of time and incidentally of the taxpayer's money'. On 28 October he said, 'I made a longish speech in the committee the other day (about ¾ hour), but don't suppose any of it will have reached *The Times*. The *NY Times* gave an account of it, which as usual was rather misleading. It described me as Winston Churchill's Colonial Office adviser.'

John underestimated *The Times*, which printed a summary of his speech under the title 'British Reply to UN Critics' in a report dated 26 October.

A British reply to misinformed criticism of conditions in the trust territories was given to-day in the Assembly's trusteeship committee.

In the British view misapprehension is apparent in four resolutions already adopted by the committee on such matters as flying the United Nations flag, submitting information to the Trusteeship Council, admitting the local population to foreign-owned industries, and abolishing child marriages. The local administrative unions set up in West Africa, to the obvious benefit of the trust territories, are regarded by many members of the committee as a first step to incorporation into adjacent colonies.

Patient reassurances were forthcoming from Mr J. M.

Martin, the British delegate, who, commenting on a motion tabled by Cuba and Guatemala, firmly rejected the idea that administering authorities could not extend the scope of an administrative union without first submitting its plans for the approval of the Trusteeship Council. Such a requirement, he said, was contrary to the provisions of the trusteeship agreements, and the British Government could only 'regretfully decline'.

Mr Martin pointed out that fragmentary strips of the Cameroons and Togoland could not be administered as separate political entities, and he explained the advantages they received from being treated for administrative purposes as integral parts of Nigeria and the Gold Coast, as was, indeed, required by the trusteeship agreements. This arrangement did not prejudice their status as trust territories; but members who said 'Spend more on education and health services' should remember that even the present services could not have been provided from the two territories' unaided resources, and that budgetary autonomy seemed meaningless in territories that had to meet half their expenditure from external subsidies.

A different situation, he said, existed in the establishment of common services between Tanganyika and the neighbouring territories of Kenya and Uganda, all of which formed a homogeneous block. The British Government had made it abundantly clear that they did not regard trusteeship agreements as conferring power to annex a trust territory or to extinguish its status, and he protested against the unwarranted questioning of their good faith. Nor, he added, could his Government agree to supervision by the Trusteeship Council of any aspect of the administration of territories that had not been placed under the trusteeship system — a reference to the colonies concerned in these administrative unions.

In a letter of 28 October, he reported the departure of the UN visiting mission to West Africa. 'Our exercise of our stewardship there is to be inspected by an Iraqi (the Chairman), an American, a Mexican (who has no knowledge of colonial administration or probably of any kind) and a Belgian. The head of their secretariat is a Chinese, assisted by a Russian. Queen Victoria must turn in her grave.'

'Our committee plods slowly on,' John wrote on 11 November. 'I had a very nice encouraging telegram from the SofS, Creech Jones ... realizing what "an unpleasant and uphill task you are having in the Committee. I should however like you to know that I much appreciate the way you are handling things and that you have my full support".'

In his address at Cambridge John emphasized the emptiness and futility of much of the discussion in the fourth committee. Each of the resolutions was a case study of the difficulties the UN imposed on the colonial powers.

On the first Resolution, 'voluntary transmission of information', he said 'we are not prepared to see the internal constitutional affairs of the non-self-governing territories bandied about in this Committee.' Mr Grantley Adams of Barbados assured the Assembly in 1948 that nothing would be more generally resented in the territories themselves.

The second Resolution invited the Administering States ... to establish equal treatment in ... education between inhabitants of the non-self-governing territories whether indigenous or not. ... The United Kingdom was alone in voting against the Resolution, though seven Members abstained. ... It was a step on the road ... leading to interference by the UN in all aspects of the domestic affairs of non-self-governing territories. I was therefore instructed in voting against the Resolution to make it clear that the vote was not cast against the principle of equal education as such, but was cast because a vote in favour would have implied an admission that the UN has a *locus standi* for interfering in British Colonial administration in a way which the UN Charter does not support. Article 2(7) states that nothing contained in the Charter 'shall authorise the United Nations to intervene in matters which are essentially within the domestic jurisdiction of any State' and we regard educational policy as one of those matters.

The third Resolution invited Administering States to promote the use of indigenous languages ... in schools. On this I pointed out that a great deal of thought had already been given by us to the subject and that our policy was to use the vernacular in the first stages of education and encourage its development thereafter, but in the later stages to use English as a medium of instruction in order to give access to world culture. I explained the difficulties arising from the large number of vernaculars in many territories — this obviously came as a surprise to many Delegates, who had apparently been thinking in terms of a singular vernacular in each — and the impossibility of providing teachers, authors and translators for them all.

Next came a Resolution on illiteracy. ... It plainly overlooked the fact that illiteracy is not a problem confined to non-self-governing territories and also seemed to have been proposed in ignorance of the immense activity that has been taking place in this field in these territories in recent years. We pointed out that its result could only be unprofitable and unnecessary 'paper pushing'. ...

The Assembly next debated a long Resolution on 'international cooperation' ... and drew attention to a number of problems which are already being studied and called on international organizations to perform functions which they are already performing. It was, however, adopted by 39 to 2 with 8 abstentions.

The sixth Resolution was that of reconstituting the Special Committee for a three-year period. It was adopted by 44 to 5 with 4 abstentions. We could see no justification for prolonging the Committee's life even for as much as three years. Once procedural questions relating to the technique of transmission have been resolved, we see no further need for a Special Committee.

Yet another Resolution ... invited the Special Committee at its 1950 session to give special attention to the problems of education in non-self-governing territories. This shows clearly the direction in which the Special Committee is developing. Though in no way technically qualified for such a specialist study, this political committee is to examine and discuss the educational problems of the non-self-governing territories. Past experience suggests that it will concentrate on shortcomings and be used largely as a forum for irresponsible criticism.

The United Kingdom was unable to vote for any of these 10 Resolutions: it cast its vote against 8 of them. Yet all were carried by large majorities. How does it come about that the United Kingdom, whose Colonial policy is in such complete harmony with the principles embodied in Chapter XI, has felt compelled to stand in such firm and often lonely opposition to the views of the majority of States regarding its interpretation?

To understand these proceedings it is necessary to bear in mind the composition and voting rules in the General Assembly. There are 59 Member States and each of these has one vote. The vote of Costa Rica or Liberia thus equals the vote of the United States or the United Kingdom. Of the 59 only 8 count as Administering Members (Australia, Belgium, Denmark, France, the Netherlands, New Zealand, United Kingdom, USA). The remaining 51 have no Colonial responsibilities. The vote on Colonial questions is thus a striking example of power without responsibility. The 51 can pass Resolutions laying down policies for Colonial administration in the happy knowledge that they will have no responsibility for meeting the financial or political consequences.

Further, these 51 Members include the Soviet bloc, who are out to make mischief and to exploit every opportunity of weakening the influence of the Colonial Powers, and most of the others start with a strong anti-Colonial bias. The Latin-American States (numbering 20) look back with emotion to the chapter of their own history when they achieved liberation from the Colonial Empires of Spain or Portugal: some of them too dislike and fear the competition of Colonial producers. The Arab States cannot forget their recent emancipation from foreign tutelage and resent the continued rule of a foreign Power in North Africa. India and Pakistan, the Philippines and even at times the United States are swayed by similar emotions springing from their own historic[al] memories.

With the malevolence of the Soviet bloc and the prejudice of many States goes a general ignorance of existing conditions which is perhaps not surprising but is certainly profound.

It is because we have not been prepared to accept the principle of international accountability or to compromise on it that we have found ourselves in constant collision with the majority at Lake Success. . . . [Our] first and most important reason is that acceptance by HMG of a system under which Colonial policy would be determined by the UN would be a retrograde step. With the steady constitutional development in the Colonial Empire effective control over an ever-increasing sphere of public affairs is passing into the hands of the Colonial Executive and Legislative bodies. Indeed the peoples of many of our Colonial territories already exercise greater control over their own destinies than the peoples of some Member States of the United Nations. Their progress towards self-government could not continue smoothly and successfully if we were to put the clock back and allow their domestic affairs to be regulated by remote control from Lake Success in a political body whose members, whatever their intentions, cannot have first-hand knowledge of the needs and aspirations of the peoples in the territories concerned. There is in many territories already a strong sense of local nationalism and the local Governments would not be prepared to submit their domestic affairs to any greater degree of international supervision or interference than sovereign States are prepared to accept for themselves. To subject them to such international supervision would . . . engender that very sense of inferiority among Colonial peoples which it should be the aim of any enlightened Colonial policy to remove.

At this point, John mentioned colonial application articles in international agreements, which enabled a colonial power to accede to the agreement on behalf of its metropolitan territory and to apply the agreement to some or all of its dependent territories after consultation with the local governments concerned, a procedure the UK was careful to adopt. The UN succeeded in eliminating the colonial application article from an international agreement. This results in less freedom for colonial peoples, who lose any power to say whether or not they agreed with an international agreement. John pointed out that 'Cuba or the Phillipines or Liberia are free to decide for themselves whether they can accede to an agreement: but Jamaica, the Gold Coast, the Federation of Malaya are to have no choice and be bound by acceptance by the United Kingdom.'

John went on to show that the stage of political development already reached by several colonial territories and the trend of such development elsewhere made it inappropriate to submit them to remote control from Lake Success.

> Further, the Delegates at Lake Success are simply not qualified to exercise such control ... the countries they represent have had no experience, or at least no recent experience, of Colonial administration. ... At one moment they are sternly critical of development of economic resources as exploitation and at another demand immediate increases of expenditure on social services for which only such development can provide the basis. ... One of the Delegates at the last Assembly pointed out in a critical tone that there was no daily newspaper in the British Cameroons and no old age pensions. In replying I expressed regret that there was even no television and reminded him that in the United Kingdom, which does not consider itself backward in social services, old age pensions had only been introduced within the lifetime of my own generation.
>
> A further disadvantage of the Assembly as a body to entrust with supervision of Colonial Administration is the fact that votes ... can be affected by all sorts of diplomatic and political considerations which have no bearing on the well-being of Colonial peoples.

In spite of these criticisms of the United Nations, John Martin went on to make it clear that it was the government's policy to support the UN, of which Britain had been one of the creators. However, huge difficulties stood in the way of creating an international civil service of high standard.

It cannot be pretended that our experience of the branches

of the Secretariat concerned with Colonial matters has been a very happy one. In particular, we have had to contend with what have seemed like efforts of 'Empire building' and there has certainly been a tendency to turn what should have been a comparatively small section for handling the information transmitted under Article 73(e) into a sort of international Colonial Office. There have been occasions when we have known that speeches strongly critical of the Colonial Powers have been drafted for Delegates by members of the Secretariat and often critical questions have been prompted from the same source.

John recognized that some of these faults and difficulties were the mark of a young and inexperienced organization. None the less, it was in the colonies' interest to support the UN; first, because of the benefits they could derive from UN agencies; second, because of what colonial governments could contribute in skill and experience to the development of backward territories, many of them sovereign states; and third, because it was important to show no signs of hanging back in international cooperation. In enlarging upon this third point, John used a moral argument. Britain and its colonies should be in a position to give moral leadership to the large number of those in the world who recoil from the tyranny of Soviet communism and yet equally fail to find satisfaction in all aspects of the American way of life. It was important therefore to overcome prejudice against colonialism.

Now our claim to be one of the leaders of the forces of progress in the world is undoubtedly weakened in many eyes by the fact that we are regarded as reactionary as a Colonial Power ... the prejudice against what is called Colonialism is strong and widespread and ... we should do what we can to show the world in a positive way the character of our Colonial achievement and ... avoid anything that serves to confirm the impression that we resent and repel outside interest in the Colonies because we have something to conceal or that we hang back from bringing them into the field of international collaboration because we wish to cling to their possession for reasons of self-interest.

In his April address, John drew attention to the fact that 'on Colonial topics we have acquired at Lake Success the reputation of saying "no" as often as Molotov.' This was done on the grounds that Britain had certain responsibilities, which could not be shared and which the charter did not require us to share. This policy, though correct, could be misunderstood as defensive and hiding what should be open. In an address to a second colonial service weekend conference at Cambridge in September of the same year, 1950, John told his audience that a different tactical approach was to be adopted in votes on colonial affairs at the UN.

> Where the principle embodied in the Resolution is good, we shall in future generally vote for it, making any necessary reservation with regard to specific points or abstain in the voting, with a suitable explanation for our reasons for doing so. But however the United Kingdom vote is cast, the principal object will be to avoid the impression that we are adopting a negative or unprogressive attitude. At the same time, while standing fast on the principle that there is no right of international supervision, we shall take the opportunity to state in a vigorous and positive way our actual aims and achievements in the particular field under discussion. We believe we have a good story to tell and we shall use the meetings of the Assembly as an opportunity to proclaim it to the world.

John found the infant UN's fourth committee a parliament of anti-colonialists, both high and low-minded, a would-be world office of decolonialization. It was a relief for him to turn from the UN to practical cooperation between colonial powers, putting into effect his Burkean principle of dealing with circumstances.

Informal cooperation between colonial powers had existed for some time, notably between Britain and France. Cooperation in Africa, apart from the Mediterranean north, was put on a formal basis in 1949 through an Anglo–French initiative. A meeting of British and French officials at the end of April, which John Martin chaired, put forward proposals for technical cooperation. In a lengthy letter to Michael Wright of the Foreign Office, John recounted what had been done in the meeting and what was proposed. The letter, of 12 May 1949, mentioned other interested parties in the two governments who were to be consulted and also other countries to be invited to be founder members. The French team had been led by M. Laurentie, a former French colonial governor and then French alternate delegate on the UN Trusteeship Council. He brought with him representatives of the Quai d'Orsay and of the Ministry of Overseas France. The French, like the British, had a strong desire to keep some of the UN and US initiatives at arm's length. The proposals were duly approved.

John's diary for 7 September 1949 records the opening of a 'Conference with Belgians, French, Portuguese, South Africans and South Rhodesians on proposed Committee for technical cooperation in Africa south of the Sahara'. Thus, the Commission de Coopération Technique pour l'Afrique du Sud (CCTA) was set up. John referred to the old informal cooperation as 'The Club'. 'The Club' it continued to be with the CCTA.

> There is now extremely close liaison between the Colonial Offices in London, Paris and Brussels — and also Lisbon. We ... have frequent telephone conversations and meetings. Although we often approach matters from different points of view ... we have always found it possible to work together with the utmost friendliness and frankness. I often feel that, apart from language difference, our meetings are indistinguishable from a conference between two or three Whitehall departments. ... We have elaborated a programme of joint technical conferences — e.g. a Rinderpest Conference at Nairobi, a Phyto-Sanitary Conference in London and a Soils Conference in the Belgian Congo. Last year there was a Conference on Food and Nutrition in the French Cameroons and a Conference on Indigenous Rural Economy at Jos in Nigeria. Last year also there was a Transport Conference in Lisbon. ... The general object of these Conferences is the pooling of information and promoting of a joint approach to the problems common to the various Governments concerned, so that, for example, French and British medical teams are found assisting one another in West Africa in combatting yellow fever and smallpox without regard to national frontiers.

For the more effective organization of these technical Conferences and of the permanent bureaux created by some of them (Tsetse and Trypanosomiasis Bureau at Leopoldville, The Soils Bureau in Paris, and we hope that there will shortly be a Bureau to deal with Epizootics in Mugugua near Nairobi that will deal with all major cattle diseases in Africa) we have recently joined with the Belgians, French, Portuguese, Southern Rhodesians and South Africans in setting up the Commission for Technical Cooperation in Africa South of the Sahara. We are trying to keep this a very simple piece of machinery and, to avoid creating an elaborate new Secretariat, we undertook to service it from the Colonial Office. It consists of representatives of the six Governments and meets twice a year to review existing activities and agree on the programme of forthcoming Conferences.

Side by side with the CCTA is the Scientific Council for Africa South of the Sahara which was born at the Johannesburg Scientific Conference last October. The Council is advisory and consultative and composed of scientists representative of both the subjects and the regions concerned. ... The purpose of this Council is generally to promote scientific research.

We have also entered into agreements with the French and Belgians for the exchange of information about the administration of our African territories and, to further this liaison, the French have attached administrative officers from their Colonies as Colonial Vice Consuls in their Consulates at Nairobi and Accra, while we on our side have appointed Colonial Vice Consuls at Dakar and Libreville. Close liaison is also encouraged by an ever increasing exchange of visits and staff. For example a Jamaican Fisheries Officer has been doing a course of study in the Congo and we have agreed with the Belgian Government that there should be occasional exchanges of administrative staff. In fact in facing our common problems we are coming to them with less regard to differences of nationality than to their effective solution. For example, a Belgian is head of the Locust Service established at Abercorn in Northern Rhodesia. The important cooperation is not so much between

Governments as between the officers facing the same problems in the field.

The Club provided John with work and friends. The CCTA was a particular interest of his for the next few years. He was the leader of the British representatives and held in high regard by the other representatives. Conveniently for him, the CCTA had its small secretariat in London. His diary, and the papers he collected on the CCTA, mention his own journeys and the CCTA's undertakings. On 9 June 1950, he dined with Belgian Minister of Colonies, de Wigny, near Waterloo and also had a short meeting later with other delegates, Dupont, Grojean of Belgium and Monod of France. He was in Paris on 26 and 27 June for a meeting with the French and Belgians at the Quai d'Orsay.

On 10 and 11 January 1951, John had talks in London with the French on the third CCTA conference, which was to be in Lisbon from 19 to 28 January; John was accompanied by Galsworthy, Lambert and Cotton, after which he stayed with Jock Colville in the embassy at Estoril, where he had earlier met Moiseiwitsch and Yehudi Menuhin. He wrote home on 28 January to say:

> We have had a week of pretty hard work at our conference and only finished at last today by holding a long Sunday morning session. On the whole we are satisfied with the results, though in this sort of international discussion it is seldom possible to get anything near 100% of what one wants. You can imagine the difficulty of getting agreement on detailed resolutions between British, French, Belgians, Portuguese, S. Africans and S. Rhodesians — with indifferent interpreters. We managed to keep good friends with the French in spite of considerable differences of opinion, but unfortunately at the end came into collision with the S. Africans with whom we had till then maintained the best relations.

The fourth CCTA conference was in London, from 25 to 30 June, with John in the chair. He entertained his guests with a supper party at Hampton Court. He had Dupont to lunch at his club and Pierre Kresser and Peyronnet to dinner at Pelham Place. On 5 November, the diary reports John's first meeting with one whom he was to get to know well and much admire: 'talk with new Minister of State (Lennox-Boyd)'. Alan Lennox-Boyd (later Viscount Boyd) was Minister of State for six months, but returned to the Colonial Office as Secretary of State in July 1954 to serve for more than five years.

At the beginning of 1952, John Martin was knighted. The KCMG came in the first New Year's honours of the second Churchill government. It gave much pleasure to John's many friends. Letters and congratulations came in from the church and state, from present and former colleagues in the colonial service dispersed around the empire and Commonwealth, from friends in other government departments and from Oxford. The expressions of pleasure at the honour were coupled with the conviction that it was thoroughly deserved.

He made a lengthy tour of southern Africa from 20 January to 13 February. He visited Brazzaville on 21 January, Leopoldville on the 22nd and Cape Town on the 25th, where the fifth CCTA conference was to run from 28 January to 2 February with Andrews of the South African Department of External Affairs in the chair. After the conference, John visited Johannesburg and Nairobi. Conversations between Secretary of State Oliver Lyttelton (later Viscount Chandos) and French Minister of Overseas France Pflimlin took place in London at the end of March. At the end of May, John was in Brussels for consultation on UN affairs, with Louwers of the Ministry for Foreign Affairs in the chair and Dupont, Nandé and Delteil present. The sixth CCTA conference took place in Paris from 23 to 28 June with Laurentie in the chair. John mentioned a reception at the Elysée by President Vincent Auriol. At the end of September, there were more talks with the Americans in Washington. On 27 September 1952, he wrote:

The days here have rushed breathlessly past and our talks finished yesterday, though I have still a last call to make at the State Department this morning. They seem to me to have gone very well and have certainly brought the Americans to a very clear understanding of our point of view (and us of them), though we can never hope to bring them to look at Colonial questions quite as we do and our old friend appeasement flourishes here under the form of saying that 'we must roll with the punch'. Personal relations could not be better and various members of our Embassy staff — the Ambassador himself is not here — and of the New York Delegation, including Gladwyn Jebb, have been a great help.

In 1953, the seventh and eighth CCTA conferences took place at Brussels from 19 to 24 January and at Lisbon from 25 June to 4 July, both of which John attended. In the middle of March, there was a joint CCTA/Commission Scientifique pour l'Afrique du Sud (CSA) working party in London. John took part on 27 March in conversations with the Belgians, van den Abeele, Grojean and de Quidt, about sites for oil installations at Kigoma and Dar es Salaam. On 5 and 6 May, John talked to the French and Belgians about colonial questions raised in the UN. Selwyn-Lloyd presided over a government lunch at 1 Carlton Gardens for the participants. A meeting of the Secretary of State with the Minister for Overseas France, planned for 22 May in Paris, fell through because of the fall of the French government. A meeting of officials only took place instead. John chaired the ninth session of the CCTA held in London from 18 to 25 January 1954. This was the last one he attended. For the rest of 1954 he was much taken up with Cyprus and Malaya.

This heavy round of meetings reflected the extent to which colonial powers cooperated with one another in those years. The CCTA spun off preliminary meetings to prepare and agree agendas, visits to the places and regions the CCTA served, and contacts with the UN and, as an interested party, the USA, itself in some way a colonial power. The friendships and understandings that grew up among the participants in the CCTA's work, along with the regularity with which certain names crop up in John's diary, suggest that 'The Club' was an accurate name. It was one of the more enjoyable parts of John's work.

9

Cyprus: Greeks and Turks, Enosis and the Ethnarch, 1945–60

In 1878, Cyprus became British as a result of the agreements reached between the powers at Berlin. Among these was a defensive alliance between Great Britain and Turkey, formed to prevent Russian encroachment in the Middle East.

On 12 October 1907, Winston Churchill, then parliamentary under-secretary of state in the Colonial Office in the 1905 Liberal government, spoke to the Greek elected members of the Cyprus legislative council at Nicosia. He touched on matters that were to be prominent after 1945, the Greek Cypriot desire for union with Greece, enosis, and the Muslim or Turkish Cypriot hope of protection by Turkey.

> I think it is only natural that the Cypriot people, who are of Greek descent, should regard their incorporation with what may be called their mother-country as an ideal to be earnestly, devoutly, and fervently cherished. ... I say that the views which have been put forward are opinions which His Majesty's Government do not refuse to regard with respect. On the other hand the opinion held by the Moslem population of the island, that the British occupation of Cyprus should not lead to the dismemberment of the Ottoman Empire ... nor impair the sovereignty of the Sultan, is one which His Majesty's Government are equally bound to regard with respect.

... His Majesty's Government may therefore be encouraged to hope that the people of Cyprus, while cherishing great national ideals, are content for the present at least, to be governed in accordance with British ideas of justice and freedom.

When John Martin returned to the Colonial Office in 1945 with responsibility for the Middle East, Cyprus was to occupy him for many years. The Colonial Office was somewhat constrained in relation to Cyprus, a crown colony. For a start, in the postwar period there was an expectation in the air that colonial rule would soon end and this made colonial populations restless and difficult to rule. Also, two governments, Greek and Turkish, had an interest in the Cypriot population. The Greek Cypriot majority, many of whom sought union with Greece (enosis), looked to Athens. However, during the negotiations it was by no means certain that the Greek government was a consistent supporter of enosis or that the majority of Greek Cypriots desired it. As A. S. Papadopoulos put it on 25 October 1994: 'The only test of public opinion on Enosis was in the form of a so-called referendum conducted by the Church when, on leaving church services on Sundays, the congregation was asked by the priest to sign a register affirming their desire for Enosis.' The minority, the Turkish Cypriots, looked to the Turkish government for protection. In addition, the military situation was changing in the Middle East and chiefs of staff were putting forward a strong case for retaining Cyprus as a colony, or at least keeping bases in Cyprus. To make matters worse, the Colonial Office and the Foreign Office disagreed over what should be done about Cyprus. The Colonial Office was putting forward a strong case for continuing British rule, whereas the Foreign Office was more prepared to envisage independence. This tension between government departments continued until after the Suez crisis of 1956, when the Macmillan government reviewed its Middle East and eastern Mediterranean policy. It opted for the Foreign Office preference for an independent Cyprus with arrangements for British military bases. John Martin held to the Colonial Office view until 1957 when a paper of his revealed that he had changed his mind.

In October 1946, Secretary of State Creech Jones stated:

(i) the Governor (Sir Charles Woolley, colonial servant, Governor of Cyprus and Commander-in-Chief, 1941–46) would be invited to call together a Consultative Assembly to consider the framing of proposals for constitutional reform including the re-establishment of a central legislature;

(ii) economic development would be pressed on with, through the 10-year Plan;

(iii) the 1937 Church laws would be repealed so as to facilitate elections to the Archbishopric;

(iv) the 1931 exiles would be allowed to return.[1]

Lord Winster was appointed to succeed Sir Charles Woolley as governor in October 1946. In January 1947, an agreement was reached on the main outlines of the constitutional programme. Only in March did the Colonial Office secure agreement on a clear 'no enosis' statement from the Foreign Office.

The Cyprus government decided to suspend invitations to the consultative assembly until after the archiepiscopal elections had taken place in June. On 7 July the invitations were issued. The locum tenens who had been elected archbishop died at the end of July. By September, the Turks and left-wing Greeks had accepted the invitation and the right-wing Greeks had rejected it. The assembly was nevertheless established because the left-wingers seemed to want to cooperate; abandoning it would merely have strengthened the right wing in its policy of non-cooperation.

As soon as the assembly met in November, the Greek members began to ask for responsible government in local affairs. With Lord Winster, a statement was issued to the effect that, while self-government could be recognized as a goal, there was no question of granting it immediately. This statement was referred in draft to the Cabinet committee on Commonwealth affairs, which was reluctant to contemplate such an advance and felt that attention should be turned on the development of local government.

---

1. In 1931, there had been serious disturbances in Cyprus, which included the burning of Government House. As a result, the constitution was suspended, restrictions were imposed, archiepiscopal elections were suspended and certain political figures were deported.

In May 1948, constitutional proposals falling short of complete internal self-government were communicated to the assembly; seven of the eight left-wing Greeks decided to reject them. The synod of the Orthodox Church in Cyprus also made its disapproval clear in a statement of 15 May. The actual voting in the assembly, on 21 May, was eleven in favour and seven against.

The rest of May, June and July were spent discussing whether to accept the majority vote and go ahead, the Colonial Office preference, or whether the proposals should be shelved, the course Lord Winster urged. It was decided, with the Cabinet committee's full approval, that they should be shelved. This was announced by Lord Winster on 12 August. He stated that while the offer was not withdrawn, no further steps would be taken until 'responsible and fully representative political leaders in Cyprus come forward to ask that these or comparable proposals may be re-examined and implemented, or there is any genuine manifestation of public opinion in their favour.' He said that self-government and enosis were both out of the question. He then dissolved the assembly. Lord Winster appears to have had an instinct for the less satisfactory solution to a problem and a capacity through his choice of language to turn potential friends into enemies.

Cyprus affairs could not be left at a standstill. John Martin's Middle East Department needed to act. In a private letter of 8 December 1948 to Roland Turnbull, colonial secretary in Cyprus and from time to time acting governor in the governor's absence or during vacancies, John wrote of his forthcoming visit.

> We feel in the Department that it is high time that someone from here came out to Cyprus and paid you a visit of perhaps two or three weeks; but I am not yet certain of the Secretary of State's view of this and it will of course have to be mentioned to the Governor. Assuming that there is to be an official visitor (and there would be obvious difficulties about a ministerial visitation at this juncture) it will probably be myself. It would probably be less open to misrepresentation if the visitor came out before Lord Winster's final departure. We know nothing definite about his plans, but there has been mention of return to Cyprus in January for a very short period. If so, it might be best to travel with him

and, if necessary, stay on a little after his departure. This might coincide with the visit of the Police Adviser.

John flew out with Lord Winster on 15 January 1949. By 30 January he could say that he had completed most of his 'strenuous programme', but various interviews and inspections lay ahead. His letter of 1 February recounted some of his activities.

Tuesday 24th. Visited a health centre in a small town — a unique institution providing services of a standard which it is clearly impracticable to supply throughout the island. One branch to which I was taken was the infant nursery class of very small children, where I felt that David would have been at home, playing with plasticine etc. Then on to the town of Larnaca to lunch with the Commissioner and his wife, a very nice young couple, to meet the Mayor and one or two other Cypriots. Back to Nicosia in the afternoon.

Wednesday. Drove to Limassol, the chief commercial town of the island, on the S. coast. It was a sunny morning and the climate seemed much milder: I felt comfortably warm for the first time. The Commissioner took me for a round of visits to country villages in his district. At each we sat in or outside the coffee shop and the men of the village collected round and discussed their affairs with the Commissioner. The chief complaint was the low price of wine, for that is a big wine growing district. We had a picnic lunch by the roadside. Returning to Limassol I was taken round the KEO wine factory, where brandy and other wines are made. A crowd of youths with banners chanted their Enosis slogans at me as we left, but we soon got away from them. In the evening Paul Pavlides, a wealthy Limassol man and member of the Governor's Executive Council, arranged a party in my honour. Twenty or more leading lights of the town. After introductions all round I was put in an extremely cold private room and they were led in to me, one at a time, for about five minutes each. They took full advantage of the opportunity to air their views. It was all very interesting, though I felt quite limp and half frozen at the end of it and was quite unable to do justice to the dinner with the Pavlides family which followed. Spent the night at the Commissioner's house.

Thursday. Drove to Kyperoundia, a TB sanatorium, high up among snow and sleet and shown round by Dr Bevan who runs it, a man with a great reputation in these parts. Then on up to Pano Platres, a summer resort in the mountains, where the Commissioner handed me over to the Conservator of Forests, Waterer, and we had lunch with some of the forest staff. ... We then drove up over the mountain ridge and through miles of forest roads. The views must be superb in good weather, but were largely blotted out by rain and cloud. There was snow on the higher parts of the road and several times the car stuck, so that we had to get out and shove. Spent the night at Stavros forest station — supper with the (Cypriot) forest staff and then a longish talk with Waterer, Green Bey (a retired governor of an Egyptian province, who came here as a commissioner during the war) and the very intelligent and interesting Cypriot Assistant Conservator.

Friday. Bright again. Went round the forest station, seeing a specimen of the moufflon, the unique Cyprus animal which seems to have been saved just in time from extermination. Drove through more forests and then to the Turkish town of Lefka, where I lunched with the Mayor. In the afternoon visited a copper mine and was shown round at great length by the (American) manager, including a descent to the underground workings some distance below sea level. Tea at his house, the first warm house I have met in Cyprus. Return to Nicosia in time for dinner, another large party.

Saturday. An Investiture at Government House. Lunch and dinner parties and Sir Mehmed Munir had tea with me; but otherwise a quiet day at last in which to collect myself.

Much of my time here is given up to official interviews with the Colonial Secretary (Turnbull), various heads of departments and others — with which I need not burden you. Yesterday HE took me to a picnic lunch in a tent, at which he was entertained by about 50 *mukhtar*s (village headmen) at a country village not far from here. Everybody

173

full of smiles and welcome and a small girl presented me with a bouquet of roses. HE made a speech. Printed copies of a Greek translation had been handed round beforehand and it was interesting to follow this (like a Loeb) and see how much of the vocabulary of ancient Greek survives. There was much drinking of toasts and general cheerfulness and after the meal two fiddlers played while others in Turkish trousers performed their traditional Greek and Turkish dances.

In the evening the local Greek member of the Executive Council gave a cocktail party in my honour — various leading lights of Nicosia, all very friendly and politics in the background. Today I have been to a smaller party of Turkish representatives, who lamented the unfavourable position of their minority community.

It is a lovely and interesting island: but I have now reached the stage of half-knowledge when it would be extremely difficult to write a report on its affairs.

John had a duty to report what he saw and heard in Cyprus. In tune with his reluctance to pose as an authority on the island, after three weeks there he chose to set down his impressions. These contain his assessment of its economy and possible political developments. He held strongly to the view that Cyprus should remain a British colony. He was aware also of conflicts between the minority Turkish population, 80,000 of 450,000, and the Greek majority. In his impressions he wrote at some length on enosis.

In the course of his visit, John met the ethnarch, Archbishop Makarios.[2] 'Ethnarch' was a title meaning 'leader of the nation', which the Turks accorded the archbishop of Cyprus during their years of administering the island. The Turks were happy to let the Church manage the affairs of its flock provided taxes were paid. The title therefore had political as well as ecclesiastical significance. Makarios set out the political case for union with Greece in a letter to John dated 20 January, on the morning of which John had seen him.

---

2. Makarios III, Mihail Christodoulou Mouskos, 1913–77, bishop of Kition 1948, archbishop and primate 1948, first president of Cyprus 1960.

On the opportunity of your visit, I wish, as Ethnarch of the Greek people of Cyprus, to expound anew the Pancyprian and with it the Panhellenic claim for the restoration of Cyprus to Mother Greece, a ... claim, based on the pure hellenicism of Cyprus and the national feelings of its people. ... The Greek people of Cyprus, abiding resolutely and irreconcilably with the claim of its national freedom, is firmly decided to reject any other solution. ... The extension of the occupation of Cyprus by Great Britain, in spite of the expressed will of its Greek people ... constitutes a blunt injustice and offence to the whole Greek Nation, which above any other country fought and sacrificed itself for freedom and justice.

John's own assessment of enosis was more cultural and social and did not admit political union with Greece.

The strength and real meaning of the Enosis demand is hard to measure. In the sense of a claim to be recognized as belonging to the Greek family, as children of 'Mother Greece', it is no doubt almost universal among the Greek-speaking population. A nation can be made as well as born. It was surely a mistaken policy to attempt to deny this claim ... and to attempt to banish the use of the description 'Greek' (substituting 'non-Moslem' or similar phrases) in official documents. In 'culture', in religion and indeed in many points of character these people are Hellenes and it need be no cause for wonder if they take pride in association with all 'the glory that was Greece', and resent attempts to question their title to so splendid an inheritance. Much strength might be taken out of the Enosis agitation by greater readiness on our part to recognize that the Greek-speaking Cypriots are 'Greeks' and to show our appreciation of the grounds for their pride in that fact.

Enosis in the second sense of incorporation in the modern Greek State is also widely and loudly demanded, and there are probably few Greek-speaking Cypriots who would publicly repudiate the claim. I felt, however, a curious air of unreality about this propaganda, in spite of all the noise and clatter with which it is conducted. The long-haired young men or schoolboys who parade with banners, chanting monotonously the cry for Enosis, or daub their slogans on the walls, seemed to enjoy these demonstrations; but, with few exceptions, they did not give an impression of desperate earnestness. Their hysterical performance was sometimes so ridiculous that I could not help laughing in their faces: as often as not the response was laughter from many of the demonstrators themselves. Municipal and ecclesiastical dignitaries repeated the demand at every opportunity; but it often seemed to me that these utterances were of a ritual character and that, having uttered the phrases expected of them, the speakers were prepared to pass on to other subjects: I felt that nothing would have surprised them more than if their demand had been taken seriously. Thus the left-wing Mayor of Famagusta, who had evidently organized for my benefit the largest Enosis demonstration I met, took in good part my refusal to discuss political matters and went on to show me with much pride and enthusiasm various municipal activities and installations, such as an excellently run municipal restaurant (on the lines of a 'British Restaurant'), a spacious and well kept market, electrical and water-pumping stations and a block of new flats for workmen. The atmosphere at my meeting with the Archbishop could not have been more friendly.

In conversation with many non-political Cypriots, the Enosis claim was, so far as I can recall, never once pressed upon me, though it was often mentioned with an indulgent smile and sometimes dismissed as not to be taken too seriously.

Moreover the sentimental attractions of union with Greece are seen against a very different background of economic and social conditions from 20 or even 15 years ago. 'Mother Greece' is torn by civil war. ... Meanwhile their own Island, no longer a 'Cinderella' colony, is visibly going ahead by leaps and bounds: there are all the marks of active development and rapid progress. ... The Church leaders must be conscious too that in the modern Greek

State they would not be accorded any of the privileges of 'Ethnarchy', of which they have so long resented the loss under British administration. The well-to-do — and there seem to be surprisingly many such — have no illusions about the disasters which would befall them if the British left. ... Union with Greece no doubt remains a comforting fantasy at the back of the minds of many Cypriots, who cherish vague ideas of the 'good time' which would follow it and of the revival of the supposed ancient glories of their race. But one doubts if they have any real belief that such day-dreams will come true. The ideal is one for which, particularly in youth, they will wave a flag or sport the blue and white of Hellas and, under the influence of a campaign of propaganda, they might cast their votes for it even in a secret ballot: it is not a cause for which they would give their lives.

John Martin was much in favour of social and economic development in Cyprus. He singled it out in his paper for the Secretary of State in 1960 as the British administration's main achievement on the island. It is not surprising that he thought in the immediate postwar years that the union of Cyprus with Greece was impossible. The severity of the civil war in Greece and the consequent instability of the country for years afterwards stayed in his mind. In the postwar world, as in 1878, Cyprus was a bulwark against southward penetration by Russia — though this time it would be through supplying arms through Greece rather than Turkey.

Both in his days at No. 10 and in the Colonial Office, John found that many people trusted his friendship and discretion. Men who were dissatisfied with their situation or at odds with their colleagues found that they could speak easily and frankly to him without damaging their career prospects. John did not think the worse of people who were open, and often it was the more able colonial servants who felt the frustrations of their position. Managing the retreat from empire was difficult. Roland Turnbull was one such able servant. His letters to John in 1949, after John's visit to the island, expressing his irritation with the departing governor, Lord Winster, and other frustrations of the service, illustrate well this relationship between one who must needs explode and the other who hears and encourages. In reply to one of these letters, of 12 July 1949, John had to point out that there was no evidence for Turnbull's claim that the Greek government was stirring up enosis activity in Cyprus. If Turnbull had such evidence, he should produce it and remember that Athens had a free press. Turnbull later went on to become the governor of North Borneo.

In 1950, Makarios embarrassed the pro-British Greek government by pressing it to raise the question of enosis at the United Nations and with Great Britain's close allies. When the Greek foreign secretary eventually did so in 1953, he was offended by a firm 'never' from the then British foreign secretary, Eden. The 'never' was repeated in Parliament in July 1954 by the minister of state for colonial affairs, Henry Hopkinson. It is possible to get John's later view on the 'never', which at the time created controversy. In 1983, he and Sir Eugene Melville, who had been assistant under-secretary in the Colonial Office in the 1950s and from 1961 had held various Foreign Office and diplomatic posts, helped Granada Television prepare a programme on Cyprus. They met to answer questions put by the company, Sir Eugene drafting their answers and John adding certain points and approving the whole.

Henry Hopkinson's 'Never' speech was in fact an answer to a supplementary question, an attempt to draw a distinction between colonies which could expect eventual independence and those which might 'never' reach the end of the road. This was interpreted, in the House and outside, as meaning that Cyprus could never achieve independence, even though Hopkinson added in his reply that he was not saying that, but merely restated the government's position at the time, namely that no change was contemplated in sovereignty as nothing less than continued sovereignty over the Island could enable HMG to carry out their strategic obligations in Europe and Middle East. This position had been very carefully formulated so as to avoid on the one hand giving Greek Cypriots who were pressing for Enosis any encouragement to think that the British government would yield to this pressure and on the other hand not antagonizing the Turks while not finally closing the door to later developments which might bring Cyprus back on to the usual colonial road towards independence. The reaction in the Colonial and Foreign Offices to the interpretation given to Hopkinson's reference to 'never' and the row this caused in the House was to play down the statement as containing nothing new and, later, to withdraw the 'never' in statements about the future international status of Cyprus.

The 'never' statement produced a strong reaction in the Greek world. Makarios preached an 'enosis only enosis' sermon to a large audience at Phaneromeni. There were Greek appeals to the UN for self-determination. A 'never' postage stamp was issued. Makarios and the Greek government told Grivas,[3] leader of EOKA, that the armed struggle could begin, though Makarios insisted on sabotage only. The United Nations, some months later in December, refused to pass a resolution on Cyprus for the time being. In January 1955, an arms-smuggling caique was caught red-handed. In April, the bombing campaign began with fewer explosions than expected. Makarios ordered Grivas to stop and regroup. April 1955 was the month in which Eden became Prime Minister. In the House of Commons, the press and among world opinion, there was strong pressure for a constructive solution.

In June 1955, the British government brought in the Turks by inviting the Greek and Turkish governments to a London conference, but without Cypriots, to begin at the end of August. By this time, the second wave of EOKA violence had begun. There were raids on police stations to collect arms, a policeman was killed on 28 August, the British Institute was burned down and EOKA men escaped from Kyrenia Castle. The governor, Sir Robert Armitage, was replaced by Field Marshal Sir John Harding,[4] an experienced and resolute military commander who left for Cyprus on 2 October.

Earlier, John Martin had accompanied Secretary of State Lennox-Boyd to Cyprus. They arrived on 9 July for a series of meetings at Government House with the executive council and various delegations. They met Archbishop Makarios at the Ledia

---

3. George Theodorou, 1898–1974, who was to leave Cyprus in 1959 and later return to lead another enosis terror campaign in 1971.
4. First Baron Petherton, 1896–1989, Chief of Staff Allied Army in Italy, 1944.

Palace Hotel. Meetings continued in Nicosia for the next two days. Lennox-Boyd put forward a development plan for the island, but refused to call a state of emergency. John Martin and Eugene Melville described their reaction to the bombing campaign that then started, but which had been feared for some time, as 'shock at the realization that it was the start of something more serious than we had had before in Cyprus and a sense of frustration that everything we had done to try to avoid it had come to nothing'. In August, Makarios met Grivas to plan the next stage. It was thought that this was the meeting at which Makarios agreed to start the killing.

The tripartite conference in London ran from 29 August to 6 September. Foreign Secretary Harold Macmillan presented a plan to it, which was rejected. It provoked riots in Istanbul but caused delay in the UN to the Greek appeal. The new governor started talking to Makarios on arrival and put the Macmillan plan to him.

In the Melville/Martin paper, there was a comment on the significance of the London conference.

> The London Conference of August/September 1955 broke new ground. Firstly, although the Agenda was purposely couched in wide terms — the political, defence, strategic and other problems affecting the three governments in the Eastern Mediterranean including Cyprus — the conference devoted most of its time to talking about Cyprus and therefore broke precedent in allowing foreign governments to take part in discussion of a Colonial matter which was traditionally the concern of the United Kingdom only. Secondly, it overcame Greek reluctance to see Turkey participate in discussion of a question which the Treaty of Lausanne put outside their competence. There were no fixed items on the Agenda and the idea was to provide for a wide exchange of views between the three Powers without prior commitment. This meant that the Cypriots could not appropriately be included in the Conference even if representatives of the two communities acceptable to the others present could have been found. Stephanopoulis, with Papagos in the background, and Zorlu, who needed no support, were pretty tough and yielded no ground. All the Conference achieved was to give HMG a chance to put forward some ideas

about the content of a new constitution for internal self-government and for floating the ideas that there might be a tripartate committee to watch progress, and a review of the situation in all its aspects, including the security of the Eastern Mediterranean, after the constitution was properly working. Also it made clear that Cyprus was an international question.

The paper went on to show that the enosis agitation had brought this about.

[F]rom the time that Enosis became a live and active political issue in Cyprus the Cyprus problem became an international one, with the Greek and Turkish governments each espousing the cause of 'their' community in Cyprus. In consequence, from the early 1950s onwards, no move was possible towards constitutional advance in Cyprus which did not gain the support or at least the acquiescence of both the Greek and Turkish governments which, until the Zurich agreement in 1959, it was not possible to achieve.

As soon as he arrived in Cyprus in early October 1955, Sir John Harding began to talk to Makarios and to discuss the Macmillan plan put to the London conference. Harding was allowed to come forward in the middle of the month with a suggested formula, which became known as the double negative. It was that 'it is not HMG's position that self-determination can never be applicable to Cyprus. It is their position that it is not now a practicable proposition.' However, Makarios broke off negotiations; violence was resumed; and, on 26 October, the governor called a state of emergency. In December, the political party AKEL was banned. The first EOKA clash with the army happened in December and Mouskos, a terrorist, was killed. Makarios conducted his funeral amid island-wide demonstrations of support for EOKA.

The year 1956 began with Greece putting pressure on Makarios to continue talking. Sir John Harding met Makarios again and went to London for consultation. John's diary entry for 16 January says he was 'At No. 10 late, getting home at 10 to 1 a.m.' on the day of the consultation, then had to return for more talks.

Makarios secured support from Grivas and the ethnarchy to settle. Harding found Makarios's new demands increasingly exasperating. Among these was a particular stumbling block, the control of internal security, which Grivas made a stipulation.

At this time, Francis Noel-Baker, Labour MP for Swindon, who was knowledgeable about Greek affairs, knew the language and had a home in Greece, visited the island and reported favourably to the Secretary of State on the progress of negotiations. On 26 February, the Secretary of State arrived in Cyprus with Sir John Moreton, his private secretary, and John Martin to stay at Government House. John's diary records three meetings with Archbishop Makarios. On the evening of 27 February, John called at the archbishopric with Francis Noel-Baker and, on the afternoon of 28 February, he called on the Archbishop again and had a one-and-a-half-hour discussion with him. These were preliminaries to a third meeting on neutral ground at the Anglican archdeacon's house, of which John records on 29 February 1956: 'in evening accompanied S of S and Sir John Harding to meeting with Archbishop, which ended in disagreement'. Francis Noel-Baker and A. S. Papadopoulos were present to help with language problems. On these four days of their visit, the Secretary of State's party received various callers from the Cypriot community and from the US consul. Much of the business took place to the accompaniment of bomb explosions in Nicosia. The British position in the Middle East was further weakened at this time with the dismissal of the legendary Glubb Pasha as commander of the Jordanian Army.[5]

It was not long before a decision was made to deport Makarios, along with the Bishop of Kyrenia and others. This happened on 9 March and the deportees were taken to the Seychelles (some say against the Secretary of State's advice). The EOKA campaign continued in the following months and became more bloody without such restraint as Makarios had been able to exercise on Grivas. Executions of terrorists led to demonstrations throughout the island.

In July, Lord Radcliffe[6] was appointed to draw up a constitution for Cyprus. Of all the proposals put forward for Cyprus, these were the most significant. It came as a surprise that the

5. Sir John Bagot Glubb, 1897–1986, had been the symbol of British paramountcy in the Middle East.
6. The eminent constitutional lawyer, Lord Radcliffe (1899–1978).

Turks accepted them while the Greek Cypriot leaders, prompted by Athens, rejected them out of hand.

Yet, the Turkish Cypriot part in the internal self-government proposals was limited to what their numbers, about one-fifth of the population, could justify. It is said that many Greek Cypriots still regret having rejected Radcliffe's proposals and see it as the single biggest mistake they made among many. The ethnarchy fought Radcliffe because they feared that once the Cypriots tasted the benefits of self-government they would forget about enosis.

In August, Grivas offered a truce and the government responded by demanding a surrender, which Grivas refused. The government had secured Grivas's diaries and now published them. The anti-terrorist campaign was weakened in November when troops were withdrawn from Cyprus to serve in Suez. Grivas declared any Englishman in Cyprus a target and the governor made the death penalty mandatory for carrying firearms.

After the disastrous Suez campaign, the new Macmillan government needed to rethink its Middle Eastern policy and its position in Cyprus. Much of its political thinking had been based on a military reassessment. Was it still necessary to treat Cyprus as a 'fortress island' or would bases in an independent Cyprus be sufficient? Further, the Ministry of Defence was seeking to reduce military expenditure.

The Melville/Martin paper contains comments on the changing positions of the chiefs of staff.

> Since the Chiefs of Staff gave their first ruling in 1950 against the 'bases only' option, the strategic and political situation had changed substantially. At the Ministry of Defence, Mr Macmillan's[7] mind had already moved to the idea of limiting our strategic needs to sovereign bases, and negotiations with the Greeks and Turks had led to a softening of our attitude towards self-determination for political reasons. Ideas of partition and tridominium had been broached. For the Chiefs of Staff their essential criterion was, of course, the security of retained bases and the absolute freedom to use them as required. Better to have secure bases in

---

7. Minister of Defence October 1954–April 1955.

a friendly country than the responsibility of keeping the peace in the whole island as a pre-condition of using the bases.

In April 1957, John Martin accompanied Minister of Defence Duncan Sandys to Cyprus, along with Marshal of the RAF Sir William Dickson, Mr Rippon MP and Colonel Strickland, to stay at Government House. The main purpose of the visit was to see the military establishments there. Following the visit, John wrote a paper dated 29 April on British military requirements in Cyprus and possible political developments:

> I conclude that ... from the military point of view, our first aim should be to secure a settlement which will guarantee our continued sovereignty over the whole island, at least so long as the present situation of international insecurity persists; but this cannot be at the price of an indefinitely prolonged international security commitment. ... It would, in my view, be reasonable to accept a period of trial of a Radcliffe-type constitution, to see whether it led to such an inter-communal *détente* as would reduce the internal security commitment to a reasonable level. If ... we cannot secure such a reduction ... it will be necessary to accept the alternative of limitation of our sovereignty to one or more enclaves, even if this means (1) uncomfortable restriction of the facilities available and (2) the risk of exacerbating and perpetuating the conflict between the two main communities in the island and the dispute over Cyprus between Greece and Turkey.

As a result of the tour of inspection, Duncan Sandys preferred the policy of a base in Cyprus rather than all of Cyprus as a base, which was to become British policy.

Meanwhile, reinforced by troops withdrawn from Suez, Major-General Douglas Kendrew[8] was pursuing EOKA with vigour. In March, the United Nations passed a resolution calling for talks. In response to this the Greeks encouraged Grivas to declare a truce,

---

8. GOC Cyprus 1956–58, KCMG 1963, later governor of Western Australia.

which he did on condition Makarios was released. The government agreed provided Makarios renounce violence. Though Makarios's reply was ambiguous, under pressure from Eisenhower at the Bermuda conference in March 1957, Macmillan decided to release him. This provoked Lord Salisbury's resignation from the government. Makarios returned to Athens in triumph on 17 April.

In July 1957, the Cabinet agreed a new plan for Cyprus. Britain would keep bases only; sovereignty would be a tridominium of Britain, Greece and Turkey. The constitution would be based on the Radcliffe proposals. At the Labour Party conference in October, Barbara Castle promised 'self-determination within the lifetime of the new Labour Government'.

By this time, Field-Marshal Harding's time as governor was drawing to a close. He left amid many expressions of goodwill and wrote cordially to John in thanks for support given by him.

> I am afraid I must have been maddening at times, but you have always been patient and forbearing and have shown great understanding. Believe me, I am most grateful. ... Anything I have succeeded in doing here, and I deeply regret it has not been more, has been due to the efforts of those who work with me here, and to the unfailing support and encouragement that you and those who work with you in the Colonial Office have given me.

In the same letter, Harding commended colleagues who had served him well in Cyprus. Harding was created a baron in 1958. He was succeeded by Sir Hugh Foot, later Lord Caradon, former colonial secretary of Cyprus and acting governor, and holder of various other governorships and government appointments at the UN.

The new governor came with a new plan, which he called his 'first initiative'. When it failed, he turned to a second plan. Each of them is mentioned in the Melville/Martin paper.

> Sir Hugh Foot's plan of January 1958 was stopped short in its tracks by a blank refusal by the Turks to discuss it and a lukewarm reception from the Greeks. Foot was gravely disappointed. His mind then turned to the idea of imposing the plan. ... The Colonial Office doubted whether any solu-

tion could be imposed against the wishes of the other parties. The result of trying to do so could only lead to an increase in terrorism in Cyprus and possibly to further troubles in Turkey and maybe in Greece. In the event no action was taken to force the Foot plan through. Instead further discussions led to the formulation of a second initiative which came to be called the Macmillan plan. The main elements of this plan, as announced in June 1958, were:

(a) A proposed new constitution on the lines of the Foot plan, which could be presented as holding prospects of eventual internal self-government.

(b) A proposal for a partnership of the Greek and Turkish governments with the UK to bring peace and prosperity to the Island.

Although the plan was presented as offering a provisional solution we did not look upon it as a first step towards partition. Partition was an alternative which the Turks kept coming back to and which proved to be a useful lever with the Greeks, but experience of partition elsewhere (in the case of Palestine partition was never given a chance under the Mandate) made it a most unattractive idea for most of us in the Colonial Office.

Between the two initiatives, the campaign against the terrorists continued. Grivas declared a boycott of British goods. Cypriot businessmen complained to Makarios, who failed to restrain Grivas. Hugh Foot sought a secret meeting with Grivas, who refused it but ordered a temporary ceasefire. Attacks began again when Foot's advisers insisted on renewing emergency legislation to make a final push against EOKA. John took part in a discussion on Cyprus on 10 May at Chequers with the Secretary of State, Selwyn-Lloyd (Foreign Secretary) and Sir Hugh Foot. On 7 June, fighting broke out between Greeks and Turks in Nicosia, fierce intercommunal violence that continued until 6 August; by this time 100 Greeks and Turks had been killed. On 19 June, when the second initiative, the Macmillan plan, was announced, the fighting was at its peak. It proposed a condominium. It advocated no change in sovereignty for seven years, a separate house of representatives, a joint council of ministers, and dual nationality Cypriot/Turk and Cypriot/Greek. The Greek government rejected the plan; a week later the Turkish government accepted it. Sir Hugh Foot was sufficiently unsettled by this partial acceptance of the plan to write a private letter to John on 24 July, not only complaining about the views and actions of some of his immediate colleagues but to offer his resignation.

From 8 to 11 August, the Prime Minister went to Athens, Ankara and Cyprus to discuss his plan. In the Melville/Martin paper, Sir Eugene Melville reported: 'My main memories of the Macmillan odyssey are of his monumental calm and patience. ... The Greek reservations ... could probably have been made negotiable but the Turks refused categorically to agree to any negotiation taking place.'

The British government decided to stick to the Macmillan plan. Surprisingly, in September Makarios decided to change his policy to independence. There was an intervention by NATO, of which Greece and Turkey were members, to mediate through Paul Spaak, the general secretary. Violence continued on the island. On 29 October, John wrote to a friend and prominent figure in the Cyprus administration, Achilles Papadopoulos, to congratulate him on escaping an attempt on his life.

> I was horrified to read of the attack on you and congratulate you on your providential escape. I cannot believe that the decent people of Cyprus are not revolted by the continued efforts of evil men to achieve their purposes by violence of this kind. Meanwhile all of us have watched with great admiration the courage and resolution of you and others who have stood in the front line.

The next developments are also described in the Melville/Martin paper.

> The Macmillan plan having been launched and having achieved support from NATO and the Americans as well as from the opposition in the House of Commons there was no disposition on the part of HMG to change tactics or to

abandon it in favour of some vague proposal for 'independence'. When the Spaak initiative to have the plan suspended while NATO conferred failed, because of Greek refusal to co-operate, we continued to stand by the plan. There was, of course, criticism in parliament and elsewhere about the lack of progress in finalizing a plan of action but we got through the UN debate in the autumn with a reasonably supportive resolution expressing the Assembly's confidence that efforts would be continued by all the parties concerned to find a solution in accordance with the UN Charter. Then out of the blue came the Greek/Turkish initiative which led to the Zurich Agreement. It seems pretty certain that our handling of the 1958 negotiations on the Macmillan plan was a catalyst to this surprising development.

What had happened? In December, the Greek and Turkish foreign secretaries approached Selwyn-Lloyd at the NATO ministerial council to ask if he would approve of their meeting to seek an agreement on Cyprus, whereby the British government would continue to hold bases in full sovereignty and the Greek and Turkish Cypriots would have independence. The government welcomed the proposal. Macmillan wrote to Hugh Foot (*Riding the Storm*, p. 692) of 'watching Zurich with crossed fingers'.

The Zurich conference brought the Greek and Turkish governments together with interested parties from Cyprus. The items of agreement reached there needed to be confirmed with the sovereign power. This was to be done at Lancaster House in London in February 1959.

John's diary recorded some of the events of the London conference. On 11 February, there was a dinner with Selwyn-Lloyd at 1 Carlton Gardens to meet the foreign ministers of Greece and Turkey (Averoff and Zorlu), who had arrived from Zurich with proposals for a Cyprus settlement — 'a soufflé which must be eaten at once otherwise it would collapse'. The Turkish ambassador, Nuri Birgi, was also in London. On 12 February, John attended the Norman Brook committee meeting on Cyprus in the morning and a meeting with the Greek and Turkish foreign ministers at the Foreign Office in the afternoon. On 13 February, he lunched with Julian Amery and Lord Perth at Eaton Square. On

17 February, at the first meetings of the Cyprus conference at Lancaster House at which Selwyn-Lloyd made his declaration, there came news of the crash of the plane bringing Menderes (he survived). Afterwards there was dinner with the Greek prime minister (Karamanlis) and other Greeks at No. 10. On 18 February, there was a meeting at Lancaster House in the evening, at which it was agreed to give Makarios further time to decide 'yes' or 'no' on acceptance of Zurich agreements and Britain's declaration. The next day, 19 February, George Chryssafinis gave John Archbishop Makarios's 'yes', after which there was a meeting at the Foreign Office, followed by the final plenary meeting of the Lancaster House conference.

Makarios's hesitation provoked Karamanlis, the Greek prime minister, to fly to London to stiffen his and the Cypriot delegation's resolve. The point Selwyn-Lloyd, the chairman, had been driving home on the evening of 18 February, was that the Zurich agreements were a foundation on which a settlement could be built; unless all parties agreed on the foundation, no settlement would be possible. Furthermore, the London conference had been called because all parties had previously shown their willingness to sign. Zorlu expressed the position effectively: 'The essence of our compromise, of our agreement is that ... this is the foundation, and nothing can be taken out of this foundation. On this basis something can be built.'

The signing took place on 19 February. At a reception that night, Makarios said to Karamanlis: 'Did you really imagine that I would not sign?' Karamanlis answered indignantly: 'Then why all the fuss?' Makarios replied: 'I had my reasons!' Karamanlis asked what they were. Makarios replied: 'I will tell you later.' But he never did. The Melville/Martin paper showed how this appeared to the civil servants.

By the time the London Conference met in February 1959 we all thought that Makarios had been finally coralled. Knowing his tactics however we expected him to wriggle hard and long. ... The Governor and the Whitehall officials attending the Conference were, of course, active throughout in lobbying Makarios and the delegation and Selwyn-Lloyd in the Chair handled him with the skill of a trout fisherman.

It was a relief, therefore, but not a surprise when the message came from Makarios's hotel on the last day of the Conference that he had said 'yes'. The Greeks and Turks, on the other hand, were entirely helpful throughout the Conference.

Various matters had to be dealt with before independence, especially the bases. The Melville/Martin paper records Julian Amery's handling of the negotiations lasting six months.

The main — and indeed the only important — sticking point was the size of the Sovereign Base Areas (SBAs). The early negotiations included arrangements for training areas, demolitions, claims for damage, customs procedures and exemptions for NAAFI stores etc., nationality and the assumption by the new Cyprus government of various obligations and liabilities outstanding at the time of the hand-over, including civil pensions. The larger question of official aid was reserved for counter-bargaining on the SBAs. Agreement on the constitution, which was tied in with the Treaty of Establishment but was negotiated in Cyprus by the Joint Commission (on which HMG was not represented), was reached in early April. Agreement on the outstanding matters in the Treaty of Establishment was not reached until the end of June. Most of the going on the Cyprus side was made by Makarios who showed all the characteristics of brinkmanship and Byzantine subtlety which he had displayed in earlier negotiations. The final settlement was for a total SBA of 99 square miles and a financial aid programme for over £13,000,000 for the Cyprus government with an additional £1,500,000 for the Turkish community. Julian Amery's negotiating tactics were in the end successful. He had carried the support of his delegation throughout but Hugh Foot, who sat in at all the meetings, expressed strong doubts from time to time as to whether the slow bargaining method would work. He regarded delay as dangerous for a number of reasons including the possibility of the local situation deteriorating rapidly. In the event Julian Amery stayed on for another two months and brought the negotiations to a successful conclusion following his own preferred tactics of wearing the other side down by refusing to concede points until he had got what he wanted.

Independence Day for Cyprus was 16 August 1960. Makarios was now head of state. Turbulent years lay ahead for him until his death in 1977. When he died *The Times* leader under the heading 'A Leader, not a Statesman', called him 'one of the foreign leaders whose image in the postwar period has most firmly imprinted itself in the consciousness of this country'.

Sir Hugh Foot had abandoned his earlier thoughts of resignation and continued as governor until independence. When the various negotiations had reached a successful conclusion and before the date of independence, John wrote to congratulate him and received a cordial reply dated 9 July.

> The past few months have been as difficult and anxious as they could be. I feared that we might lose all the advantages of the settlement made in London in February of last year. But now a solution of all the outstanding difficulties has been found which is, I believe, as good as we could possibly have hoped for. ... I thank you more than I can say for all the comfort which you have given me. It was a great consolation to know that we could always turn to you for understanding and help.

The Granada television programme, in the preparation of which they had given much assistance, did not entirely please the two retired colonial servants. Sir Eugene remarked in a letter to John:

> There was no attempt to analyse, far less to assess, the issues of policy that lay behind the events they dramatized — I expect that, in the end, they came to the conclusion that what we — especially you — lived through and worried ourselves sick about was just not any good for television and that things like the agricultural and forestry development that we gave Cyprus were irrelevant to the story of the EOKA rebellion.

John said he found it hard to accept 'the self-satisfied, self-confessed murderers'. He thought:

> the choice of dates for the narrative left out too much at the beginning and too much at the end — the painstaking efforts of the British to devise and sell a democratic constitution (which in accordance with all the precedents, as Makarios should have seen, would have led to genuine self-government and, in the end, to self-determination) and, after Zurich, the disastrous failure of Makarios to operate the new constitution with wisdom and magnanimity.

10

The Federation of Malaya and Malaysia, 1954–62

M alaya returned to British control in 1945 on the defeat of the Japanese. In the early years after the war, John Martin had no direct responsibility for Malaya. Yet he kept his affection for Malaya and its people; he valued those who corresponded with him during the occupation and in the period of reconstruction after the war. Newspaper articles and correspondence were carefully filed. After the war, recriminations continued over the conduct of the administration and of the armed services during the fall of Malaya and Singapore. John's view of this was put succinctly in a letter much later.

> For some years before 1941 Japan had been regarded as a potential enemy; but it was assumed that any attack would be on Singapore from the sea ... and the Japanese could not be expected to cross the 'impenetrable' barrier of mountain and jungle running down the centre of the Peninsula. ... When the war came the principal reason for the rapid collapse was ... the inadequacy of the forces available to the British defence ... the inevitable result of the over-commitment of the UK to theatres nearer home.

The British government had to set about reconstruction in Malaya after the war. Not all who served there were happy about what was happening. John replied carefully on 27 March 1946 to the wife of one such anxious Malayan civil servant.

I am quite sure that any suggestions of cynicism, hypocrisy or conscious bad faith on the part of the authorities are without any foundation in fact. I know the people concerned and know that they are singleminded in their determination to find the right course and pursue it. You may disagree with their conclusions or their methods; but not their spirit or intention.

[Further], the situation with which we have to deal now is utterly different from that in 1939. The Japanese flood has swept over the land, obliterating and changing, and we have to build afresh and not on the old foundations only, because some of these have been shaken or washed away. In particular, the claims of the non-Malay inhabitants which, in ordinary times, might gradually have been asserted over a long period of years, have suddenly taken on an entirely new aspect. For nothing so attaches a man to a place or people to a country as the memory of a deep experience, suffering and struggle. These people fought and suffered for their adopted home and could never accept the position of tolerated resident aliens, excluded from the privileges and responsibilities of citizenship.

To recognize this is not to be false to the Malays. It would be much more false to delude them into thinking that the facts are otherwise. But where our duty, as I see it, does lie is to ensure that in this new Malaya the Malay has his reasonable place, his padi lands preserved for himself and his children, his customs and religion undisturbed, and opportunity and encouragement to play his part in the public affairs of his country.

But I doubt if E, and those who share his anxieties, really dispute the ends in view — that Chinese and Indians settled in Malaya should have the full rights of sons of the soil and help with the Malays to create a Malayan community, living happily together as before but growing up to a more adult political stature; that the inefficiency of excessively decentralized administration should be replaced by a more economical system.

In 1948 a new constitution created a Federation of Malaya with considerable powers of local and central government, leaving security and external affairs to Great Britain. That year, John received a letter dated 1 February from a businessman in Kuala Lumpur, gloomy about the prospects of self-government in Malaya.

> The situation out here has improved considerably recently, both in public order ... and in the hope of progress and stability under the new constitution. One can hope rather little in the long run I think from the introduction of self-government in a country like this, but a sensible compromise between that and real and firm 'colonial administration' may be practicable. ... I feel it rather difficult to be patient with Governors General and such who talk of the coming of self-government as if it meant the beginning of the millennium. However the fairly even balance between the Malays with their tradition of paramountcy, and the Chinese with all the cash, may prevent a too rapid withdrawal of British influence.

Later in the year, a very critical letter dated 23 September 1948 came to him from David Gray, then of the Federal Labour Department in Kuala Lumpur, targeting the governor, the policies of the British government and its advisers, as well as the administration in Malaya.

Gray thought the former governor, Sir Edward Gent, had not taken note of the evidence given him of a likely communist insurrection. He felt that the government did not trust the colonial service. He charged the commissioner general for the UK in Southeast Asia, Malcolm MacDonald, son of Ramsey MacDonald, with interfering in the domestic affairs of Malaya, although he had no executive powers, and thus weakening the Malayan administration. He thought that talk of democracy in Malaya was premature and unsettling to the rulers. His main message was the approaching trouble, the signs of which he listed as the Singapore harbour dock strike, the Kedah riots, the formation of the Pan-Malayan Federation of Trade Unions and the meeting of the communist-controlled unions in Singapore in March 1948. These were the warning lights that were being ignored. He hoped that the new governor, Sir Henry Gurney, would be allowed to rule and to cope effectively with the coming crisis.

The forecast of trouble was only too accurate. The emergency in Malaya began in 1948; the communist insurgents made progress, which was only halted by the firm measures of the high commissioner and director of operations, Field Marshal Sir Gerald Templer, in the years between 1952 and 1954, which denied the insurgents supplies and recruits.

John visited the federation at the end of 1954 and saw evidence of the emergency and of the success of Templer's policies. His tour began in the Borneo territories, which he had not previously seen. It was to end in Malaya and Singapore, where more than twenty years before he had spent three happy years of attachment. He now returned as assistant under-secretary of state with a knighthood. His arrival was inconvenienced by an unfriendly meringue eaten in Calcutta to celebrate his birthday on 15 October. He quickly recovered. His first main stop was at Jesselton, capital of North Borneo.

> Arrival from the air, circling twice round before landing, gave a good birds-eye view of Jesselton — a small town along the sea-edge, with a few houses on hill ridges behind and a backscreen of jungle-covered mountains. A launch took me to the jetty, where Roland Turnbull (Governor, formerly of Cyprus) was waiting for me with the acting Chief Secretary (David Gray), the Resident, West Coast (Combe) and the acting Chief of Police (Plunkett).

His next stop was at Sandakan, where he visited two sawmills, a kutch factory, an electric power station and a hospital. On 23 October:

> After the round of factories I had a glass of beer at the house of the boss of one of the companies in an immense room overlooking the port. . . . One of the ships in the port was Japanese. Only the Captain and No. 2 are allowed ashore: the people have such bitter memories of the occupation that the police couldn't guarantee the safety of any other members of the crew if they landed.

Back in Jesselton I was taken on a round of Government Offices and quarters. The towns of N. Borneo were almost completely destroyed by the end of the war (partly by our own forces in the operations for its recapture) and the administration had to start in a scratch collection of temporary buildings. ... Senior Civil Servants had been invited to ask to see me if they wanted to raise any personal matters with me and I sat in the secretariat in the afternoon receiving those who had applied — mostly enquiries about possibility of transfer.

Next was Brunei where, on 26 October, the governor showed him a great deal of new construction, some completed, some in hand.

I visited a well-kept War Graves cemetery with rows and rows of graves and long lists of Australian dead whose graves are not known. It is an impressive place.

Brunei, once a poor state, has recently become immensely wealthy on account of its oil wells and the place looked like a boom city, with a great deal of building and road-making going on — bulldozers pushing the mud about and the hammer of pile-drivers, a new airfield being surfaced, mosque foundations, sites for a big new school, a girls' hostel and so on. In the evening the Resident gave a big cocktail party, to which the Sultan came as well as a good many Malays (with their wives, who sat apart and were very dumb), a few Chinese and all the principal European officials. I sat down with HH and had a short conversation with him — in Malay, which surprised him!

In Sarawak, John's base was at Kuching where he participated in a Borneo defence advisory committee meeting, a conference on Brunei and other consultations. On 31 October 1954, he wrote:

The Astana is across the river, reached only by a little covered boat paddled by three Malays. ... I had a spacious bedroom, used by the Duchess of Kent, with weird Chinese ceiling decorations — dragons, birds and so on. Tony Abell

... is an excellent host — and also an excellent Governor, exactly the right man in the right place. Roland Turnbull and Malcolm MacDonald were staying too, the latter as youthful and spritely as ever — turned two cart-wheels when we came into the drawingroom before dinner one evening.

Most of Wednesday afternoon was taken up with a meeting of the Borneo Defence Advisory Committee (Malcolm, the Governors, the Brunei Resident, the Manager of the Oil Company and Officials) in the newly opened air-conditioned Secretariat. I broke away before the end and was taken by the ADC (improbably named MacSporran) on a sightseeing round of the town, finishing at the new Broadcasting Station. There was a dinner-party at the Astana to which Tony had asked 2 leading local Malays and 2 Chinese, also Lord Rowallan, the Chief Scout. After dinner we had a hilarious game of darts with a blow-pipe.

The Brunei Conference took the whole of Thursday morning — Malcolm presiding over the Governors and other representatives in the three territories for discussion of various matters of common interest.

Before leaving Sarawak John was taken up the Rajang river by Dennis White, the Resident, to spend the night in a Dyak long house. On 1 November 1954, he wrote:

A 'long-house' is really a covered street of houses. Running the length of the front is an open verandah. Parallel with this, but inside and under the roof, is a broad passage way, in which much of the day's business is done and on which the young men sleep. Behind and opening off this is a series of rooms, each the home of a family and the sleeping place of the women (and, I think, the older men), with a kitchen connected to it at the back. The house is built of bamboo and plaited palm leaf etc. and raised on pillars above the grounds. Pigs rout about underneath and are the scavengers. Dogs and hens seem to be everywhere. Some long houses have well over 20 rooms. The one we visited was only half built and had eight; but for this occasion a good many neighbours had come to join the party. The men mostly wear only a sort of loincloth and have their legs, arms and bodies elaborately tattoed. Some have tunics or vests of sorts and the chiefs wear funny little straw hats with feathers. ... The women have skirts and the older ones also have a sort of bodice or little jacket above. The men wear their black hair long and have large holes in their earlobes.

... On climbing on to the open verandah we were invited to squat on mats on the floor for the offering of food to the spirits. A lot of little plates of rice, popped corn and other tit-bits were placed in front of me. More *tuak* was ceremoniously drunk and I poured most of the food from the little plates into one big dish, sticking eggs into the heap and also a small dish of *tuak*. A cock was waved over the offering with a prayer for good crops and other forms of good luck. Blood was taken from its comb and smeared on a feather with which several people asked me to touch the palms of their hands. I then stuck it in the dish, like holly on a plum-pudding, and the offering was lifted up and placed on a high bamboo holder.

The chief next showed us round the house. In his own family room, besides some old Chinese jars, bedding, pictures of the Royal Family etc. there was a rifle which he proudly said he had taken from a Japanese he had killed. I asked if he had also taken the Japanese's head and was shown this gruesome relic hanging in a basket from the roof, along with several other old dried heads. (Malcolm MacDonald was once offered the head of the former Japanese Director of Education, complete with spectacles.)

It was now dark and lamps were lit, the light and shadow making the scene even more strange as the people squatted in groups along the floor. ... After dinner we returned to the inner verandah. Everyone crowded round and the chief made a little speech of welcome, hoping that I would take their troubles away with me to England, where we were cleverer at finding cures for them. Dennis gave them a talk in their own language, which he seemed to speak very fluently, and this was followed by a long discussion of their problems. The next item on the programme was dancing — by men, one at a time, dressing up in plumed hat and coat, to the accompaniment of a monotonous orchestra of drums and gongs. An effort was made to make the women dance, but they were coy and refused. This went on and on. Meanwhile three men whom I took to be a kind of priest paraded up and down noisily thumping the floor with staves and chanting a sort of litany to drive away evil spirits. When we had had enough of the dancing we withdrew into one of the rooms and tried to go to sleep on camp beds; but the party continued noisily for some time and the litany was kept up relentlessly all night. I slept very little and as dawn came was awakened by a flirtatious young woman taking hold of my hand and putting my fingers in her mouth!

Two days later, on 3 November, he wrote:

I learnt a lot and (the Borneo territories) have come alive for me in a way they never had before. They are much less developed than Malaya and in many ways none the worse for that, though they are all going ahead visibly — Brunei perhaps too fast, with its fantastic wealth poured on a tiny state of some 50,000 people, and North Borneo, owing to lack of money and population, perhaps too slowly. Sarawak is lucky to have Tony as Governor — emphatically the right man in the right place. Everybody is delighted that his appointment has been extended: as I told him, I have never seen a happier ship.

Moving on to Malaya, John Martin saw evidence of the emergency — military briefings, escorts on his journeys and provisions for containing insurgents. Despite all this and the experiences the country had gone through with the Japanese invasion and occupation, John recognized the Malaya he had known and loved in the early 1930s.

He stayed first at the high commissioner's house at Kuala Lumpur (the King's House), the high commissioner being his old friend Sir Donald MacGillivray. He called on the Sultan of Selangor and had 'a particularly interesting talk' with the director of operations,

General Bourne.[1] Bourne believed that time for ending the emergency was limited, not more than two years, that a stalemate had been reached and that there was no possibility of a purely military solution. He believed that Asians had to be induced to come down off the fence by being convinced that the British meant to stay in Malaya and by taking responsibility for the campaign as theirs and not just British. He hoped to achieve this by inviting their leaders to become members of his advisory committee, which they had accepted. He complained to John of slowness and inefficiency of administration in certain states, especially in those with the worst trouble spots. He described to John the tactics of putting troops into the jungle to control particular areas. John was also given at this early stage a 'VIP briefing' on the emergency by the police commanders.

Thursday 4 November was a typical day of visits with the British adviser and *Mentri Besar* (Prime Minister) of Selangor. On 6 November, he wrote:

> Our first stop was at Petaling Jaya, a 'new town' a few miles outside KL, in an airy and attractive situation, where the Town Adminstrator showed us round and explained his plans. We visited the first so-called 'national type' school to be started in the country, where children of all races are taught together in English (and also in another vernacular if sufficient parents request it). ... On from there to the vast new Connaught Bridge Power Station, where we were shown the good accommodation for their labour and made a rapid and very hot tour of the station itself. I always find large electrical machinery rather baffling and am tongue-tied when trying to express suitable sentiments to its keepers. Meeting the District Officer of Klang (Hamer) we drove on with him to Port Swettenham. It had been intended that we should watch the embarkation of a large party of Chinese detainees banished to China; but there had been threats of rioting and the Police asked us not to enter

---

1. Geoffrey Kemp Bourne, GCB 1960, baron and life peer 1964, GOC Malaya 1954–56.

the port area. Instead, we left our flagged car and the escort of armoured cars which had accompanied us from KL and drove inconspicuously in the DO's car to a small jetty, from which we toured the port from the seaward side in a launch. Lunch with the DO and his wife. ... We then drove on to Jenjarum, one of the 'new villages' in which Chinese squatters were concentrated — behind wire, to protect them from intimidation by the communist terrorists and keep them from supplying the latter.

While in Negri Sembilan, John visited 'food denial check-points', where all cars leaving Malacca were searched to make sure they were not taking food for the insurgents. Volunteers helped the police in this task. He was irritated by having to travel to his much-loved Kuala Pilah under escort. 'Tiresomely there was again a strong military escort and they made me travel inside a "Saracen", a large 6-wheel heavily armoured car, while going over the pass between Seremban and KP.' On 9 November, he wrote:

We went off on bicycles along a bridle path through the rice fields and past Malay houses — the characteristic Negri Sembilan scene — to a small Kampong, Rembang Panas, where we lunched with a Malay headman — squatting shoeless on the verandah of his little house and eating the curry with our fingers. We sat there quite a long time gossiping with him and his friends and then went out to watch a game of spinning tops between Rembang Panas and a neighbouring village. I cycled back well content with the day. ... A cocktail party to meet local people of all races, dinner with the DO, the headmaster of the English school and a planter — and so to bed.

On the following day the district officer at Alor Gajah produced Mat Nor, 'my faithful syce. He was as much affected as I was by this meeting after twenty years and said he had been unable to sleep with excitement the night before.'

John's tour in Malaya was taking him to most of the states. His letterheads mention the residencies of Seremban, Kilantan, Kuala Trengganu, Penang and Malacca.

He attended the legislative council proceedings in Kuala Lumpar. He wrote on 22 November 1954, that they began with:

> a formal session with an excellent speech by MacGillivray (in blue uniform), followed by the Financial Secretary Hainsworth's budget speech, and on the next day a free for all general debate on the budget. The proceedings follow closely those of the House of Commons, with a bewigged Malay speaker, procession with mace, prayers in English and Malay, oaths by new members and so on. Some of the speeches were pretty good nonsense and there was a great deal of irresponsible criticism of the Government, but I was struck most by the general good-tempered atmosphere and give and take between the races and parties.

He also paid a return visit to the Sungei Buloh leprosarium.

> [This is] a huge place with a population of over 2000, some in hospital, some in a boarding school and the rest living in houses as a small village community, complete with churches, clubs etc. I visited it 22 years ago. ... Now with the discovery of the cure by sulphone injection the cloud has lifted and it seemed wonderfully cheerful, especially the school. It obviously owes much to the fine doctor who runs it and is completely devoted to his work for the patients (Dr Molesworth).

To revisit Penang was a particular delight to John. He went across by launch:

> It was a bright sunny morning, with a light wind and the view crossing the strait most lovely. I almost wept at the beauty of the morning and the return to this magic place where I first landed over 23 years ago. Penang has been British longer than Australia and has an atmosphere comparable in this part of the world only with that of Malacca.

In Perak, John went 'by speedboat down the Perak river to inspect a new irrigation scheme. It was hot and sunny, but it was very pleasant to rush along at a great pace past the riverside Kampongs, sometimes narrowly escaping grounding on sandbanks.' John returned to Kuala Lumpur for more talks with the high commissioner and for the St Andrew's feast, 'celebrated with tremendous gusto at the Selangor club last night and until 3.30 a.m. this morning — haggis and all, pipers, much Scottish dancing'. He also had the opportunity to visit a jungle fort, Fort Iskander, in Pahang, as he described on 3 December.

> A number of these forts have been established in the heart of the jungle as centres for the protection of the aborigines, who are otherwise apt to be dominated by communist terrorists and made to help them with supplies and intelligence. They are inaccessible on the ground but fed with men and supplies by air — by pioneers and helicopters. Armed police under British officers man them. From the air it was difficult to believe that there was room to land, but the pilot took us in without misadventure and again in a remarkably short distance on departure. Weather was deteriorating so the pilot wouldn't stay long, but there was time to see round the camp (some 70 men) and the adjoining aborigine village — all enclosed within barbed wire fences.

Although the military and security aspects of Malayan life were continually before John's eyes, his visits covered many other aspects, education, commerce and industry, medicine and health. He visited schools and colleges, various enterprises and public services, hospitals and other agencies for the care of the sick. He gave attention to the processes of government under the new constitution. His skill lay in making new friends and in remembering and cultivating old friendships.

John's last day in the federation, 4 December 1954, was spent in Johore.

> Johore is a very black area for terrorist activities and we drove down to Johore Bahru with my usual heavy escort (which was perhaps less unnecessary this time) but saw nothing untoward. At urgent police request we missed out a

visit to an estate on the way but looked in at a police field force training school, where they staged a mock riot — complete with soap box Malay orators and real tear gas.

Wednesday morning was spent on a round of visits — to the Operations room at defence HQ for the latest news and a review of the emergency situation in the state, to the depot of the Marine Dept on a muddy creek, to a large pineapple-canning factory (much modern machinery but also surprisingly much handling by bare hand) and to a really first-class primary school for blind children in beautiful new buildings. Then to a large lunch party with the Regent. I'm afraid he must have thought me a dull fish for he asked me if I knew name after name in Debrett with almost invariably negative result and his other interests appeared to be hunting and racing. ... A tea party at the Government offices and I said goodbye to the Federation, driving into Singapore with Somerville.

Ten days in Singapore and a week in Hong Kong completed the tour. Singapore in 1954 still had a governor but was developing some self-governing institutions. It was still part of the Malayan federation. Hong Kong was to remain a crown colony until 1997. In each of these, John Martin's programme was much the same as in the Borneo territories and Malaya, a careful look at the colony's life and prospects. In Singapore, heavy rain hindered some of his activities.

He spent the morning of 9 December 1954, which was a fairly typical day, at the governor's weekly staff meeting. In the afternoon, he was at the education department with its director and at the Royal Malayan Navy headquarters for a 'stirring parade, at which the Governor presented their swords to the first Malay officers'. In the evening, he dined with Loke Wan Tho, a wealthy young Chinese, 'a public-spirited person, intelligent, a keen bird-watcher and a collector of porcelain, of which he showed me some lovely pieces. We had a Chinese dinner of many courses, each delicious, shark's fin soup, roasted skin of sucking pig, duck skin and so on — in a seventh floor verandah-room looking out over the lights of Singapore.'

He had various talks with Malcolm MacDonald; on one

occasion he lunched with him in 'a party including the authoress of
A Many Splendoured Thing, the Indonesian Consul, John Keswick,
the head of Jardine Matheson, the chief merchant firm in Hong
Kong and a Chinese woman from New York'. In talk with
MacDonald afterwards, John and he 'agreed on the comforting
conclusion that Malaya is unlike Palestine in that the problems
here are not (or need not be) insoluble.'

John was back in London on 22 December after an energetic ten
weeks. His presence and interest in what he saw won him many
friends. Donald MacGillivray wrote to him on 5 January 1955 to
let him know 'how very greatly your visit was appreciated. You
may not realize it,' he said, 'but it did a great deal of good. Too
often visits by senior Colonial Office officials leave behind a
feeling of disappointment and sometimes an impression on the part
of the "locals" of a lack of understanding of their difficulties. Your
visit was a tonic.'

The movement towards Malaysia took a sharp step forward in
1961 when Tunku Abdul Rahman, the Malayan prime minister,
made proposals that led to its creation. In addition to Malaya,
Singapore and the North Borneo territories were to be members.
Malaya had become independent in 1957 and by 1960 the
emergency was considered to be over.

Tunku Abdul Rahman had for a long time taken a close interest
in Brunei and, to a lesser extent, in the other Borneo territories. He
was interested in the possibility of a closer association between
them and the Federation of Malaya, but had looked coldly on the
suggestion of a merger with Singapore, which had been put
forward by Lee Kuan Yew.[2] In Malaya, people were suspicious of
Lee's party, which was seen as a left-wing party that might open
the door to communism in Singapore. Moreover, the greatest
problem for the Malayan administration was the existence within
the federation of a large Chinese minority, which in some areas of
the west coast and in nearly all the large towns constituted a
majority, dominating the economic life of the country. Although
the Chinese in the federation were for the most part anti-
communist, the Chinese community was susceptible to communist

---

2. Founder of the People's Action Party in 1954 and prime minister of Singapore
   from 1959.

indoctrination. The Malays' reluctance to add the 1.25 million Chinese of Singapore to the federation's population was understandable. The Malays would become a minority in a predominantly Chinese state.

The Singapore ministers' proposals for a merger were therefore rebuffed in Kuala Lumpur until May 1961, when Tunku Abdul changed his mind, apparently because of the increasing danger of the communists obtaining control in Singapore. The Tunku said:

> Malaya today as a nation realizes that she cannot stand alone and in isolation. Outside of international politics the national one must be broad-based. Sooner or later she should have an understanding with Britain and the peoples of the territories of Singapore, Borneo, Brunei and Sarawak. ... We should look ahead ... and think of a plan whereby these territories can be brought closer together in a political and economic co-operation.

The Tunku's proposals were immediately welcomed by Lee Kuan Yew, and also by British Prime Minister Harold Macmillan as a 'constructive suggestion'.

The Tunku's statement was in general terms, but an essential point in it was that he contemplated an association not just with Singapore but also with the Borneo territories. In a merger between Malaya and Singapore, the Chinese would predominate, but if the Borneo territories were brought in, their non-Chinese majorities would redress the balance and these non-Chinese majorities were largely made up of Malays or of communities regarded as racially akin to the Malays.

The Tunku's general ideas had to be worked into the shape of a detailed plan that would be practicable and would be acceptable to Singapore and the Borneo territories. It had to be a plan the British government could endorse as safeguarding the interests of the peoples for whose welfare it was still responsible. It was also necessary to ensure that essential defence requirements in Southeast Asia were not prejudiced.

Talks with the Tunku and other Malayan ministers took place in London in November 1961, reaching the conclusion that 'the British and Malayan Governments are convinced that this

[Malaysia] is a desirable aim ... before coming to any decision it is necessary to ascertain the views of North Borneo and Sarawak'. In North Borneo and Sarawak, there was a careful process of consultation with local opinion. This was the purpose of John Martin's first visit in January and early February 1962. At the same time, a commission of inquiry under Lord Cobbold[3] was set up. The Cobbold Commission was to visit Borneo in spring 1962.

On his first visit, John was accompanied by a Colonial Office colleague, Ian Wallace.[4] They had much preliminary documentation to absorb, especially on the Borneo territories, on their demography, education, economics and political development. There was correspondence with the governors and Residents. In addition to assessing the likely impact of a Malaysian federation on the countries as a whole, they had to look to the sort of administration needed to run newly independent countries within a federal framework. An indigenous civil service had to be developed quickly, with consequences for the existing European service, raising problems of the sort John had met in Nigeria. A new political elite had to be brought forward. There was urgency in these questions, which were being asked in situations where quick answers could not be found, or, if found, were likely to be wrong. While John's letters usually strike an optimistic note, there is in them a counterpoint of anxiety.

Early in their tour, John wrote from Sarawak to Christopher Eastwood at the Colonial Office of the difficulty of putting over the policy of Malaysia to the native, namely non-Malay, races.

> The attractions of Malaysia are not at all obvious to people who are very content with their present lot. Further — and this was new to both Ian and to me — there is little doubt that at least the Sea Dyaks (Ibans), and probably the other native peoples also, prefer the local Chinese to the local Malays. The latter, unlike the former, not only carry with them memories of old oppressions, but renewed them (at least in some cases) through collaboration with the Japan-

---

3. Cameron Fromanteel Cobbold, First Baron of Knebworth 1960, Governor of the Bank of England 1949–61.
4. W. I. J. Wallace, formerly serving in Burma, transferred to Colonial Office in 1947, head of the Far East division, assistant under-secretary 1962.

ese. All this makes the Tunku's repeated remarks about Ibans and Malays being one people, with one language and culture, etc., etc., look absolutely nonsensical when seen from this end. It also makes them dangerous because of the way they can be misrepresented. We have so often heard it said in this country that the Tunku is his own worst enemy insofar as putting Malaysia over here is concerned. However that may be, the fact is that whatever certain natives may say when they are invited over to Malaya, the idea is very far from being accepted by the Ibans and other native peoples.

The first visit took in the five territories but concentrated on the Borneo ones. It was a preparation for the commission, the membership of which was a matter of some importance. In Sarawak, John got a careful opinion from the Roman Catholic bishop, who believed that all non-Malays would at that time reject a Greater Malaysia; patience and time would be needed to persuade them.

In Singapore, on 16 January John talked with the prime minister, Lee Kuan Yew, who thought that the people in the Borneo territories could be brought to accept a Greater Malaysia. It had to be put to them by someone they trusted such as Tony Abell. He also said that, in Brunei, the Sultan was for it and Azahari (leader of the Party Rakyat) would be unable to stand against him. This was an optimistic assumption.

Lee Kuan Yew thought that the present process of juggling could not go on for long. The Tunku could be persuaded to accept Singapore right away while waiting for Sarawak and North Borneo in 1963, provided there was a firm agreement about this and that Brunei came in at once as a guarantee of British good faith. Lee was mistrustful of British intentions. He would be prepared to make the Malayan representative chairman of the internal security commission or add further Malay members. He also said that he was determined to have a referendum but not one of a simple yes or no to the merger. The questions would be loaded and he would be sure of the answers.

John recorded his own views on this conversation.

Greater Malaysia had for long been in the back of our

minds as our long-term objective in the area. Its advancement to the foreground of policy in 1961 was untimely in the Borneo territories, which were not yet ready for it and could usefully have been left in peace to develop on the usual Colonial lines for another ten years or so; but it had to be brought forward now because it was essential to meet pressing dangers in Singapore. Our immediate task is to secure acceptance in the Borneo Territories. They are not in the bag; there is danger in haste.

While in Jesselton, on 31 January 1962 John sent a telegram to Minister of State Lord Perth in response to one received from him. In its first paragraph, he said:

In our tour we have discussed Malaysia with a great many people of all races. It seems clear that apart from [the] Malays in Sarawak[, a] great majority of [the] population of both colonies is at present opposed to acceptance of Malaysia now. This goes even for some of the Muslims in North Borneo. What is said by hospitably entertained delegations in Kuala Lumpur is no safe indication of opinion in the territories and I fear that some of these spokesmen have little claim to be regarded as representative leaders. [The o]nly hope of reconciling opinion to Malaysia is for [the] commission to listen patiently to people's fears and objections and try to devise safeguards and special conditions of association with the new federation to meet them.

He went on to warn that people in Sarawak and North Borneo felt they were being rushed, but added that governors and their senior officials believed in the policy of Greater Malaysia. It was important for people to feel they were being heard. He also said that Lord Cobbold's announcement as chairman of the commission of inquiry had been well received.

A few paragraphs of a letter towards the end of his tour, of 3 February 1962, gives some idea of the rapidity of John's movements about these territories and of the number of his meetings and consultations.

I wrote last in Jesselton. The flight on via Brunei (a short talk with the High Commissioner at the airport) to Singapore was uneventful. ... In the morning I had visited the UK Commissioner's office and listened to the speeches at the opening meeting of the Malaya Consultative Committee — a sort of CPA meeting of representation of Malaya, Singapore and the 3 Borneo territories to discuss Greater Malaysia. ...

On Thursday afternoon I flew up to KL ... and spent 2 nights with the Troys in Carcosa. ... Geoffrey Troy and I dined with Abdul Razak, the Deputy PM and a very friendly party of Malays, one or two of whom I knew. An interesting talk with Razak and a very pleasant and convivial curry dinner.

Yesterday I started the day with a visit to the operations room of the Rural Development Scheme ... then called on Abdul Aziz, Permanent Secretary to the PM, who gave us those Malay spoons, and then on the Tunku himself — quite a long and useful talk. Abdul Aziz then drove me off to Kuala Pilah, where I had a very happy afternoon in my home of exactly 30 years ago. Back rather late for another Malay dinner party. After which I was taken on to a Malayan Civil Service dance (almost all Malays now) and got to bed at 2. A rather bumpy flight back to Singapore this morning via Malacca. I took the Allens and 2 others to lunch at a Chinese restaurant and have since had a meeting with Selkirk.[5]

As he flew out, John wrote up his notes on the interview with the Tunku on BOAC notepaper. He recorded that, on Brunei, the Tunku seemed prepared to accept that there was substantial opposition to Greater Malaysia, for the Brunei Malays were difficult people. But the decision would be made by the Sultan, who long ago indicated that he was in favour of a merger. John told the Tunku of the impression he had gained during his visits to North Borneo and Sarawak. The governors and senior officials fully

---

5. Lord Selkirk was UK commissioner for Singapore and commissioner-general for Southeast Asia from 1959 to 1963.

accepted and supported the policy, yet, apart from the Sarawak Malays, the great majority of the population was at that time opposed to immediate Greater Malaysia, though generally accepting it in principle. It would be necessary for the commission to listen to their objections and fears and to try to work out safeguards to meet them.

On the question of safeguards, John referred to control of immigration by the states, which the Tunku had already conceded, and mentioned the local insistence that any such safeguards must be entrenched, for example by requiring a two-thirds majority in the states as well as in the central government for amendment. The Tunku said it was impossible to provide for state control of immigration in the constitution. It could be confirmed in an exchange of letters, which would *not* be published. John said that the safeguards for the Malays' special position in the civil service was provided for in the constitution and there could be no objection to providing similar safeguards for the position of Borneans in the civil service. The Tunku seemed to accept this; if the commission reported that there was a majority against Greater Malaysia and it was not possible to arrange a merger of the Borneo territories, he could not accept responsibility for Singapore.

On his way home, John spent two days in India with his sister Peggy at her medical practice in the village of Dhapewada, with a population of about 1000, some miles out of Nagpur. In 1962, the village had electricity but transport was difficult, especially in the rainy season. Peggy was often taken to cases by bullock cart and a whole night could be spent on such an expedition. Later, roads were improved and access to the large hospitals of Nagpur became much easier.

Immediately on return to London, John saw Lord Cobbold and members of the commission of inquiry in North Borneo and Sarawak regarding Malaysian federation. Its other members were Sir Anthony Abell and Sir David Watherston, appointed by the British government, and Date Wong Pow Nee and Euche Muhammed Gazali bin Shafie, appointed by the Federation of Malaya government. The commission reported that one-third of the population of North Borneo and Sarawak strongly favoured the early realization of Malaysia; one-third either preferred British rule to continue or would prefer to have independence before Malaysia; and one-third, while favourable to the Malaysia project, asked for conditions and safeguards. The commissioners themselves concluded that a federation of Malaysia was an attractive and workable project and was in the best interests of the Borneo territories.

In the autumn, an intergovernmental committee sitting in Borneo and Malaya worked out in great detail the future constitutional arrangements and necessary safeguards for North Borneo and Sarawak. These meetings of the committee were the purpose of John's second visit to the territories from October to a few days before Christmas.

The committee's first meeting was in Jesselton. John flew via Kuching, for a short meeting at the airport with the acting governor, and Brunei, for lunch and a hurried discussion with the high commissioner about the difficulties that had arisen over Brunei's acceptance of the new federation.

> Bill Goode,[6] Henry Hall[7] and others were there to greet me and I was soon settled in this familiar and comfortable guest room at Government House.
>
> The tempo here is very different from what I am accustomed to in London and it is not going to be at all easy to get our negotiations moving at the pace expected by Ministers. ... One seems to work in a slight fog and there are many practical inconveniences and difficulties, particularly arising from the difficulty of getting together representatives of the different governments concerned. Besides the main committee normally to be taken by Lansdowne[8] we have at least five sub-committees.

The committee's work proceeded at the sort of pace at which the car John managed to hire in Jesselton, an ancient Wolsey 1550, travelled. He acquired a police driver, 'a smart and pleasant

---

6. Sir William, GCMG 1963, Governor and Commander-in-Chief North Borneo 1960–63.
7. Harold Percival Henry Hall, Assistant Secretary, Colonial Office 1955–62, seconded to office of UK Commissioner General for Southeast Asia 1962–63, British deputy high commissioner for Eastern Malaysia, Kuching and Sarawak 1963–64.
8. Eighth Marquess, Minister of State for Colonial Affairs.

Malay', who, he said, 'drives with extreme caution and I make a stately progress, like a dowager, generally in low gear and seldom at more than 20 m.p.h.' The committee then moved on to Kuala Lumpur in mid-November for a strenuous week.

Our first meeting — on finance — did not go particularly well and the Malayan Minister gave the Borneo representatives a nasty jolt by saying that if they wanted improved services they would have to pay for them themselves. This is of course quite the opposite of what Malayan propaganda about the benefits to come from Malaysia had led them to expect. After that, however, we went on to discuss constitutional questions, with Razak as the Malayan Minister, and we made excellent progress, which would have been greater if we had not had to cut the meeting short on the last day to enable the N. Borneo people to jet back to Jesselton to be ready for the Tunku's visit.

As I feared, the meetings were accompanied by much hospitality, but though exhausting — I found KL very hot — the parties were enjoyable in themselves. One evening there was a mammoth housewarming party at Tun Razak's new official residence as Deputy Prime Minister — more of a palace than a house. There was a buffet supper and dancing. The Tunku, in very cheerful mood, invited me to his table and talked a great deal about Malaysia, especially his decision to offer the Borneo territories 40 seats in Parliament — against 104 for the existing federation, which has several times the population. It seems to me a wise and timely proposal and should go a long way to reassure the Borneo people if they can understand how political power works. But it is a bit of a gamble for the Malayans to accept such a large Irish vote and it won't make things any easier for Lee Kuan Yew, who has secured only 15 seats for Singapore.

There followed another round of meetings at Jesselton.

The outcome is that we are now planning to hold our final meetings in Kuala Lumpur on 18th and 19th December ... so there is no question of having to return here after Christmas, though a short visit some time in 1963 is not excluded. Meanwhile we shall have to work hard to produce a draft report and tie up various loose ends before the KL meeting and there will be some sub-committee meetings.

John had reason to think that trouble was brewing at Limbang, which was close to the border of Brunei, and that he should go to see the place. On Saturday 3 December at 5.00 a.m. he set out.

I travelled down the railway in state in a private rail car to Beaufort, where a Chinese ADO took me ... across the ferry to the funny little Emett railway to Weston, the oldest bit of railway in the Colony and the invasion route in turn for Japanese and Australians. Here I travelled the 20-odd miles in a jeep with railway wheels, the driver sitting beside me to work the gears and brakes, but of course with no need to steer. It was a very bumpy journey, through some pretty dull country. At Weston, the Resident of the Fifth Division (Limbang), Dick Morris, was waiting for me with his launch and we set out on our 6-hour journey across Brunei Bay and up the Limbang river. There was a strong head wind and we had a fairly rough passage, which kept us most of the time in the cabin. Morris is a great talker and had much of interest to tell me, especially about some rather disquieting political developments in these parts — secret drilling by a 'Liberation Army' with dummy rifles (real ones evidently expected from an unknown external source) and uniform. The Sultan of Brunei has been demanding the return of Limbang which the Rajah of Sarawak took from his predecessor seventy years ago and this is an irredentist anti-British anti-Malaysia movement. I'm afraid we are likely to hear more of Limbang in coming months, which is one of the reasons why I wanted to pay this visit and get the picture in focus.

Limbang itself is a small town with a bazaar of Chinese shop houses on the river bank and the Residency on a high site overlooking it.

On Sunday morning, the Resident took me for a rough drive in a Land-Rover, visiting a new school, along one of the old two roads — some 8 miles along. We passed a place where there were a great many men's bicycles and on our return, suspecting illegal activities, alerted the police: but it turned out to be just a betrothal ceremony.

In the early evening there was a drinks party to meet the small local community of officials. ... Afterwards we went to a Chinese dinner party with the leading Chinese merchant — about 9 courses, all very good. ... Then return by launch to Labuan — 4 hours and pretty rough, but we were able to sit on deck, holding on as the boat lurched, and it was very exhilarating. The DO gave me a mug of beer while waiting for the daily plane for Jesselton. And so back to the Office.

All appeared calm from this letter. The next letter of 9 December reported trouble.

I hope the news from Borneo over the weekend has not been causing you concern. If I had chosen this weekend instead of last for my visit to Limbang I should have been in the thick of the trouble. I knew it was likely to be a trouble spot — which was the main reason why I wanted to see it — but I did not suppose that the trouble would come so soon.

Most of the detailed news has been about the insurrection in Brunei and there have been some clashes in the neighbouring part of N. Borneo, including a land and sea engagement at the jetty at Weston, where I embarked. But about Limbang there has been ominous lack of news. The telephone is dead and air reconnaissance reports no sign of life in the town apart from men with shot-guns (i.e. rebels) patrolling the main road and no flags flying. A police launch trying to get up the river from the sea was met with small arms fire from the bank and had to withdraw. I have a sick feeling of anxiety for the Morrises with whom I stayed and the other members of the little British community whom I met a week ago today.

There has been no trouble in any part of North Borneo except the border district where there are Brunei Malays. Police reinforcements have been flown from Jesselton, but otherwise life here is normal.

I hope that the preoccupation of governments with this situation will not be used as an excuse for postponing the KL meetings. It seems to me all the more important to button up our plans for Malaysia as quickly as we can. We had further meetings here this last week — and also meetings with the staff associates about compensation — and there should now be a lull until we meet in KL on Monday week.

John's last letter from the tour was written on 14 December.

I had four very unhappy days and nights waiting for news of my friends in Limbang. At last came news that Royal Marine Commandos had broken through up the river (though at a cost of 5 lives) and relieved them. I have so far heard no details of their ordeal except a report that the rebels had put a rope round the neck of the Resident, Dick Morris, and were choosing a tree from which to hang him when a flight of RAF planes zoomed low overhead. Breaking up in disorder they abandoned him with the rope still tied round his neck. Some of the European hostages in Brunei had a nasty time too, especially those who were tied together and pushed forward as a shield in front of men attacking a police station. I might very easily (because of the St Andrews dinner) have postponed my visit by a week and so coincided with the day when the balloon went up.

Naturally everyone in the Government here and in Sarawak has been very much taken up by those events and it seemed for a while that our meetings in KL might be cancelled. But there is a general wish not to allow the revolt to delay progress towards Malaysia. So we are to meet after all, but it will not be possible to field full teams and there won't have been much time for preparation.

What had happened on 8 December had been a revolt against the Sultan of Brunei and not opposition to Malaysia. The prime cause of the revolt seemed to have been the frustration of Azahari and the Party Rakyat, which, though having won all the elected seats, did not, under the constitution, control the government. Dissatisfaction with the corruption and inadequacy of the Sultan's regime and Azahari's ambition to set up a union of Brunei, North Borneo and Sarawak were further factors. The revolt was quickly suppressed and the Sultan resumed negotiations with Malaya.

The intergovernmental committee duly finished its work and reported. It had cleared the way for North Borneo and Sarawak to enter Malaysia. Meanwhile, Brunei and Singapore were negotiating separately with Malaya. John took part in London meetings in 1962 with Malayan and Singapore ministers in the final preparatory stage of Malaysia, which came into being in 1963. The 8 December revolt took place after Brunei's first round of talks with Malaya. Singapore became part of Malaysia in 1963 but withdrew two years later. Brunei never became part of it. Britain secured the defence agreements it required.

The early years of Malaysia were difficult. In correspondence with L. S. Dixon in 1966, with whom he had stayed in Jesselton in 1962, John defended its creation. It came too soon, he wrote, but:

> the timing of the policy was decided not by HMG but by the Tunku. When he was converted to the principle of the thing, he began to press for its early implementation with an embarrassing impetuosity which was as unexpected as it was unwise. Several more years of expatriate guidance were needed to produce in the Borneo States a Civil Service, an electorate and experienced political leaders able to bring their countries into the partnership on reasonably equal terms.

He also argued that the importance of bringing Singapore into the federation quickly as an alternative to communism made a 'rush job' in Borneo inevitable.

John ended this letter of 18 January 1966 with observations on the process of ending empire.

> It has not been fun to have had to play a part over the last few years in the dismemberment of the old British Empire, though I believe that in its broad lines the process was inevitable and, given the circumstances, right. But I was in the Colonial Office long enough to know that the old Colonial rule was one of the best British gifts to the world.

11

Troubleshooting in Nigeria, 1958–60

I n 1958 John was sent on a troubleshooting mission to Nigeria, a mission which was at some cost to his health. Turning colonies into self-governing states was not an easy task and, in the 1950s, the process was moving forward rapidly. Many of the difficulties of decolonization in Africa lay in what Harold Macmillan described as 'the careless, some might say even criminal, methods by which the different portions of the newly discovered parts of Africa were divided during the grab for colonies by the rival European powers' (*Pointing the Way*, p. 125). In the case of Nigeria, the problem of retaining sufficient Colonial Service officers to see the country through the period of transition had become urgent.

By 1949, there was general agreement on federal government for Nigeria with regional legislatures. Under the 1951 constitution, there was an elected majority in the central legislature with the British governor-general holding certain reserved powers. Troubles in Nigeria in 1953 caused the constitution to break down. Following the constitutional conference in London in 1954, the British government went ahead with plans for further regionalization and self-government. This divided the unitary public service into four separate public services. By 1958, the Western and Eastern regions were self-governing, the Northern region was to become self-governing in 1959 and the country as a whole under its federal administration was to become independent in 1960. The Eastern and Western regions were building up their Nigerian administrative officers; the Northern region and the federation were not far advanced in this. In this uncertain period, British officers had been offered a compensation scheme of a lump sum on retirement or the opportunity to put their names on a special list to stay on and later be found a post elsewhere. Being on the special list was not, however, binding; a man could at any time take his lump sum. By the time John went to Nigeria, the lump sum scheme was very popular and many proposed to take it while the names on the special list were few and uncertain.

The Secretary of State sent a telegram to the three regions and the federation on 30 December 1957 announcing his intention to send John Martin, who was responsible for overseas service matters, for 'informal discussions on the staff position with the Nigerian governments and also ... informal talks with overseas officers about the operation of the Special List Agreement'. John received a careful briefing on many of those whom he was to meet.

He described his task in the opening paragraph of his report.

> I was sent to Nigeria by the Secretary of State to examine the position resulting from the rapid exodus of expatriate officers from the Eastern and Western Regions and the small initial response to the invitation to apply for admission to the Special List. I was instructed to consider any alternative arrangements, either within the framework of the Special List or outside it, which might help to ensure that overseas officers will remain in Nigeria, so long as their services are required, in order to assist in the difficult period before and after the attainment of self-government and until African civil servants are available to take their places.

His diary and letters reveal the thorough programme of visits and talks he undertook. His first letter home, written on 9 January, described a pattern of work he was to follow throughout the month's tour.

> We arrived at Kano on January 8th in the dark about 5.30, but the Resident, Oliver Hunt, was at the airport to meet

me along with Sam Moore,[1] who is going to accompany me throughout the tour of the Northern Region. Once more I benefit from following in the footsteps of royalty, for I was shown to a most pleasant bedroom, with bright modern bathroom, which had been put in its present order for the Queen's visit. Hunt is the acting Resident. He has arranged an excellent programme to enable me to meet a number of European Officers in small informal groups, besides seeing something of various Government activities in and round Kano.

This was interrupted yesterday by departure on a visit to the Emir of Kano, who received me in his Council Chamber surrounded by the members of his inner Council. In voluminous robes and turbans, they made an exotic picture. Conversation was through an interpreter and went rather heavily, though friendly. After this I was taken for a drive through Kano City — a very large walled, mud-built city with no obvious plan and a good deal of open space. At one point we climbed a minaret for a general view of the city stretching in every direction as far as the eye could see. We stopped to look at one or two industries — a ground-nut oil mill (owned by a Cypriot), a scent factory (run by a Swiss) and native dyeing in deep vats in the open air.

The morning ended at the house of one of the district officers, who had invited a number of younger British Officers to meet, and we had a long discussion, over mugs of beer. Back to lunch in the Residency at 2.30, followed by a much-needed siesta until tea time. Then watched polo (mixed Europeans and Africans) and later returned for a talk with more officials over more beer. A district officer to dinner. And so to bed and a solid night's sleep.

Today I started before breakfast with an hour's visit to a Trade School, where carpentry, cabinet-making, electric work, diesel-engine repairing and other trades are taught by European instructors. There was an opportunity for some discussion of staff matters and especially the difficulties of the (low paid) European instructors with children to educate

---

1. The former 'beachcomber' Nigerian officer seconded to the Colonial Office.

at home. The rest of the morning was occupied by a visit to a district headquarters in the country and, on return to the Residency, another long discussion with another group of officers.

So you can see that I am having plenty of opportunity to pursue my enquiry about service feeling, as well as seeing something of the country and its administration. It is a great help to have Sam Moore's guidance and the Hunts are excellent hosts. The climate here is a delightful change from the English winter — sunny (though with a dust haze) and dry. It is distinctly cool morning and evening, but very comfortably warm at midday.

In his next letter, of 11 January 1958, John added a comment on education in Northern Nigeria.

The last afternoon at Kano (Thursday) was partly taken up by a visit to the Provincial Secondary Boys' School (at present doubling up in one building with the Teachers' Training College). It is only very lately that education in Northern Nigeria has developed from a very small affair covering only a tiny fraction of the child population. In this conservatively Moslem Region there has been a strong prejudice against it and parents had virtually to be compelled to send their children to school, even paying bribes to escape the unwanted school places. In the last very few years there has been a slight change and there is now a steadily increasing demand but it is still small and this secondary school is the only one for boys in an Administration with a population of over 3 million. It has to take almost all candidates who offer themselves and has not yet worked up to a high standard. Shortage of staff is another difficulty. But the masters I met (all Europeans) did not seem discouraged and in fact were obviously cheered by the evidence that the tide is at last rising.

Visits followed to Maiduguri, Yola, Jos and Kaduna. At Kaduna John visited the emir in his palace who asked:

why the British were in such a hurry to hand over responsibility before we had had time to put anything in place of
the 500 years' old system which we had destroyed. He is
obviously much concerned about the future of the country
under the new constitution. A picturesque old diehard. ...
An hour's talk (alone) with Premier and four other African
Ministers. I told them very frankly of my impressions and
proposals. They took the latter much better than I had
expected and promised to discuss further at the Lagos
Conference.

His travels then took him westward to Ilorin, Benin, Sapele,
Warri and Ibadan. On 25 January he reported from Ibadan,
finding

this hot, moist climate very wearing — you would hate it —
and the programme is non-stop. ...
   My first morning here (Thursday) was given up to discussions with the Governor, the Deputy Governor ('Satan'
Mooring — well named, for he is the split image of Auld
Nick) and Mr Adebo, the Permanent Secretary of the
Ministry of Finance and one of the ablest African Civil
Servants (whom I had met at the Lancaster House Conference). In the afternoon I had a not very easy meeting with
the Council of 'the Bolshie Society' (the Civil Services Association), followed by a drinks party at Mr Adebo's house to
meet a number of junior officers (Africans and Europeans)
and their wives, followed by dinner until midnight at the
Moorings' — at which I was under persistent and relentless
attack by a rather disgruntled civil servant, John O'Regan.
   Friday began with a meeting with the Public Service Commission and then an hour with Gardner-Brown the Deputy
Governor-General of the Federation, who had kindly flown
up as he will have gone on leave by the time I reach Lagos.
Then a meeting with various Departmental Heads. In the
afternoon I drove (about 1¾ hours) to Igebu-Ode (pro-
nounced Jebode) to spend the night with the District
Adviser, a bachelor called Partridge. ... A late dinner party,
followed by a short night during which I was frightfully

bitten in various sensitive parts. The lack of electricity in this climate is a great drawback.

Returning early to Ibadan, I began yesterday with a talk with the Minister of Finance, who was at first rather difficult but became more friendly, followed by a meeting with Permanent Secretaries of Departments. In the afternoon I visited the University College — wonderful buildings in the Festival of Britain style, mostly good I thought. Shown round by the Principal after tea, at which we discussed the Biobaku affair.[2]

Back to change for a drinks party of people invited to meet me in the garden at Government House. Biobaku and his very charming wife stayed on to dinner and I was able to tell him how ashamed I had been of the club exclusion and that this was due to the power placed in the hands of a few unrepresentative blimps by the Club members.

John then flew eastwards to Enugu. On 28 January 1958, he wrote of his encounter with the local branch of the 'Bolshie Society, but they had made it a social occasion — drinks and joining the wives later — and it was not unfriendly, though the position in this Region is particularly difficult, with an impossible and insolvent government and a crumbling administration — e.g. 2 Europeans trying to run a province where three years ago there were 10.'

After meeting the Eastern region's various political and ecclesiastical authorities, John moved on to Onitsha and Owerri where the district officer, Andy Urquhart, had been coping with a demonstration of 10,000 women against school fees. On 5 February, John wrote:

He is ... the best sort of Scot abroad, and had obviously dealt very well with this formidable invasion. He had an old house without electricity or water, which quite took me

2. Two years earlier, Mr Biobaku, a Cambridge graduate and registrar of Ibadan University, had been proposed for membership of John's London club, the United University Club; the chairman had insisted his name be withdrawn to avoid the 'embarrassment' of his 'inevitable' blackballing by the club's committee. John, appalled, had fought a spirited campaign on his behalf before resigning from the club in protest.

back to Malayan days. The local Shell manager and his wife and a visiting Shell manager from Lagos came to dinner. Apart from an English ADO and Maltese doctor we were all Scots and the party included 3 sons of the manse and 2 Edinburgh Academicals.

He next went south to Oron and Calabar and then Buea in the southern Cameroons. His tour ended with several days in Lagos. By this time John could write: 'I am now pretty clear about what ought to be done but whether it can be done is another question.'

Near the time of his departure, the Governor General, Sir James Robertson, wrote to the Minister of State, the Earl of Perth on 7 February 1958.

From our point of view Martin has had a very useful tour round the country. He has seen a large number of the expatriate staff, both individually and as represented by their staff associations. He has had very useful discussions and conversations with them; I am informed that his sympathetic and friendly approach has been greatly appreciated, and has impressed the expatriate staff generally with the Secretary of State's anxiety on their behalf and of HMG's interest in their future welfare.

During his tour Martin has also had lengthy conversations with Ministers, both in the Regions and here at the centre, where he had a two-hour meeting yesterday with the Prime Minister, the Northern Premier and Minister of Finance, Bell and myself, about expatriate staff in the Federal and Northern Regional services. Later he had another meeting, at which we Governors were not present, with the National Council on Establishments, which under the Chairmanship of the Prime Minister discussed the question of expatriate staff generally with him.

Martin has therefore got a very good idea of the fears and feelings of the expatriate staff, of the reasons why officers have left and are still leaving the Eastern and Western Regions, and also of the outlook of the Nigerian politicians, and can now give you and the Secretary of State a fully up-to-date account of the whole position.

Sir John Macpherson, the permanent under-secretary, wrote in the margin: 'a very well worth-while visit — as I knew it would be'.

In his report, John set out the position in the three regions and the federation. In the two self-governing regions, Eastern and Western, which had already instituted lump-sum compensation schemes, about 25 per cent of the 'entitled' expatriate officers had gone by the end of 1957; from the Eastern region 59 out of 220 and from the Western 68 out of 287. It was expected that another 35 would retire during 1958 in the Western region and a similar number in the Eastern. In these two regions, Nigerianization had progressed with a stream of new recruits from Ibadan and universities overseas. The new recruits were bringing paper qualifications but lacked experience. John saw the problem as a short-term one of 'retaining sufficient expatriates during the next six or seven years to train these young Africans and maintain the machinery of government during the transition from a European-directed to an African service'. Yet, the exodus of expatriates on the scale he found would endanger this process of training and could lead to a breakdown of administration. He was more hopeful of success in the Western than in the Eastern region.

The situation was different in the Northern region. The great majority of senior posts were held by expatriates. The administrative staff had 300 expatriates and only 21 Northerners. Also, there were 164 expatriate medical staff and only five Northerners qualified to hold these posts. Social development in this region had been much slower than in the others. John concluded that 'withdrawal of expatriates in proportions comparable to the present exodus in the Eastern and Western Regions would lead to a collapse of the governmental machine, administrative and technical'. At the time of the report, the lump-sum scheme had not come into force in the Northern region, but was proposed for 15 March 1959. A questionnaire circulated to officers in the north, returned by 60 per cent, revealed that half of these would elect to retire with lump-sum compensation. Such a scheme for the federation would not come into effect until independence in 1960, but 'any large and immediate exodus on independence' would be very damaging to the federal government.

Why then was there such an exodus of expatriate officers? John found three reasons in 'political difficulties', in the attractions of the lump sum and in dissatisfaction with present emoluments. His report sets them out.

'Political' difficulties. By 'political' difficulties I refer to such matters as the frustrations of working with inexperienced and often inefficient African ministers, the attempts of some ministers to influence executive action or even judicial processes for reasons of personal or partisan interest, the fear that 'Nigerianization' will be pressed faster and further than justified, to the detriment of the promotion prospects of expatriates (and with the result of placing professional and technical officers under the directions of young and inexperienced African administrative heads), and the uncertainty of the expatriate whether he is any longer really wanted by the Nigerian Ministers. The expatriate feels that he is being squeezed out and is in danger of prostituting his personal or professional integrity by service to an inefficient and corrupt regime. This is most true in the Eastern Region, where ministerial standards are particularly deplorable; but even in the North, although full self-government has not yet come, some officers have already found grounds for such fears and expect to see deteriorating standards follow the next constitutional advance. By and large, the expatriate officers appreciate the constitutional changes which have taken place and are prepared to co-operate with their African masters in trying to make a success of the new system, but they are not prepared to lower their personal or professional standards. This is all the more true of those, perhaps more numerous than is sometimes recognized, for whom there was an element of the missionary spirit in their original choice of a career in the public service overseas.

Effects of lump sum compensation scheme. These 'intangibles' are the principal cause of the lowering of Service morale. In such a situation the lump sum compensation scheme offers a way of escape to the harassed expatriate. It is in itself an inducement to go. Few officers can hope to accumulate so much in the course of a Service career. The compensation money may provide the means of meeting educational or other family commitments which, whatever

227

his personal feelings about leaving the Service, an officer may feel that he owes it to his family to accept. In the prevailing uncertainty about career prospects in Nigeria or in the contracting field of pensionable employment for expatriates in the Overseas Service elsewhere, many officers feel the urge to start a new career outside the Service before it is too late and the compensation may help to start a farm or a business at home. Further, unless 'freezing' is allowed there is an additional temptation to leave as soon as maximum entitlement is reached and before the amount of the lump sum begins to decline with advancing age. This of course affects the most experienced and therefore, in general, most valuable officers. Further, the fear is often expressed that, for financial or political reasons, Nigerian Governments may at a later stage default on the promise of compensation (and even on payment of pensions) and some officers believe for this reason that it is prudent to 'go while the going is good'. It is also widely believed that, with the prospect of large-scale discharges of officers of the Armed Forces and of continuing retirements from Nigeria, it will be easier now than later to find good jobs in the United Kingdom.

Dissatisfaction with present emoluments. The frustrations of the expatriate's position in working under his African masters (not to mention the strain of life in a tropical climate) make him feel all the more keenly dissatisfaction with his material conditions of service. It is clear that the Nigerian Governments are not at present paying the market price for their expatriates.

John produced figures to show that before the war salaries in Nigeria, with its less attractive climate and other amenities, were always considerably higher than in East and central Africa. He also pointed out that, in many posts, Nigerian salaries no longer offered any element of inducement over those in the United Kingdom. He was convinced that there were grounds for service dissatisfaction with remuneration at that time and that some of the younger men with families were suffering real hardship.

John next dealt with the failure of the special list to attract. He put it down to the 'belief that those who join it thereby lose their freedom to escape from Nigeria even if conditions became intolerable and, secondly, lack of confidence in the undertaking that, if they have to leave Nigeria, every endeavour will be made to find them equivalent appointments elsewhere'.

John put a number of paragraphs in his report on the United Kingdom's stake in Nigerian stability and prosperity. It was clear to him that some funding by the British government was necessary to the solution of the problems his report was considering. He wrote that 'the whole achievement of the British people in Nigeria over the last half century and more ... may be largely destroyed if, at this final stage of our responsibility, British staffs are allowed to melt away before the transference of administration to African hands is safely complete'. He quoted Sir Francis Drake: when it is given to us 'to endeavour any great matter ... it is not the beginning, but the continuing of the same, until it be throughly finished, which yieldeth the true glory'.

John recommended urgent action in these areas. The first was to do with the special list. The British government should place all pensionable expatriate officers on a new special list, should take responsibility for payments of emoluments at present rates and of lump-sum payments for loss of career as well as pensions and other benefits allowed under Nigerian governments. These governments should refund these payments to the British government. In addition, the British government should provide an extra inducement allowance and an additional allowance for the education of children in the United Kingdom on the foreign service scale — and the necessary funds for these.

Second, the Nigerian governments should provide 'counter-inducements' in their compensation schemes in the form of generous provision for 'freezing' advances at a low rate of interest up to three-quarters of entitlement to lump-sum compensation and commutation of part of pensions.

Third, John recommended setting up an Overseas Service Officers' Resettlement Bureau.

John's report was in the Secretary of State's hands within a few days. By 19 February, the Secretary of State was able to send copies of the report to the Governor General and to the three regional governors. He commented: 'I have read Martin's report

... and am very greatly attracted by his recommendations. Subject to your detailed comments and those of the other governors and to any modification necessary of these and of study at the official level here I am prepared to put them to the Chancellor [of the Exchequer] with my strongest personal support.'

On the same day, John sent a personal letter to the Governor General with certain queries about the report to be considered by him and the regional governors, and with recommendations on handling the report.

John also sent a copy of the report to Sir Ivo Stourton, Inspector-General of Colonial Police, with a comment on the expatriate police in Nigeria.

Mr Bovell[3] was present at a large meeting at which I discussed the position with Heads of Departments in Lagos. Subsequently, at his request, I had a short private talk with him. The uncertainty about the future and concentration of interest on questions of lump sum compensation, which are general throughout the Service in Nigeria with inevitable effect on morale, seem to be particularly prevalent among some of the Police. (In their case the lump sum schemes will not come into force until independence, i.e. on the present assumption some date in 1960.) The Police are perhaps as much affected as anybody by what I have called in my report the 'political' factors and some of them are much concerned at the prospect of becoming the agents of corrupt Ministers, expected for example to take action against their political opponents (e.g. by banning processions etc.) or refraining from proper action against their supporters. I was told a story, of which I could not check the facts but which is worth mentioning as the sort of thing people have in mind, about an incident in one of the Regions where a Minister and some thugs under his control held up and robbed a lorry: the Police had an absolutely cast iron case for prosecution but word came down from on high that the case was to be dropped.

Some of the younger married Police are also much

---

3. C. S. K. Bovell, Inspector-General of Police in Nigeria.

affected by financial difficulties. I met one young ASP (whose name I forget) in his second tour, with a wife and child, who said he could only make ends meet by drawing on savings accumulated in a job he had had before joining the Police. He struck me as a very good type of young officer and the District Officer assured me that he was a man who lived very quietly and that what he had said could be taken as correct.

Mr Bovell mentioned that he had been reluctant to agree to any transfers of Police from Nigeria, in view of his present staff difficulties, but I said I thought it would be a mistake to let the Police have the impression that they are caught in an enclosed pond in Nigeria and that a certain amount of movement could have a very good effect on morale.

I can only hope that my recommendations, if accepted, will help. The importance of retaining a substantial expatriate element in the Nigerian Police is sufficiently obvious.

Sir Ivo replied on 1 April:

With the troubles in Eastern Nigeria of January/February and now those in the West, any exodus from the police even in 1960 will undoubtedly have a very serious effect on law and order. Between now and then expatriate officers in the force will be worrying over their future which will inevitably, even though unconsciously, affect their work — so I hope something will be done very soon on the lines you recommend in your report. The police are particularly vulnerable to what you call 'political factors'.

John had time to prepare his report before he was struck down by an unwelcome Nigerian gift, a form of poliomyelitis, which put him in St Thomas's Hospital, after a few days in bed at home, from 1 to 31 March. He did not return to the Colonial Office until 5 May. He was thus out of the discussions and action that followed his report. People did pursue him to his bedside in St Thomas's, among them Philip Mason on 17 March, secretary of the Board of Studies in Race Relations, whom he had met on his

231

Nigerian tour. Mason wanted to know what the report said. John was able to give a clear account. Mason summarized it and sent the summary back for checking. Although John had spoken to Mason of 'being out of the battle', his mind was working effectively.

The hopes the Secretary of State expressed when he sent the report to the Nigerian governments were not fulfilled. The federation and the Northern region accepted the report's recommendations. The Eastern and Western regions both put forward alternative recommendations, which the Secretary of State somewhat reluctantly agreed to accept. The Secretary of State came to the House of Commons on 1 August to report at a stage when he was considering these two regions' alternative suggestions. He accepted fully the arguments of the report and reported that the government had put forward proposals along the lines recommended there. Two former secretaries of state in the House, Creech Jones and James Griffiths, gave full support to the action being taken by the government.

A constitutional conference on Nigeria was to take place in London in the autumn of 1958 when the final arrangements for Nigerian independence were to be considered. A leader in *The Times* on 7 August referred to this conference and spoke of the expatriate officers in Nigeria.

> One matter which concerns both parties (the British government and the Nigerian governments) is the terms on which British civil servants can stay on in Nigeria after independence has been granted. Here many of the difficulties have been smoothed out of the way by the fruitful recommendations of Sir John Martin, who visited Nigeria on a tour of inquiry earlier in the year.

John Martin's visit and the recommendations put into effect as a result of his report improved the position of colonial service officers and encouraged many to remain to ease Nigeria into independence, achieved on 1 October 1960. Yet the new federation of regions was not stable. Tensions between the regions were to lead to political murders and the nightmare of civil war.

12

Federations in Africa and the Caribbean, 1959–62

Federations were made possible by two gifts of colonialism. The colonial power brought a common language to unite members of the federation. In the case of Great Britain this was a language on its way to becoming the common language of the world. The colonial power also provided in its rule improved means and methods of communication.

Many colonies, especially in the Caribbean, were too small to stand on their own, or, in much of Africa, had been drawn with artificial boundaries that disregarded geographical or tribal distributions. To group such colonies in a federation would, it was hoped, create a new and larger loyalty from which economic advantage would follow. Within the federation, there would be a larger internal market. The stronger parts of the federation would support its weaker parts. The federation would be able to supply common and public services on a scale its smaller parts could not. Moreover, the larger unit of the federation could defend itself more readily against external attack and internal subversion. This point was felt most strongly in Malaysia, where the North Borneo territories had suffered attack by Indonesia and where Malaya had endured the long emergency created by communist subversion.

Federation worked through a supreme authority covering all the territories within it and through local or regional authorities, allowing for different balances of power between central and local authorities.

There were, however, many serious problems. One with which John was much concerned was the protection of minorities. At the time of the Kenya conference in 1960, Julian Amery[1] asked for John's views on this matter in the three territories in the East African Federation (Kenya, Uganda and Tanganyika). His reply of 21 January showed how difficult it was to provide such protection through legal formulations and Commonwealth guardianship.

> 'Capitulations' suggest the machinery of Consular Courts and the like, but nothing of that sort would be acceptable to the independent African Governments and it is difficult to see what sanctions there could be or how they could be applied. Mr Gorell Barnes's[2] suggestion of Commonwealth guardianship seems to be open to the same question and is not very attractive when one considers the composition of the Commonwealth as it is now and as it may well develop.

This was the airing of a problem and the rejection of two possible solutions. It was a particular problem of Kenya and attention was paid to it in the Kenya constitutional conferences. A form of regionalism was brought in to protect the minorities of the East African coastal strip at the Lancaster House conference in March/April 1962, the coastal strip being Zanzibari territory. This conference was a preliminary to the union of Tanganyika and Zanzibar, which came into effect in 1964 to form Tanzania.

Another major problem with federation was distance. The 1000 miles between Jamaica and Trinidad created difficulties. When, in 1962, after a referendum Jamaica opted out of the West Indian Federation, Eric Williams, Prime Minister of Trinidad and Tobago from 1961, remarked that 'one out of ten leaves nought'. Without its strongest member, the federation fell apart. Federations also tended to underestimate the power of nationalism. States and territories preferred to stand on their own. Even in the most successful federation, Malaysia, oil-rich Brunei never entered and Singapore left within two years. In the Caribbean, the islands moved at their own speed to independence, retaining many of the common services set up by the federation but without a federal government. In East Africa, enthusiasm for federation waned in

---

1. Parliamentary Under-Secretary of State for the Colonies, 1958–70.
2. KCMG 1961, Assistant Under-Secretary of State in Colonial Office, 1959–63.

the 1950s. The Mau Mau rebellion and civil war in Kenya, beginning in 1952 and fought largely over land, cast a shadow not only over Kenya but more generally over Africa. They revealed not only the power of Africans but also the terror of a situation out of control. It was a factor in weakening the East African Federation. By the time of the independence of the three territories, it had faded away. What common services the independent countries required, they negotiated themselves.

The history of the Central African Federation, consisting of the two Rhodesias and Nyasaland, exemplifies the nationalist case against federation. Macmillan, in *Pointing the Way* and writing after the federation had fallen apart, speaks of 'his collective responsibility' as a member of the government that set up the federation. He goes on to say (p. 133): 'Had I then realized, or had indeed any of us realized, the almost revolutionary way in which the situation would develop and the rapid growth of African Nationalism throughout the whole African continent, I think I should have opposed the putting together of three countries so opposite in their character and so different in their history.'

Three out of four federations in operation at this time failed. In the British government's defence, it can be said that it was meeting expectations of the time and drawing on its own best experience. The former colonial nations expected Britain to pass on to them at independence their best forms of government and administration; anything else or less would be insulting. Federation had worked admirably for the white dominions of Australia and Canada, as it had for the former American colonies. Parliamentary democracy had served Britain well and had been adopted by many independent countries. India was an example of a most successful transplant. Yet, 'the wind of change' was blowing rapidly through Africa and elsewhere and was not to stop blowing. Whatever institutions were planted at independence might soon be uprooted.

From 1959, John Martin had responsibility for African departments. A complication was that the Commonwealth Relations Office (CRO) had an interest in Southern Rhodesia, a self-governing colony since 1923, being CRO territory. Federation for Northern and Southern Rhodesia with Nyasaland had been proposed in the last years of the postwar Labour government, and had been taken up by the succeeding Churchill government. From the beginning it appeared to African opinion that federation was a process by which the Africans of the three territories would be subjugated to the white population of Southern Rhodesia. Critics also deplored the absence of provision for educated Africans to play a part in its administration. In addition, Africans themselves felt that in the lengthy negotiations over the future of the three territories their views were not adequately taken into account. In 1957, the powers of the federal government were enlarged but, by the end of the year, the African National Congresses in the three countries had affirmed their opposition to federation and proposed to boycott the federal elections of 1958, which they did. Macmillan described the dilemma that faced the British government. 'If federation remained, how could progress of Africans come about in the two countries, Northern Rhodesia and Nyasaland, where they were dominant? If it went, European-controlled Southern Rhodesia would go independent or join South Africa' (p. 134). Meanwhile, in 1958 and 1959 there were states of emergency in Nyasaland and Northern Rhodesia and, in 1959 and 1960, in Southern Rhodesia. Macmillan's solution was to appoint a Royal Commission under Lord Monckton with Sir Donald MacGillivray as one of its members to enquire into the working of the federation.

In these years, John Martin was much engaged in the last stages of preparing a number of countries for independence, mainly in Africa but not exclusively. His diary gives an outline of meetings and conferences in this process. On 17 January 1960, he lunched at Chequers with the Secretary of State, Macleod, and the Governor of Kenya, Sir Patrick Renison, in preparation for the Kenya conference at Lancaster House, which opened the following day and ran to 21 February. On 12 February, he had a consultation with Macleod and Lord Home, the Commonwealth Relations secretary.

In June 1960, John Martin visited the countries of the Central African Federation. He spent ten days in Nyasaland, five in Southern Rhodesia and six in Northern Rhodesia. He had consultations with leaders of the federation and of Southern Rhodesia in Salisbury; he met Northern Rhodesian officials in Lusaka and saw the dam and developments at Kariba. Nyasaland was the most difficult country in which to travel, which explains the longer time allowed, and also the country at the sharpest point of crisis. Macmillan had passed through it in January on his way to South Africa and commented on the sense of strain there.

Dr Hastings Banda and his Malawi African Congress were causing unrest in Nyasaland. Banda had had a successful London medical practice, which he gave up in 1955 to return via Ghana to Nyasaland to campaign against the Central African Federation and for the independence of Nyasaland (Malawi). He was imprisoned in 1959, but at the time of John's visit had been released. Macmillan had arranged for him to be released a few days before the Monckton Commission left the country so that he could give evidence as a free man. Macmillan grew to like Banda, but his campaign was causing difficulties for the administration. Banda later became minister of national resources in 1961, prime minister in 1963, president of the Malawi republic in 1966 and life president in 1971.

On 4 July, John made a full report of his visit. He began with a parable.

The African headmaster of a secondary school at Blantyre, a released detainee, dismissed some of the boys for indiscipline. There was an immediate storm of protests and the Malawi Party (including Orton Chirwa) joined in pressing for a reversal of his decision. But the headmaster stood firm, declaring that he must have discipline in his school; the boys have not been taken back. As Mr Doig, the Church of Scotland Missionary, said in telling me the story, neither he nor any other European could have got away with such a decision. It was only possible for an African.

This is a parable, for the Nyasaland Administration have almost everywhere lost the power of authoritative leadership — in education, in agricultural development (which must be the first priority in Nyasaland) and generally over the whole field of their relations with the African community — and only association of Africans in responsibility for government seems to offer the possibility of escape from this impasse. The hold of the Malawi Party is almost universal, though by no means universally popular (e.g. among many of the Chiefs, who resent the loss of their personal authority) and maintained by ruthless intimidation (which is indeed the most outstanding feature as it is the least pleasant in the present situation). The fact must be faced that without African cooperation, which is not now forthcoming, the Government plans for social and economic development are completely frustrated. The refusal of the £90,000 offer for improvement of coffee cultivation by small farmers is a spectacular example, but there are many others. Even the ordinary processes of administration, such as collection of taxation, are becoming increasingly difficult. Meanwhile anti-European emotions are being aroused which, if there were a call from the African leaders for more positive opposition, would quickly produce disorders which the present woefully thin and extended Security Forces could not contain.

In the Northern and Central Provinces I followed only a few days behind Banda, Chiume and Orton Chirwa and heard much of the results of their incitement. I will give only the example of Kota Kota. Order at the Doctor's meeting, attended by thousands of Africans, was maintained by a force of Malawi police in a sort of uniform, with the letters MG (for 'Malawi Government') on their caps and some carrying wooden model rifles. I myself witnessed a squad drilling openly in the street with an officer calling out 'left right, left right', as they marched past, and saluting the District Commissioner, who was in the car with me. In the absence on this occasion of police recording apparatus, the speeches contained attacks on the Government, missionaries and Europeans generally of exceptional violence. Banda himself fiercely attacked the UMCA Mission (the Universities Mission to Central Africa), saying that the first Bishop had murdered Africans and the present Bishop had given information to the Government during the emergency: the missionaries must go 'now, now, now'.[3] One of the speakers repeated what seems to be a stock declaration that

---

3. This attack on the missions was particularly repellent to John, who knew how much of a contribution churches had made in Africa. Although the UMCA, which was an Anglican mission, is mentioned here, it was the Presbyterian churches that had served Nyasaland so well.

after independence Europeans would only be retained to dig latrines. School children were instructed to defy authority and insult Europeans. The results of all this had been considerable excitement in the town on the following day. Europeans were jostled and insulted while shopping and there was pandemonium in the Mission School. Subsequently, following a meeting with the District Commissioner, the Malawi leaders gave orders for restraint and it was significant of the extent of their authority that the worst excesses immediately ceased, though (at the time of my visit several days later) insulting shouting at Europeans still continued. In this District, with an African population of several thousands, the forces of law and order consist of 12 African policemen under a young European officer.

The authorities were exercising the greatest restraint, so as to avoid any incident which might prejudice the Conference, but no Government could continue in a position of such obvious impotence for more than a few weeks and it is generally assumed that, if there is no agreement at the Conference, there must be a 'showdown' and the Government must re-assert its authority. It seems to be generally believed that this will be possible if there is the necessary 'firmness' and if the Malawi leaders are removed to detention. Such an operation would call for military reinforcements. The re-assertion of authority would be much more readily accepted if these were supplied from the United Kingdom and not by the Federal Government. In any case, opinions differ as to whether 'firm' Government could be indefinitely maintained and how far the present non-cooperation of the African population would be effectively broken; but elsewhere it is recognized that the awakening of national emotion has now gone too far to be arrested by the detention of a few leaders, that a policy of repression would lead nowhere and that, in fact, Government without African cooperation is no longer possible. This is the lesson of the parable with which I started and I believe it to be broadly true.

If so, there is really no acceptable alternative to an agreed settlement and everything depends on the success of the

Conference. There are many excuses for pessimism. The speeches of the Malawi leaders could hardly be more extreme and uncompromising. The violence of their attacks on Europeans are hard to forgive, even when allowance is made for the Eatanswill atmosphere of a barn-storming campaign of this kind and though it may be said on behalf of Orton Chirwa that he is under a compulsion to prove that he is as good a Nationalist as the rest. I had tape recordings of two of Banda's speeches played back to me: there was a bitterness and venom in his references to Europeans which no transcript can reproduce. The general belief is that the source of this extremist attitude is Chiume (whose return to Nyasaland at large was repeatedly described to me as a disaster), that he has had an evil effect on Orton Chirwa (who is said to have been a changed man — Pretorius said that even his face had changed — since meeting Chiume in England) and that Banda is (as suggested by the Devlin account of the situation before the emergency) simply a puppet made use of because of his popular appeal. Banda's subordinate role is thought by some to be confirmed by the fact that he always speaks third at the campaign meetings — when the audience is already exhausted and beginning to trickle away; but it may be (as Mr Finney of the Special Branch holds) that this is only an example of African incompetence in managing such things.

It is however beyond question Banda and not Chiume who enjoys outstanding popularity and prestige. He is the Gandhi of Nyasaland nationalism and he has no rival. Although every pressure will be brought upon him by Chiume to refuse a reasonable settlement, my conclusion from the many opinions I heard expressed is that, if Banda himself commends any agreement reached in London, he will be able to secure its general acceptance and would not immediately be overthrown by Chiume and the other extremists, though they might possibly form a strong splinter group in opposition. Banda's instability, vanity and limited understanding of Government generally and in particular of Nyasaland affairs may seem to make him an unsatisfactory negotiator, but these are defects which will render him vulnerable rather than strong in negotiation, and we have one solid and perhaps decisive advantage in his undoubted confidence in the Secretary of State personally (a confidence which, I gather, also extends to Scots generally!) (This was made very clear by him in conversations with the District Commissioner of his home town, Kasungu, with whom and his doctor wife Banda is on terms of intimacy and friendship.)

In spite of the difficulty and frustration of their position I found the District Administration generally in wonderfully good heart. Throughout many conversations with these men in the field I was struck by the absence of 'belly-aching'. The Governor has won their sympathy, loyalty and even admiration and I believe that his sudden removal at an earlier stage would have come as a severe jolt. The appointment of Mr Jones[4] as Chief Secretary has been well received. They describe him as 'one of ourselves' and it is evident that he quickly established his grip on the machine. I doubt if we can find a better successor to Sir Robert Armitage. Mr Jones is not a man whose goods are in the shop window and I could wish that I had been able to see more of him (he was taken up with a long meeting of Executive Council during the only day I spent in Zomba), but he gives the impression of one who thoroughly understands the situation and has all the necessary firmness of resolution. Sir Evelyn Hone assured me that he could also be relied upon to be tactful in his handling of politicians like Banda. His appointment would be popular in the Service and would give them understanding leadership. (Sir Robert Armitage is himself anxious to be given an early decision regarding his own position.)

There are as yet only a handful of Africans ready for appointment to positions of any responsibility in the Administration — and these only in the lower grades. The retention of an expatriate Civil Service will be essential for years to come. Fortunately there is a general appreciation

---

4. Glyn Jones, KCMG 1960, Governor of Nyasaland 1961.

among expatriate officers of the climate in which we now live and I believe that they can be relied upon to support loyally a settlement on the line contemplated and make it work. There is however naturally much uncertainty among them about their own prospects and future security. An early announcement of the kind now under consideration in relation to HMOCS generally would have a most salutary effect in Nyasaland, and would do much to ensure success in the difficult transition to African responsibility.

If the Conference succeeds, we shall have one further asset to assist in the next phase. There is no doubt that a fair volume of private investment is at present held back by the prevailing political uncertainty. Once our course is set, this will be released to swell our sails, supplemented by the resources generated by a resumption of Government development.

The conference did succeed and, once the principles derived from John's parabolic story were put into effect, the future of Nyasaland, now Malawi, was to be in the hands of Dr Banda for many years.

On 25 July, the Nyasaland constitutional conference opened at Lancaster House and concluded on 4 August.

The year 1961 opened with the East African governors' conference from 4 to 9 January. On 30 January, the resumed Northern Rhodesia conference opened, which the United Federal and Dominion parties boycotted, and this ran to 17 February. On 15 June, John recorded the first of a series of talks with East African governors. This was followed on 19 June with an open meeting of talks on relations between Tanganyika and the East African high commission. On 30 September, the Uganda constitutional conference began at Lancaster House, ending on 9 October. During this year the names of Gambia and Sierra Leone pass through the pages of John's diary.

In 1962, John's time was much taken up with Malaysia, but he was also involved in the Kenya conference from February to early April. On 13 March, there was a government dinner at Carlton Gardens for the Sultan of Zanzibar before the coastal strip conference, which ended on 7 April, and the Uganda independence conference ran from 12 to 29 June. Aden crops up throughout John's 1962 diary.

The roll call of African countries achieving independence in John's last years at the Colonial Office is long. Ghana (1957), Nigeria (1960), Sierra Leone and Tanganyika (1961), Uganda (1962), Kenya and Zanzibar (1963), and Nyasaland and Northern Rhodesia (1964). To follow were Gambia (1965) and Botswana (1966).

John had one brief experience of the short-lived West Indian Federation, which was very different from his prolonged involvement with central Africa and Malaysia. Harold Macmillan, on a tour of the Caribbean in spring 1961 during the short period of the West Indian Federation, invited John to be in his party.

The Prime Minister had come to see the federation and meet some personalities in the main islands in preparation for talks on independence in 1962. The federation was to survive for little more than two years. The tour of the federation was planned as a preliminary to Macmillan's first meeting with Kennedy, victor in the US presidential election, who had taken up office in January 1961.

After the party's arrival in Trinidad, instead of accompanying the PM on his trip to Florida, John went to the morning service in the cathedral at Port of Spain. He was impressed by the warmth of the West Indian welcome. 'A round of parties, receptions, drives and interviews. It is a wonderfully friendly place and everywhere there are smiles and waves, so unlike the reception a British Minister might receive in Africa.' The three other islands visited were Barbados, Antigua and Jamaica.

> We had two rather hectic days in Barbados and Antigua and it was rather a comfort to be able to settle down again in this large well-run Government House (and incidentally to have some laundry done). Each island seems completely different from the others. Barbados is flat and very English, quite like Sussex from the air, and bursting with people, especially children, who gave the PM a wonderful welcome. Over 10,000 school children were marshalled in the main square and he spoke to them from the balcony (after receiving the freedom of the city from a red-robed Negro mayor). Each child received a frozen coca cola.

In the afternoon we visited the deep water harbour, just completed, and saw an immense mountain of sugar awaiting shipment.

On 3 April John wrote from Jamaica: 'The West Indian part of the tour is virtually over. The Prime Minister goes on to Washington tomorrow morning and I leave for New York in the afternoon. We have had various meetings with Ministers and visited the University Colleges. . . . I have exhausted myself in writing (for the PM) a letter to the Queen!'

The letter to the Queen hoped that the constitutional conferences in May and June would lead to the independence of the islands, pointing out that the future of the federation was a matter for the islands themselves. It praised race relations there:

> Certainly it is in the field of race relations that the West Indies, as they move forward to independence, seem to offer their greatest contribution to the Commonwealth family. There are no doubt tensions, and in Jamaica there is some anxiety about the repercussion of events in Africa on relations between white and coloured here; but in general it was impressive to see the free, friendly and tolerant intermingling in public life of people of all races and creeds. In this, as in much else, the West Indies give the impression of a civilized and sophisticated community, not unready to take their place among the independent countries of the world.

Economic stability and progress caused anxiety, a fundamental problem being over-population. There was fear 'lest we closed the door against further immigration into the United Kingdom. Here I have made no promises, but I have shown our sympathy,' wrote Macmillan.

The Prime Minister departed to Washington and John to New York. The conferences of May and June were 'acrimonious', in Macmillan's word. Jamaica in September voted to leave the federation, which fell apart. In April 1962, Parliament dissolved the federation. In August, Jamaica and Trinidad achieved full independence.

13

Malta: Crown Colony to Independence, 1945–67

Malta's heroic role in the Second World War matched its defence of the Maltese islands in the great siege of 1565. Small though these islands were, in population no larger than Nottingham, they were strategically important for British arms both within the Mediterranean and in the seaborne route to Southeast Asia. The immediate task for the British government after the war was reconstruction and repair of property and facilities damaged by frequent and heavy bombing. It was in this connection that the name of Dom Mintoff first appeared in John Martin's diary; he was minister of reconstruction in the Maltese administration in the postwar years and was later to play a strong part in negotiations over the country's future.

Malta had become a British crown colony in 1802 at the request of the Maltese after four years of French occupation. The relationship was defined in a Declaration of Rights of the Inhabitants of the Islands of Malta and Gozo. The opening paragraphs stated:

> We, the members of the Congress of the Islands of Malta and Gozo and their dependencies ... make the following declaration
>
> That the King of the United Kingdom of Great Britain and Ireland is our Sovereign Lord, and his lawful successors shall, in all times to come, be acknowledged as our lawful Sovereigns.
>
> That his said Majesty has no right to cede these Islands to any power. That if he chooses to withdraw his protection,

and abandon his sovereignty, the right of electing another sovereign, or of governing these Islands, belongs to us the inhabitants and aborigines alone and without control.

John Martin retained responsibility for Malta throughout his postwar service in the Colonial Office until early in 1965 when he took up the post of British high commissioner there, an appointment under the Commonwealth Relations Office, for two years.

John's diary is almost silent on Malta in the early postwar years, apart from a mention of Mintoff in 1946 and of meetings with the governor. In 1947, Malta received a constitution that gave the Maltese control over their internal but not their external affairs, the latter being retained by the Crown. In 1951, John went on from a CCTA conference in Portugal for an extended stay in Malta, from 31 January to 10 February, with Governor Sir Gerald Creasy[1] and Lieutenant Governor Sir Donald Campbell to deal with a political crisis. The visit gave John an opportunity to visit the islands thoroughly and meet those who were influential, but his main task was a political one. While Malta already had self-government, the politicians, inexperienced as they were bound to be, were caught in the difficult situation of no party enjoying an absolute majority. This had led to a failure either to make or to execute decisions. John was sent out to report and to recommend political or other changes that might ease matters. In his report, he spoke well of the governor and lieutenant governor, the former having an additional anxiety about the safety of Princess Elizabeth whose husband was serving in the navy there. He commented that Michael Gonzi, who had been Archbishop of Malta since 1943, supported the British connection, but was bitterly opposed to Mintoff, whom he saw as 'a corrupter of youth' and as suspected of communism. He was disappointed in the politicians.

They are not an impressive lot and naturally are lacking in experience and the sense of responsibility. ... In private conversation the members of the Nationalist, Constitutional and 'Workers' [Dr Boffa's] Parties appeared to show a fairly clear appreciation of realities and, in particular, of the

---

1. Governor from 1949 to 1954.

difficulties by which any Government in Malta is at present confronted; but they are quite unprepared to take any public responsibility or attempt to get unpleasant truths across to the electorate. This is made all the more difficult for them, particularly with the prospect of another General Election in the immediate future, by the irresponsibility of Mr Mintoff. The latter seems determined to exploit all possible grievances against the British Government and demands a lowering of the cost of living by subsidies and the provision of new social services on the United Kingdom scale, leaving the financial consequences to be met by HMG. ... It is unfortunate that such a line is taken by a leader of such obvious ability and, as his record in connection with reconstruction shows, drive and effectiveness as an administrator. ... The Prime Minister himself[2] gives an impression of alert intelligence. ... I imagine that his Finance Minister, Dr Azzopardi (a water-polo player and soccer enthusiast), is a stronger character.

In his political assessment, he mentioned the Italian issue, that the Maltese would exchange the Italian flag for the Union Jack, but thought it to be 'largely dead'. He had heard from some who thought that self-government had come too soon, a view he could not support, there being no reason to despair of the present constitution. He added: 'It is necessarily a matter of time before a tradition of responsibility amongst the political leaders can be built up and in the meantime it may be necessary for HMG to intervene occasionally, to avoid a breakdown, without definitely withdrawing the constitution.'

John thought a general election would not alter the balance of power and would fail to give one party an overall majority. It was important for Britain to nurse Malta through a period in which it was unlikely to enjoy stable government. John signed his report on 15 February. He notes in his diary of 25 February that consideration was being given to 'constitutional instruments', in other words to ways and means of making the constitution effective. He records a year later the arrival of Maltese ministers led by Borg

---

2. Dr George Borg Olivier 1911–80, Prime Minister 1950–55, 1965–71.

Olivier for talks, which took place over two days in the following week. On 6 August, John mentioned a talk with Borg Olivier to try to make him consent to a financial agreement. Talks took place a year later in June 1953. Borg Olivier asked for dominion status for Malta under the Commonwealth Relations Office, which Oliver Lyttelton, as secretary of state, turned down. Lyttelton put forward 'the Home Office offer', which was to transfer responsibility for Maltese affairs to the Home Secretary and place Malta in the position of the Channel Islands and Isle of Man. There was no enthusiasm for this.

In 1955, a general election brought Mintoff and a Labour administration to power. The following year, a series of negotiations began in which John was to take an active part. They were to run on almost until he took up his post as high commissioner.

Mintoff quickly put forward proposals for integration with the United Kingdom, which the Malta Labour Party had begun to advocate at recent elections. He and Borg Olivier came to London for private talks with the Secretary of State, at which the Secretary of State agreed that, although dominion status was ruled out, the existing constitution should be revised. John Martin took part in the preparations with the Secretary of State for these preliminary talks on 19 June and with the Maltese delegations from 20 to 24 June. At the conclusion of the talks, in July, an agreed statement on social and economic policy was issued saying that economic and social development was a necessity and calling for a joint and sustained effort by both countries. It was later agreed to hold a round-table conference under the chairmanship of the Lord Chancellor, Lord Kilmuir, which met in London and in Malta and reported in December 1955. It favoured representation at Westminister by three Maltese elected under the same electoral laws as members from the UK.

In announcing publication of the report in December, the government gave an undertaking that it would be considered with all speed, but that no action would be taken until the House of Commons had had an opportunity to debate it. Without waiting for the debate in Parliament, Mintoff went ahead with a referendum on the proposals in Malta in February 1956. From a register of 152,000, votes were cast by 90,000 (59 per cent), of whom 67,000 (74 per cent of those voting and 44 per cent of the electorate) were in favour of integration. The large number of abstentions may have reflected the strong advice given by the Church, which had misgivings about closer association of Catholic Malta with Protestant UK. Efforts were made by the Governor and the Secretary of State to halt the split between Mr Mintoff's government and the Church.

In the Commons debate on the report on 26 March, the Secretary of State made it plain that the government favoured the recommendations put forward by the round-table conference.

A series of meetings averted a crisis. John records that there were over 50 meetings in these negotiations. An economic commission was appointed and there were talks on constitutional and financial principles. However, in June, a disagreement over economic assistance slowed down negotiations over integration. By the end of 1957, Mintoff had lost interest in integration. There were anxieties about the future of the dockyard after 1960 and about employment. There was another financial dispute over the grant for the 1958/9 budget.

Relations with Mintoff deteriorated in 1958. He came to London in March to ask for more large financial commitments from Britain or independence. Since the prospect of integration was disappearing HMG offered an interim constitution for a five-year review period.

On 21 April, Mintoff resigned over the specific issue of the level of UK aid during the period necessary to hold a general election. When Borg Olivier, the leader of the opposition, refused to form a caretaker government, Mintoff agreed to carry on in a caretaker capacity. There were riots, during which Mintoff issued orders to the Commissioner of Police, which the latter referred to the Governor because, if they were carried out, he could no longer accept responsibility for public safety. The Governor countermanded the orders. On 24 April, he informed Mintoff that HMG was prepared to give financial assistance for the period of the election at an annual rate of £5 million and asked him for assurances that he would carry out his responsibilities for maintaining law and order. Mr Mintoff would not give these and the Governor accepted his resignation. A general strike followed and, on 30 April, a state of emergency was declared.

A constitutional conference was called in London for November and December. John's diary of 17 November duly records: 'Nominal opening of Maltese Constitutional Conference'. Nominal it was and remained. No plenary sessions were held; there was no common ground on which the parties could meet. In this situation, HMG decided that the only alternative was to introduce, as a temporary measure, a constitution enabling the governor to administer Malta with the assistance of a nominated executive council (in which the Maltese participated). In introducing the necessary legislation in February 1959, Lennox-Boyd in effect said, 'This is where I came in,' recalling that as a junior member he had listened to the almost identical bill in 1936, when the 1921 constitution (a form of parliamentary self-government) had to be withdrawn and replaced by 'Crown colony rule'.

Meanwhile, with HMG's support, the Governor would press on with economic development, the aim being to attract new industries and reduce Maltese dependence on service department expenditure. A strong industrial development committee for Malta under Lord Hives's chairmanship had been set up in November 1957 to assist in this. HMG undertook to contribute £29 million over the next five years towards the cost of converting the Valletta dockyard to commercial use, the encouragement of new industries and other capital development. Work was begun on constructing a deep-water wharf in Grand Harbour.

The new constitution came into operation in April 1959. The Governor's executive council was composed of six officials, including two (later) Maltese and four 'unofficial' Maltese. In June, Sir Guy Grantham[3] succeeded Sir Robert Laycock on completion of the latter's term as governor. Lennox-Boyd retired from office as secretary of state in October 1959.

Malta obtained independence in 1964. A commission was appointed under the chairmanship of Sir Hilary Blood, to formulate detailed proposals for the restoration of representative government. Their recommendations, accepted by HMG, gave the Maltese parliament and government responsibility for domestic affairs, and 'concurrent powers' in relation to external affairs and defence (in which HMG would have overriding legislative powers). The new constitution was promulgated in October 1961

---

3. Admiral, Governor and Commander-in-Chief 1959–62.

and elections were held under it in February 1962. The result was a victory for Borg Olivier's Nationalist Party. In August, Olivier wrote to the secretary of state (now Duncan Sandys) asking that Malta be granted independence. Duncan Sandys asked the Malta government to draft a constitution as a basis for discussion. A conference met in July and August 1963, attended by representatives of all the Maltese political parties. (For John the conference was like No. 10 over again in the late hours it kept; he recorded getting home at 2.30 and 3.00 a.m. frequently.) There was no agreement among the parties either on the terms of a constitution for independence or on the holding of a referendum. However, HMG decided that independence would be granted not later than 31 May 1964. Meanwhile, the Maltese prime minister was invited to hold discussions in Malta on joint constitutional proposals. Dr Borg Olivier submitted his draft constitution to a referendum. In a 74 per cent vote it was approved by 51 per cent of those voting and opposed by 43 per cent. Duncan Sandys decided to press forward to independence (for which the target date had already passed), though amending the Maltese government's draft on certain points. The necessary legislation was passed in July (second reading, committee and third reading in the House of Commons in a single day) after an undertaking by the Maltese prime minister to sign linked agreements on defence and finance. Malta became independent at midnight on 20/1 September 1964.

Though out of office, Mintoff maintained his hostility to the Church. He sought to establish civil marriage, to make the teaching of religion in schools a voluntary parental decision and to establish a common right of burial in cemeteries maintained by the state. In addition, he felt that the police should have the right to enter churches if bell ringing or other disturbances interfered with public meetings. Also, he wanted standards of public morality, decency and public order to be determined by generally accepted principles and not by one particular faith.

In January 1965, John arrived in Malta with Rosalind to serve for two years as British high commissioner.

Malta was now an independent member of the Commonwealth and, under the 1964 constitution, came under the Commonwealth

Relations Office (CRO). Sir Maurice Dorman[4] became governor general, a post he held until 1971. British interests in Malta were represented by the high commissioner. John Martin was now a member of the diplomatic corps but with a special position through Malta's long connection with Great Britain and through his own long service to Malta through the Colonial Office.

The high commissioner had a house overlooking St Paul's Bay near Naxxar, the Villa di Giorgio, and an office in Floriana. A large part of his and his wife's day consisted of paying visits, exchanging hospitality, and attending functions and special events. There were also consultations with the Maltese government, with other diplomats and with London.

John and Rosalind arrived on 26 January, but the following day he returned to London for Winston Churchill's funeral, having recorded a tribute to him in Malta. It was a magnificent state funeral in St Paul's. More than the funeral of a great statesman it appeared to be a funeral of the British Empire itself.

In Malta John was delighted by:

> the richness of its architectural detail ... the historic interest ... but ... the greatest glory of Valletta is its unity and the fulfilled completeness of its grand design. The magnificent whole is greater than the sum of the parts.
>
> Climbing from sea-level one approaches the majesty of the city with a proper humility, pausing on the way to rest for a time in the Upper Barracca Gardens and enjoy one of Europe's finest views — beautiful in form and space, in colour and perspective. It is the noble setting of a heroic story, reminding the visitor that in Malta he is on historic ground, the scene of sacrifice and endurance which will be held in honoured remembrance as long as history is told.

In 1965, Malta celebrated the fourth centenary of the great siege in which the Knights of St John successfully defended Valletta against the forces of Suleiman II of Constantinople The celebrations focused on 8 September with Pontifical High Mass and Te Deum with a regatta in Grand Harbour. The American Sixth Fleet

---

4. Governor and Commander-in-Chief 1962–64.

was present during this period. John was invested by the Governor-General as a Knight of the Order of St John in the Palace of Valletta on 29 April 1966.

In mid-1965, John Martin prepared a review of how he had found Malta in his first months, which he sent to the CRO on 15 August. He summarized his findings and first impressions:

> A happy people, united as a small nation by language, race and religion, maintaining, however, the institutions appropriate to a larger country.
>
> Outwardly prosperous, but rising unemployment aggravated by the Services' run-down. Emigration provides a safety valve; diversification of the economy with the development of tourism is being attempted with the £50 million provided by Britain under the Financial Agreement.
>
> The Defence Agreement has been running smoothly.
>
> Malta has not stepped on to the international scene with any great flourish; economic and domestic affairs are likely to dominate the elections which must be held before July 1966; there are difficulties and dangers for Britain and the West if Mintoff should come to power.
>
> The population is only 320,000, but the pretensions and the trappings are those of a national State. The curious visitor may ask whether Government institutions such as the High Court with its Chief Justice and six other Judges should not be on a scale more appropriate to the country's resources. It is, however, unlikely that he would find much reflection of these doubts among the Maltese.
>
> The visitor is indeed at once struck by many outward signs of prosperity. The roads are crowded, often overcrowded, with cars. There is much new building. A dense forest of television masts sprouts from the roofs. Shops are stuffed with consumer goods.

He thought that the attempt to attract new industry and to develop tourism had to a large extent compensated for the rundown of British services.

The run-down has indeed been a severe blow and, as the

figures for unemployment show, it has borne heavily on many individuals. Indeed the hardship has been greater than the unemployment totals may suggest, since the older men are generally too old to seek new careers by joining the wave of emigration which has removed such large numbers from the labour market. Nor do they gain from the expansion of industry and tourism, which have provided employment principally for women and young men. Thus, while in some directions there is modest economic growth, its benefits are not equally shared. If many are now enjoying their motor cars, refrigerators and television sets, there are many more for whom life is hard and the future unpromising.

Some progress is therefore being made in assisting the country to develop a viable economy dependent as little as possible on aid from Britain. There is a general feeling that progress would have been greater under a more effective Administration and there are many complaints of delay in obtaining necessary decisions from the Government. In fairness, it must be remembered that much is being demanded of a small administrative machine, lacking in experience in the sort of responsibilities now crowding upon it; but it cannot be denied that the lawyer politicians now in control show little of the qualities of energy and decisiveness which the situation demands. My personal relations with them and particularly with the Prime Minister have been most friendly ... and they are duly appreciative of the generosity of our financial assistance. In return they have in all important respects faithfully carried out their undertakings under the Defence Agreement.

John added comments on the defence agreement and on Malta's external relations.

It is only fair to record that since independence relations between the Government and people of Malta and the British forces have been singularly free from acrimony. Even Mr Mintoff now seems to accept that the defence arrangements with Britain should continue in some form, although he takes the line that the terms should be made more favourable to Malta. .... In other spheres of its international relations Malta has so far been content to assume a sensibly modest role. .... Perhaps, wisely, the Maltese are trying to make their main mark in the Council of Europe and to a lesser extent in the United Nations. .... Malta's apparent lack of ambition in this field can be welcomed as indicating her readiness to cut her coat according to the cloth.

At the end of July 1966, the Colonial Office closed. Such colonies as remained in the much run-down British Empire were to be under the wing of the Foreign and Commonwealth Office (FCO). John Martin was pleased to find in *The Maltese Observer* of 14 August an appreciative article by Dr Herbert Ganado, 'An Honest Post-Mortem on the Passing of the Colonial Office', in which the author said:

The list of benefits, accruing from Colonialism is a long one. There was a cessation of tribal warfare; an abolition of slavery; the establishment of a generally paternal central government; the introduction of railways; a continuous fight against disease; the building of Schools, Colleges and Universities; the training of an efficient Civil Service; the upholding of democratic principles; the forming of economic relations; the spreading of technical knowledge; the teaching of modern European languages — all these made possible a passage from Colonial rule to Independence without too much travail. The spreading of the true faith, the Christian religion has benefitted too, from sympathetic Colonial administration.

In a letter of thanks to the author dated 1 September 1966, John wrote:

The Colonial relationship with Malta, a country with a long history of civilization, was always difficult; but as you recognize, the modern 'Colonial' task was in those other territories, mainly in Africa, where the Colonial Administrator established the rule of law over vast areas which had never known it, laid the foundations of civilized life in

education, health and other spheres, and provided the infra-
structure for economic development.

*Tu regere imperio populos, Romane, memento (Hae tibi
erunt artes) pacisque imponere morem, Parcere subjectis et
debellare superbos.*

Colonialism is out of fashion now, but I believe that the
ultimate verdict of history will be that this was one of the
greatest British contributions to the world. In travelling
through the three regions of Nigeria some years ago, to discuss Service conditions with expatriate officers, I was
repeatedly struck by the idealism which had led to many of
these young men to choose their career overseas. They had
gone into the Colonial Administration because they believed
that this provided outstanding opportunities for constructive public service.

After two relatively serene years, a crisis came to a head in
January 1967, the very week of John's departure. It had its origins
in negotiations in August. The British government intended to
reduce the number of servicemen stationed in Malta over a period
of two years. The proposal met strong opposition in Malta on
account of loss of revenue and of increased unemployment.
Further discussion had Britain agreeing to lengthen the run-down
period to four years. A joint communiqué of talks between Secretary of State for Commonwealth Affairs Herbert Bowden and
Prime Minister Borg Olivier, dated 17 January 1967, indicated the
British government's intention to go ahead and reported Borg
Olivier's great concern over the impact on Malta. On 27 January,
Borg Olivier told the Malta house of representatives that, in so
doing, the British government was in breach of the 1964 defence
agreement. The British government replied the following day that
the agreement did not mention numbers of servicemen. There were
threats of violence on the island.

In the midst of this, John was saying goodbye and packing. Borg
Olivier had dined him out on 18 January. In his letter of thanks
the next day, John wrote:

You know that I have done my best not only to represent
the interest of my country in Malta but also to ensure that

the interests of Malta were appreciated and borne in mind in any decisions affecting them taken by the British Government. It is sad indeed that at the very end of my term as High Commissioner the good relations between Malta and Britain should be disturbed by disagreement over the Services' economies. However serious the disagreement may be and however painful the immediate consequences I cannot believe that they will in the long run shake a friendship so deeply rooted in shared history and common interest.

Before Christmas 1966, Harrison Lewis, the American chargé d'affaires, who had met him at the airport on his arrival and with whom he formed a close friendship, wrote: 'Malta has been fortunate in its first years of independence to have had as British High Commissioner, one, like yourself, who has been able to strike such a happy balance in handling Great Britain's relations with it. You have been respected and loved for your understanding and patience combined with a forthright assessment of Malta's responsibilities and requirements.' In reply, John wrote:

Since my school-days I have believed passionately in the importance of friendship between Britain and the United States as the foundation for peace and progress in the world. I was therefore delighted in my first and only diplomatic appointment to find, from the moment of arrival in Malta (when you gave me such a friendly welcome at the Airport), that I had an American colleague with whom cooperation was easy and natural.

On 23 January, an exchange of telegrams began between Sir Saville Garner, later Baron Garner, head of the diplomatic service from 1965 to 1968, and John. 'S of S is rather concerned at position which may arise next month if there is serious trouble in Malta as result of Defence Run-down. Do you in fact apprehend serious trouble which will require control in the High Commission?' John's reply of 24 January said:

My intelligence which I believe is reliable is that violence is neither intended nor likely though we cannot of course be certain that there will not be isolated incidents or that situation may not deteriorate.

... I should be most reluctant to stay on after 31st. We have been saying goodbyes. Packing will be completed tomorrow. I am very tired and frankly ashamed of the policy I have to represent. If however I thought public interest so required I should stay. I do not.

Sooner Troy[5] can be introduced to problems here the better. ... Meanwhile I do not recommend appointment of stopgap. This would suggest lack of confidence in Brown and appear alarmist.

John's final dispatch on the day he left Malta, 31 January, was coloured by crisis over the services rundown. His views had been made clear earlier.

In my despatch of 17th August, 1965, submitting the traditional 'first impressions' of a newly appointed High Commissioner, I gave a picture of the Maltese people as I found them — a happy and friendly nation, outwardly prosperous ... achieving some progress in development of a viable economy and faithfully carrying out its undertakings in the Defence Agreement.

It was, on the whole, a happy sun-lit picture. So it remained until the very last weeks of my term in Malta. Anglo–Maltese relations were maintained at a higher level of close friendship than ever before in living memory. The fruits of British aid were increasingly shown in consolidation and expansion of new industries and the development of facilities to match a rapidly mounting flood of tourists. The Services continued to enjoy their rights under the Defence Agreement in an atmosphere of good will. It seemed that, given a few years — perhaps six or seven — the economy would have developed to a point when it would no longer be dependent on Services expenditure.

Then, with startling suddenness, announcement of the details of the British Government's defence cuts brought a

---

5. John's successor at Malta, Geoffrey Troy.

dark cloud of dismay and resentment across the scene — a resentment shared by all classes and parties, and all the fiercer because of the depth of the trust and friendship for Britain which seemed to have been betrayed.

This reaction came as no surprise. I myself gave repeated warnings of the 'catastrophic' effect on the Maltese economy of reductions in Defence expenditure on the scale and at the speed proposed and of the bitter Maltese resentment to be expected. Subsequent modifications of the original British proposals were insufficient to affect their reception, since they still involve a level of discharges in the first two years too high to be cushioned by any possible development of new employment in the same period or by 'natural wastage'.

I leave Malta today at the height of the storm ... of which the incidents have been or will be separately reported to you. It is impossible to forecast its future course. The storm may soon pass ... or it may rage on. ... In the circumstances it is impossible for me to submit a valedictory appreciation of the normal pattern. I can only express the hope that the quarrel will be mended before too late and my horror in contemplating the alternative — that the friendship of the Maltese people, so deeply rooted in the shared experiences of many years of peace and, especially, war, will be cast away; that thousands who have served Britain long and loyally will be abandoned to the hopelessness of unemployment (for which, for most, there can be no remedy); that the millions already spent in aid will be frustrated through the collapse of confidence and consequent blighting of the hopeful growth of industrial and tourist development; and that we shall lose for ever this foothold in the central Mediterranean. The Battle of the Atlantic — and with it the last war — was almost lost through lack of the Irish bases. Who can say, as the Libyan oil-field develops into one of the most productive in the world and as Communist military 'hardware' is poured into Algiers, what price we and our allies may have to pay for abandonment of Malta?

Most of my public service was in the Colonial Office,

where the guiding principle was the welfare of the wards for whom the British Government were trustees. For two years I have been a temporary diplomat, in a sphere in which the general guiding principle is the maintenance of British interests. The latter seem more difficult to calculate; but I believe that the fulfilment of moral commitments is not inconsistent with a proper estimate of British interests and, with respect, I submit that the British people have a moral commitment to see the Maltese people through their present difficulties.

Cordial relations remained with Borg Olivier, who wrote on 14 February 1967:

> In all sincerity I must tell you that I was very sorry to see your term of office as British High Commissioner coming to an end. I doubt if there is anyone who could appreciate, better than I, how lucky we all were to have you as High Commissioner. The unpleasant fact that these differences with the British Government had to come to a head at the very end of your career, has not in any way affected my deep respect for your fine qualities. If anything, the whole matter has served to strengthen the real bonds of friendship between us. It is, after all, in adversity that the real character of a person becomes so evident.

Further negotiations eased the position. On 15 March 1967, John wrote to congratulate Borg Olivier on their conclusion.

> You must be flooded with messages, but I cannot resist the urge to add my warmest congratulations on the outcome of the London talks. 'A man's reach should exceed his grasp,' but if I had been pleading your case I could not have expected more.
> The hard human problem of the older men among the discharged civilians remains, though reduced and mitigated; but the overall problem of unemployment will now be manageable if tourism and industry develop as we have every reason to believe they will. Above all — and in the

long run this may be what matters most — the friendship between the people of Malta and Britain, which shone like a rainbow across those troubled weeks, has been preserved and perhaps even strengthened.

Borg Olivier replied on 25 March: 'I, too, am satisfied that the result of my discussions with the British Government was, all in all, a happy one. Your remark on the friendship between the two countries is a very true one; in fact I am convinced that it was this real bond that kept the talks going on more than one occasion.'

John Martin, with Rosalind, was summoned to Buckingham Palace to attend a farewell audience with the Queen. The audience took place on 21 March. So, John entered retirement, with friendships made in many parts of the world, to speak and write in defence of the reputations of Churchill and his wartime colleagues and of the British Empire and its colonial policy, to be a source of information and encouragement to scholars who sought his help, to continue his biblical studies and to serve his Oxford college and many other people and institutions over more than 20 years. His home at Watlington was the scene of an active retirement.

14

L'Accomplissement

I n elegant and austere French prose, a letter from Paris after
John Martin's death by Jacqueline Chatenet, sister of Alexandre
Parodi, minister of labour in de Gaulle's postwar government,
contained the phrase *'l'accomplissement de sa vie'*. 'Accomplissement' is rich in meaning. It means both the bringing of a life to a
good end and the achievement of a life taken as a whole.

Having spent three years absorbed in John Martin's letters and
papers and in seeking to discover some of the background and
context of his work, I am overwhelmed by his devotion to long
hours of demanding work in service to his country. His wife
remarked that she often thought she should have camped outside
No. 10 in the postwar period to demand more staff for the
Colonial Office. Just as long and late hours were the order of the
day in wartime No. 10, so they were too in the postwar Colonial
Office. The sort of itinerary John had to keep in the prewar days is
well illustrated in his year with the Singapore shipping inquiry and
in the Palestine Royal Commission.

There was no lack of delegation. John was able to attract staff
to work for him, who enjoyed the experience and profited from it.
Will Mathieson, a son of the manse and later of the Overseas
Development Ministry and UNESCO, entered the Colonial Office
Middle East Department, of which John was then head, in 1945.
He wrote:

> I was fortunate in my early days to work for him on
> Palestine and he patiently taught me my first lessons in how
> to be an effective public servant. ... He was also the most
> liked senior officer in that friendly company of the Colonial

262

Office, the finest department in Whitehall. He could gently correct without seeming to punish. He inspired maximum response and indeed affection.

Another Colonial Office man, Peter Whitley, described some of the pleasures of working with and for John at the Colonial Office in the early 1960s.

He was a Deputy Secretary and I was (three grades lower) a mere Principal. We were engaged in some distinctly complex negotiations for a new university in Basutoland (as it then was) and, for reasons which escape me, I worked for quite a lot of the time direct to Sir John. It stands out as a happy time. His ability and experience were an education to me and, even more important, it was so extraordinarily pleasant. He made everything seem easy; and otherwise rather punishing work became fun. All in all, he was the most human, good-humoured, equable and approachable Deputy Secretary that I encountered in the Civil Service.

These pages have also recorded the pleasures of working with John in Churchill's private office and the wide appreciation of his quiet and effective leadership there amid the pressures and demands of the war.

On his transfer to No. 10 in 1940, John remarked that the Colonial Office was his home. The qualities he brought to the private office, placed in the Prime Minister's home, and to the Colonial Office are those of a good home: efficient conduct of its affairs, hard work, friendship, care of the young and provision for their welfare, lightness of touch and good humour, recognition of wrong-doing but dealing with it gently and also the deflating of pretension.

John was a master of friendship with old and young from his earliest days, friendship without racial or religious differentiation. His kindly, rather reserved good humour drew friends from many parts of the world. He was a much-travelled man and opportunities for friendship were rarely lost. His friendships were an essential component of his Colonial Office work after the war, and had already played a part in the way in which he ran the wartime

wartime private office. It would be wrong to see these friendships as having been entered into to advance British policy. They were entered into for their own sake because they were part of John's own nature and character. What profit British policy derived from them came because his friends liked and trusted him.

John's combination of friendliness and integrity made him an admirable troubleshooter. Where difficult situations were developing John was the man to send. Before the war, his service as secretary to the Palestine Royal Commission was a sign of things to come. After the war, the difficulties in bringing the colonies to independence were manifold. The second part of this story has recounted his adventures in Malaya and the Borneo territories, Cyprus, Malta, Nigeria and central Africa, not always to the sound of gunfire but always amid considerable tension.

The reader of these pages can see that people were attracted to him because of the power of his mind, expressed modestly but with the convincingness of truth. He could put his finger on the essential point in an argument; he was not swayed by grand ideological theories, but looked for reasonable, attainable solutions to difficulties, which he could present in easily understood language. With his classicist's mind, he was irritated by the inflated ideas and impractical polices of the infant UNO after the war.

One quality that John greatly admired in others and that he himself exemplified was loyalty. There were four main loyalties in his life as well as lesser loyalties to schools, college and other institutions of which he was or had been a member. The first of these was to his family — his parents and, as the years went by, to his extended family of relations and godchildren.

John's second loyalty came from his Christian faith, acquired from his upbringing in a devout home and family. His whole life was an expression of Christianity in action. The Scottish Church laid the foundations for this, though in later years he held a dual church loyalty. He became an elder in the Church of Scotland at St Columba's in London, an office he gave up when he sold his London home. In retirement, he worshipped at the parish church of Watlington. The arrangements after his death reflected this pattern, funeral at St Leonard's, Watlington, and memorial service at St Columba's.

John kept alive the intellectual side of his faith. The five large files containing 400–500 pages of his commentary of the New Testament are impressive. They hold studies of the four gospels, of the Acts of the Apostles and of five Pauline epistles, Romans, I and II Corinthians and I and II Thessalonians. John's method is to take the Greek text, compare it with ancient Greek and occasionally with Aramaic and also to compare various English translations with each other. This gives some indication of dating. His method helps locate the historical significance of a biblical text and to establish its present meaning. It was a lifetime's work, interrupted by the war years, but then picked up again and continued until late in his retirement. The work on the gospels is particularly interesting, full of wise observations and theological insights. The reader may well think that the one that bears his own name is the most satisfying of them and of his studies. In coming to the end of his own life he too may have thought it the most fulfilling.

John's third loyalty was to his wartime master. The last of Churchill's private secretaries, Anthony Montague Browne, who served him from 1952 to his death in 1965, wrote that from Churchill's conversation over these years, he realized John's 'true distinction, his unswerving loyalty and the high quality of his service to our country in the moments of greatest peril'. In retirement, John played his part in defending Churchill's reputation. One of John's immediate assignments on retirement was to prepare his memoir for *Action This Day*, which was published in 1968. His papers have left a careful analysis of Lord Moran's *Winston Churchill: The Struggle for Survival, 1940–1965* with marked extracts. This book, containing opinions and judgements of Churchill John and his friends thought to be wrong, was the trigger for *Action This Day*. John was continually correcting mis-understandings, distortions and plain errors about Churchill's decisions and actions, through letters, some to newspapers, or by interview. Lady Soames, Churchill's youngest daughter, wrote that 'the quietness and authoritative calm of the tone of John's inter-ventions were of the utmost value.' She remembered John among the 'answerers for the honour of my father's name'.

After the war, the historians were at work, Churchill among them. A life was required after his death, begun by Randolph Churchill and continued and completed by Martin Gilbert. John was among those who assisted this work. Gilbert's two wartime volumes contain information John supplied and warm tributes to him for his help. Martin Gilbert describes in his *In Search of Churchill* (p. 182) how research led to friendship. 'I always enjoyed driving over from Oxford to spend time with John and Rosalind Martin, to absorb not only the Churchillian aspects but to relax in their friendly, cultured and wise company.' As the years went by and more documentation came to hand, revisionist historians entered the field. Late in his life, John agreed to the publishing of extracts from his diaries and letters in *Downing Street: The War Years*, not so much as a counter to revisionists but as a help to historical accuracy and a source for further studies.

John's fourth loyalty was to the British Empire and Colonial Office. Defence of the empire absorbed his working life and retirement. He learned his respect for the empire in the silver period before the war. After the war, the critics and denigrators were in the ascendant, yet the empire was not one of domination. John worked towards preparation for independence, not retention. The problems were not 'if', but 'when'. John often felt that a colony could be pushed too quickly into independence, before it was ready, but independence was always the goal. While he had misgivings about the speed of decolonization, he could see that the empire had to come to an end.

In defence of the empire, he held that it had been a great benefit to its territories. It had brought sound government and administration, economic advances and, in difficult circumstances, had prepared the way to independence. As in his defence of Churchill's reputation, he sought to establish the facts about empire, about what actually had happened, been done and been achieved. He was aware of its defects and errors, but thought these were far outweighed by its achievements. He looked upon the empire as Britain's good gift to the world. He thought that many of those who served it did so with a sense of vocation, that it was a good cause and a good way to spend one's life. This was certainly the spirit of his service. Decolonization was almost over by the time he left the Colonial Office. In his view, the empire was Britain's *accomplissement*, something good well done.

Index

267

Index

Belgium, 96, 158, 164
Bell, Mr, 225
Ben-Gurion, David, 85, 99
Benson, Sir Arthur, 29
Bernadotte, Count, 137
Bernières, 121
Bevan, Dr, 173
Bevin, Ernest, 133, 135, 138–9
Bevir, Anthony, 105
Biobaku, Mr, 224
Birgi, Nuri, 188
Blantyre, 237
Blood, Sir Hilary, 250
Board of Studies in Race
    Relations, 231
Boas, Philip, 9, 20–1
Boffa, Dr, 246
Bolshie Society, 223–4
Bolshoi, 125
Bonar family, 54
Borneo territories, 28, 196, 198,
    200, 205–14, 216, 218, 264; see
    also North Borneo
Boston Symphony Orchestra, 146
Bourguebus, 123
Bourne, Geoffrey Kemp, 201
Bovell, C. S. K., 230–1
Bowden, Herbert, 256
Bracken, Brendan, 110
Brazzaville, 166
British Institute, 179
British School, Rome, 5
Brook, Norman, 188
Brooke family, 28
Brown, Dr Graham, 88, 258
Brunei, 209, 211, 213, 215–18,
    234
Brunei Bay, 215
Buchan, John, 13–14
Bukit Mertijan, 61
Bukum, 69
Bunche, Dr, 137

Burke, Edmund, 24, 162
Burma, 25, 84
Butterworth, 61
Byrnes, James F., 136–7

Cadogan, Alec, 113, 124, 140,
    145, 147
Caen, 122–3
Cairo, 93, 118
Calabar, 225
Caledonian Club, 13–14
Callendar, 2
Cameron Highlands, 57
Cameroons, 155, 160, 163, 225
Campbell, Sir Donald, 246
Cannes, 2, 5
Canton/Cantonese, 53, 59
Cape Town, 166
Carcosa, 211
Caribbean, 22, 233–4, 243
Carlton Gardens, 167, 188, 242
Carlyle, Thomas, 5
Carstairs, Charles, 25, 28, 30,
    36–7, 77, 138–9, 148
Carter, Sir Morris, 81, 83
Casablanca, 118
Castle, Barbara, 185
Castle Mills, 73
Central African Federation, 235–7
Chamberlain, Neville, 7
Champs Elysées, 124
Chatenet, Jacqueline, 262
Chenderoh, 59
Chequers, 108–10, 128, 137, 186,
    235
Cherbourg, 123
Cherwell, Mr, 113
Cherwell, 13
Childs, Marquis, 111
Chiltern hills, 128
Chirwa, Orton, 237–8, 240
Chiume, M. W. K., 238, 240

Index

Index

Dyak, 198, 208

East Africa, 83, 228, 234, 242
East African Federation, 234–5
East India Company, 22
Eastwood, Christopher, 21, 208
Ebal, 81
Eden, Anthony, 108–9, 124, 131, 178–9
Edinburgh Academy, 2–3, 5, 12, 20 67, 107, 225
Edinburgh Association for the University Education of Women, 1
Edinburgh High School, 3
Edinburgh Medical Mission, 2
Edinburgh Social Union, 1
Edinburgh University, 5
Edward VIII, King, 80
Egypt/Egyptians, 6, 47, 79, 173
Eisenhower, President, 125, 131, 185
Elias bin Ahmad, 59
Elizabeth, Princess, 246
Emmet, Dorothy, 20
Empire Marketing Board, 36, 62
Empire State building, 140
enosis, 168–72, 174–6, 178–9, 181, 183
Enugu, 224
EOKA, 179, 181–2, 184, 186, 191
Es-Salt, 88
Estoril, 165
Evatt, Chairman, 142
Exeter College, Oxford, 3

Famagusta, 176
Farrell, 87
Feisal, Prince, 141
Ferard, Reginald Herbert, 3
Fiji, 31, 33, 75–7
Finney, Mr, 240

First World War/Great War, 4, 9, 30, 79, 94
Flanders, 103
Flandin, M. Pierre-Étienne, 109
Floriana, 252
Florida, 116, 243
Foot, Sir Hugh, later Lord Caradon, 185–8, 190–1
Flushing Meadow, 140–1
Ford Motor Company, 71
Foreign and Commonwealth Office (FCO), 130, 255
Foreign Office (FO), 26, 36, 113, 133, 138–9, 144, 162, 169–70, 178–9, 188–9
Fort Iskander, 204
Fox, Richard, 9
Fox Knowe, 69
Franks, Oliver, 20
Fraser's Hill, 56
Free French, 110–11
Free St Paul's, 1

Galilee, Sea of, 81, 86, 98, 100
Galsworthy, John, 165
Gambia, 242–3
Ganado, Dr Herbert, 255
Gandhi, Mahatma, 240
Gardner-Brown, 223
Garner, Sir Saville, 257
Gaza Strip, 137
Gazali bin Shafie, Euche Muhammed, 212
General Medical Council, 47
Gent, Sir Edward, 195
George VI, King, 80
Gerig, Mr, 153
Gerizim, 81
Ghana, 237, 243
Gibson, President, 64, 67, 73–4
Gilbert, Martin, 31, 265–6
Gilbert and Ellis Islands, 31

270

Index

Index

Index

Index

Malawi, 237–40, 242; see also Nyasaland
Malawi African Congress, 237
Malay College, 57
Malaya, 11, 31, 33, 35, 38, 41–4, 47–8, 52, 54–5, 57, 59, 63, 65, 68, 71, 74–5, 77–8, 86, 102, 128, 160, 167, 193–6, 200–2, 204–7, 209, 211–14, 218, 225, 233, 264
Malaysia, 78, 206, 208–10, 212–14, 217–18, 233–4, 242–3
Greater Malaysia, 209–12
Malta, 39, 126, 131, 245–59, 261, 264
Marburg, 18
Marlborough, 11
Marshall, General, 121, 136
Marshall Plan, 136
Martin, David Ross, 120, 125, 128, 172
Martin, Jessie (Detta), see Gulland
Martin, John (Snr), 1, 3, 14, 17–18, 20, 48, 81, 129
Martin, Peggy, 2, 112, 212
Martin, Rosalind, 117–20, 128, 130, 251–2, 261, 266
Martin, William, 2, 39, 112
Mason, Philip, 21, 231–2
Mathieson, Will, 262
Matthew, Mr, 13
Mau Mau, 235
Mecca, 55–6, 64
Melville, Sir Eugene, 178, 180, 183, 185, 187, 189–90
Menderes, Adnan, 189
Menuhin, Yehudi, 165
Mexico, 153
Miller, Edith Godwin (John's mother), 1, 3, 12, 41, 48–9, 75, 103–4, 106, 112–13, 118–20, 129, 148

Miller, Innis, 64, 66–7, 70, 74
Ministry of Overseas France, 163
Mintoff, Dom, 245–9, 251, 253–4
Moiseiwitsch, Benno, 165
Molesworth, Dr, 203
Molotov, Vyacheslav M., 125, 162
Monckton, Lord, 236
Monckton Commission, 237
Monod, 165
Montague Browne, Anthony, 265
Montgomery, Field Marshal, 121–3
Montreal, 124
Moore, Sam, 221–2
Mooring, 'Satan', 223
Moran, Lord, 102, 106, 265
Moreton, Sir John, 182
Morris, Dick, 215–17
Morris, Sir Harold, 81, 83
Morrison, Herbert, 138
Morrison–Grady plan, 135–6
Morton, Desmond, 110
Morton, H. V., 85
Moscow, 113, 117, 124–5, 127
Mount Scopus, 84
Mouskos, 181
Mugugua, 164
Muir, Edward, 11, 21
Munir, Sir Mehmed, 173
Mussolini, Benito, 119

Nablus, 85
Nagpur, 212
Nahalal, 97, 101
Naif, 90
Nairobi, 163–4, 166
Nakorosuli, 76
Nandé, M., 166
Nasser, Gamal Abdel, 131
National Council on Establishments, 225
Nationalist Party, Malta, 251

274

Index

NATO, 187–8
Naxxar, 252
Nazareth, 100
Negeb, 98, 135
Negri Sembilan, 44, 47, 54, 202
Nel, Elizabeth (née Layton), 109,
   126, 128
New Reform Club, 13
New York, 116, 136, 140–2, 149,
   152, 167, 206, 244
New Zealand, 22, 158
Newfoundland, 22, 113
Nicolson, Harold, 82–3
Nicosia, 168, 172–4, 180, 182,
   186
Nigeria, 32, 155, 163, 208,
   219–20, 222, 225–32, 243, 256,
   264
Noel-Baker, Francis, 182
Nor, Mat, 49, 53, 75, 202
Noriega, Manuel, 153
Norman-Butler, Susan, 11
Normandy, 108, 121, 123
North Africa, 109, 117–18, 158
North Borneo, 28, 44, 178, 196–7,
   200, 206, 208–14, 216, 218, 233
North Borneo Chartered
   Company, 28
Norway, 154
Nyasaland, 235–7, 240, 242–3;
   see also under Malawi

O'Regan, John, 223
Officers' Training Corps (OTC), 4
Olivier, Dr George Borg,
   247–9, 251, 256, 260–1
Onitsha, 224
opium, 31–2, 41–3, 45–6, 77
Oriel College, Oxford, 112,
   117–18, 120
Ormsby-Gore, W. G. A., later
   Lord Harlech, 81, 98

Oron, 225
Ottawa, 26–7, 36
Overseas Development Ministry,
   262
Overseas Service Officers'
   Resettlement Bureau, 229
Owerri, 224
Oxford, 3–5, 8, 9, 11–16, 18–21,
   26, 83, 107, 112, 117–18, 120,
   166, 261, 266
Oxford Academical Club, 13
Oxford Magazine, 13
Oxford University Colonial
   Records Project, 25
Oyster Bay, 147

P & O, 41, 74
Pacific, 31, 125
Pahang River, 44–5, 56, 204
Pakistan, 24, 143, 158
Palestine, 36–7, 39, 43, 79–82,
   84–5, 89–90, 92–4, 96–101,
   132–44, 146–8, 186, 206, 262
Palestine Bill, 147
Palestine Partition Commission,
   100
Palestine Royal Commission,
   35–6, 40, 64, 79–80, 82, 84,
   98–101, 133–4, 137, 147, 262,
   264
Pan Malayan Federation of Trade
   Unions, 195
Pano Platres, 173
Papadopoulos, A. S., 169, 182,
   187
Papagos, 180
Paris, 5, 123, 137, 163–7, 262
Parit forest, 58
Parkinson, Sir Cosmo, 98
Parodi, Alexandre, 262
Partridge, Mr, 223
Party Rakyat, 209, 217

275

Index

Index

Index

Index

Weizmann, Dr Chaim, 82, 84–5, 89, 91–2, 96–8, 101, 143, 146
Wellington, 26
West Africa, 154–5, 163
West Bank, 134, 137
West Indian Federation, 234, 243
Westminister, 120, 141
Weston, 215–16
White, Dennis, 198
White House, Hull, 14
White House, Washington, 115, 116
Whitehall, 27, 33, 163, 189, 263
Whitley, Peter, 263
Wild, J. H. S., 20
Williams, Dr, 3
Williams, Eric, 234
Wilson, Sir Charles, 115
Winster, Lord, 170–2, 177
Wisconsin, 111
Women's Industrial Council, 2
Women's Liberal Federation, 2

Woodhouse, Sir John, 100
Woodhouse Commission, 98, 134
Woolley, Sir Charles, 170
Worcester County Cricket Club, 11
Wright, Michael, 162

Yalta, 126–7
Yeop, Raja, 58
Yola, 222
Young Women's Christian Association (YWCA), 2
Younger, Norman, 143

Zanzibar, 234, 243
Zanzibar, Sultan of, 242
Zionist, 79, 85, 89, 91–2, 98, 138–9
Zionist Organization of America, 144
Zomba, 241
Zorlu, 180, 188–9
Zurich agreements, 181, 188–9, 192
Zvegintzov, Mr, 18